The chief glory of every people

arises from its authours.

Samuel Johnson
"Preface" to *A Dictionary of the English Language*

The Chief Glory
of Every People

Essays on Classic American Writers
Edited by Matthew J. Bruccoli

Southern Illinois University Press
Carbondale and Edwardsville

Feffer & Simons, Inc.
London and Amsterdam

Library of Congress Cataloging in Publication Data

Bruccoli, Matthew Joseph, 1931–
  The chief glory of every people.

  Includes bibliographical references.
    1. American literature—19th century—History and
criticism. I. Title.
PS201.B75   810'.9   73–1783
ISBN 0-8093-0615-8

CONTENTS

Notes on Contributors vii

Preface ix

1. Fenimore Cooper:
   The Development of the Novelist
   JAMES GROSSMAN 1

2. Stephen Crane in Our Time
   MARSTON LAFRANCE 25

3. The Relevance of John Dewey's Thought
   SIDNEY HOOK 53

4. Mr. Emerson – of Boston
   ELEANOR M. TILTON 77

5. Consistency in the Mind and Work
   of Hawthorne
   ARLIN TURNER 97

6. William Dean Howells:
   Perception and Ambivalence
   CLAYTON L. EICHELBERGER 117

7. Washington Irving: Nonsense, the Fat of the
   Land and the Dream of Indolence
   WILLIAM L. HEDGES 141

8. Herman Melville, 1972
   JAY LEYDA 161

9. William Gilmore Simms
   THOMAS L. MCHANEY 173

10. Henry Thoreau and the
    Reverend Poluphloisboios Thalassa
    JOEL PORTE   191

11. Mark Twain: The Triumph of Humor
    JAMES M. COX   211

12. Walt Whitman's Omnisexual Vision
    JAMES E. MILLER, JR.   231

    Notes   263
    Index   287

NOTES ON CONTRIBUTORS

JAMES GROSSMAN practices law in New York City. He wrote *James Fenimore Cooper* for the American Men of Letters series (William J. Sloane Associates, 1949; reissued Stanford University Press, 1967) and has written a number of articles on literary and legal subjects. His latest piece is "Vanzetti and Hawthorne" in *American Quarterly*.

MARSTON LAFRANCE, Professor of English at Carleton University, Ottawa, is a Canadian scholar whose special interests are irony and American literature. He is now at work on Evelyn Waugh and Hart Crane.

SIDNEY HOOK is Emeritus Professor of Philosophy at New York University and Senior Research Fellow, Hoover Institution. He completed his graduate work at Columbia University under the supervision of John Dewey who wrote the introduction to his first published work, *The Metaphysics of Pragmation* (Open Court Publishing Company, 1927).

MISS ELEANOR M. TILTON is Professor of English at Barnard College. She has published articles on Melville, James, and other American writers and is the author of *Amiable Autocrat* (New York, 1947), a biography of Oliver Wendell Holmes, and the editor of T. F. Currier's *Bibliography of Oliver Wendell Holmes*. She is currently editing new and uncollected letters of Ralph Waldo Emerson.

ARLIN TURNER is Professor of English at Duke University and Editor of *American Literature*. His scholarly publications have dealt with Nathaniel Hawthorne, George W. Cable, and other American authors of the nineteenth century.

CLAYTON L. EICHELBERGER is Professor of English at The University of Texas at Arlington. He is the editor of *American Literary Realism, 1870–1910*.

WILLIAM L. HEDGES is Professor of English and Chairman of the American Studies Program at Goucher College. His publications include *Washington Irving* (The Johns Hopkins Press, 1965).

JAY LEYDA, translator and historian, has published works on Herman Melville and Emily Dickinson. *Kino* is a history of Soviet cinema, and his newest work is *Dianying,* an account of the film and film audience in China. He is a Guggenheim Fellow, and is now teaching at York University in Canada.

THOMAS L. MCHANEY has published articles and reviews on nineteenth- and twentieth-century American fiction. He is Assistant Professor of English at Georgia State University in Atlanta.

JOEL PORTE is Professor of English and American literature at Harvard University. His most recent book is *The Romance in America: Studies in Cooper, Poe, Hawthorne, Melville, and James* (Wesleyan University Press, 1969).

JAMES M. COX is Professor of English at Dartmouth College. He has published studies of Twain, Frost, Poe, and Whitman. His most recent book is *Mark Twain: The Fate of Humor* (Princeton University Press, 1966).

JAMES E. MILLER, JR. is Professor of English at the University of Chicago. He has written books on Whitman, Melville, James, Fitzgerald, and Salinger. His most recent publications are *Theory and Fiction: Henry James* (University of Nebraska, 1972) and *Word, Self, Reality: The Rhetoric of Imagination* (Dodd, Mead & Co., 1972).

PREFACE

> . . . almost the most prodigious asset of a coun-
> try, and perhaps its most precious possession, is
> its native literary product—when that product
> is fine and noble and enduring.
>
> MARK TWAIN

As of February 1973, one hundred volumes in the Center for Editions of American Authors series of definitive editions have been published or sealed. They include the works of twelve American writers: James Fenimore Cooper, Stephen Crane, John Dewey, Ralph Waldo Emerson, Nathaniel Hawthorne, William Dean Howells, Washington Irving, Herman Melville, William Gilmore Simms, Henry David Thoreau, Mark Twain, and Walt Whitman. The purpose of this collection of essays on the writers whose works are being issued in CEAA editions is to salute the scholar-editors who have produced them.

This is not the place for a history of the Center for Editions of American Authors, but a few facts about it are worth noting for readers who are not familiar with its work. The CEAA is a wing of the Modern Language Association of America, and has operated since 1966 with annual grants from The National Endowment for the Humanities. Nine editions of nineteenth-century American authors are funded—for editorial work only—through the CEAA; five additional editions of nineteenth-century American authors receive no editorial grants but are associated with the CEAA and operate under the editorial standards established by the CEAA. There are two separate editions of the works of Emerson and Mark Twain. A complete listing of CEAA editions is given at the end of this volume. The completion of the editions now projected will entail the publication of some 260 volumes.

A definitive edition recovers the author's full intentions from all the evidence; it is prepared without regard to time and cost; it includes all the evidence behind the editorial decisions; a volume is awarded the CEAA seal only after inspection by an outside expert; the editors of the funded volumes have foregone all royalties; the texts of the volumes, without the apparatus, are available to reprint publishers on a nonexclusive basis at a reasonable fee within two years of original publication.

This volume is not about the CEAA, nor are the contributors in any way connected with it. *The Chief Glory of Every People* has no special editorial or critical rationale. The plan was simply to have a specialist on each of the authors whose works are being issued in the CEAA series of definitive editions prepare a new essay on his figure. They were asked to omit any consideration of the CEAA unless they found it necessary to do so, and there are only a couple of passing references to the CEAA in this volume. It was suggested to the contributors that they consider writing a reappraisal of their authors—i.e., "Stephen Crane in Our Time." But, as will be seen, those contributors who accepted the suggestion interpreted it quite differently. *The Chief Glory*, then, is intentionally unstructured—which is not necessarily a virtue, but it is deliberate. Even contributors who eschewed the "in-our-time" gambit backed into it; for example, Jay Leyda's survey of needed Melville research is a position report on the state of current scholarship. Because of their very dissimilarity these essays show that the study of American literature is thriving in 1973. A dozen scholars have written a dozen fresh essays demonstrating a variety of useful approaches to American literature. Although, as it will be argued below, literature itself is not necessarily practical, the best literary scholarship is functional: it helps us to understand the work and the author behind it. Of course, in the end the book belongs to the reader—it means to him what it means to him. Yet the professional study of literature works to expand and intensify—and to correct, where necessary—these meanings, to make better readers. To put it another way, literary scholarship is concerned with the permanence of literature.

The word relevance is used in several of these essays, and Sidney Hook's is titled "The Relevance of John Dewey." The words *relevance* and *relevant* have become loaded in the last five years or so, as Professor Hook indicates.* (I once heard a "committed" young man alibi his attendance at a Broadway entertainment by explaining that it was "surprisingly relevant.") If this loose collection of essays shows anything, it shows that great writers are always worth reading and studying and teaching—not because their work is applicable to contemporary problems, but because they provide pleasure and stimulation beyond the dimension of time. We hear nowadays that the novel is dead and even that literature isn't worth studying for its own sake. I submit that great literature is permanent because it is irrelevant to particular political-social-economic problems.

Ernest Hemingway, writing at a time when writers were under pressure to be relevant, stated the case for the permanence of literature as well as anyone: "A country, finally, erodes and the dust blows away, the people all die and none of them were of any importance permanently, except those who practised the arts, and these now wish to cease their work because it is too lonely, too hard to do, and is not fashionable. A thousand years makes economics

---

* John Dewey is the only systematic philosopher represented in this volume; therefore he represents an exception to some of the ideas about American literature expressed in this Preface. His ideas should be applicable to our contemporary problems if he is to have more than historical interest.

silly and a work endures forever, but it is very difficult to do and now it is not fashionable." * He wrote that in a book about the irrelevant activity of big-game hunting at a time when the United States of America was in the middle of the Great Depression.

There is very little difference, if any, between the cry that literature must be relevant to today's problems and the didactic heresy that literature must teach us how to be better human beings or better servants of God. It may well do these things—but that is not its prime function. It is enough that literature give us pleasure—aesthetic pleasure and intellectual pleasure and emotional pleasure and even the simple pleasure of recognition.

To be sure, writers have ideas about the problems of their times. But these ideas are of temporary value. Hawthorne's antiabolitionist sentiments do not matter today, except as they may help us to understand his work. Thoreau may or may not be a better writer than Hawthorne, but not because one was—or is—more "relevant." Writers write about the things they are moved to write about; and the marriage between an author and his material is usually far more binding than any other marriage he enters into: "But, my God! it was my material, and it was all I had to deal with." † Picture the consternation when Melville informed his publisher that he was writing a novel about a deranged captain's search for a particular whale—a white one: "It'll never sell, Herman. It isn't relevant." A writer's material is shaped by his life and his era; but his work achieves permanence only by transcending the contemporary, by doing something or saying something that will move readers forever after. *The Red Badge of Courage* is a Civil-War novel by an author who was born six years after the war ended, and it is not about the "relevant" aspects of the war at all.

* *Green Hills of Africa*. New York: Charles Scribner's Sons, 1935, p. 109.
† F. Scott Fitzgerald, introduction to *The Great Gatsby*. New York: Random House, 1934.

This is not to deny that the classics of literature are often applicable, to a greater or lesser extent, to present-day problems, as James E. Miller, Jr. demonstrates in his essay on Whitman's omnisexual vision or as William L. Hedges shows in his analysis of Irving's view of the American dream of success. Certainly the problems of conscience confronted by Emerson and Thoreau will always be with the human race. But, remember, Emerson and Thoreau were not imaginative writers: they were thinkers more than creators. Perhaps, then, the case I am making for the irrelevance of literature should be limited to Cooper, Crane, Hawthorne, Howells, Melville, Simms, Mark Twain, and possibly Whitman. Yet Emerson and Thoreau have escaped the calendars, too, because their ideas—and, more important, their expression of their ideas—were not limited to particular issues of their time.

It is my conviction—and I have not consulted the contributors on this point—that what gives great literature permanent value is its irrelevance—it is as useless as any other art form, as useless as *Swan Lake* or a Modigliani. These remarks are appropriate to this volume because the CEAA is engaged in producing definitive and therefore permanent editions of classic American writings—editions that will never have to be done all over again. The expenditure of time and money—millions of dollars and the time of some two hundred scholars and students for the first 260 volumes—can only be justified in terms of the permanence of American literature. I don't know what will seem relevant in 2073; but I am certain that these authors will be read—some more than others, as their reputations shift—and that careful readers will be reading CEAA editions to find the authors' intentions.

Matthew J. Bruccoli, Director
Center for Editions of American Authors

Columbia, S. C.
July 25, 1972

Fenimore Cooper
The Development
of the Novelist

JAMES GROSSMAN

American fortunes can be lost as well as made, and social mobility can be downward as well as upward. This is nowhere so visible as in the lives of our first great American writers. Washington Irving, Fenimore Cooper, Melville, Poe—all, at some time before taking up writing as a permanent career, suffered a serious diminution in worldly prospects.

Cooper's father, Judge William Cooper, who founded Cooperstown, New York, was at the time of his death in 1809 one of the wealthy men of America; his sons were well provided for by his will. Yet in a period of ten years the bulk of the family fortune was lost and Cooper's five brothers had died, some of them insolvent; Cooper assumed the burden of their debts and contributed to the support of their wives and children. From this background and this experience some of Cooper's main themes were to emerge.

Around the time of the death of the last of his brothers Cooper in 1819, at the age of thirty, began his writing career, seemingly by accident. "I could write you a better book than that myself," he had said to his wife in criticism of a novel of English family life that he was reading aloud to her, and on her dare proceeded to. *Precaution* (1820), the bad novel he wrote about English family life, was of course a false start, but it has an awareness of the deceptiveness of appearances, an intensity of interest in the problems of life and society, that were to reappear in his later work. As a novelist he was to be profitably interested in the practice of professions: in the complications of landholding, in the manners and morality of military and naval life, in the conduct of lawyers. His chief mistake in *Precaution* is to treat its subject, marrying off daughters, as if it too were a profession, consciously followed and with its own rules and code of ethics.

With his second book, *The Spy*, Cooper became famous, with the third, *The Pioneers*, great. He had turned from England to America for his subjects, a patriotic tale of the American Revolution, a charming, amused, loving account of life in a new settlement, Templeton, much like Cooperstown, with a founder, Judge Temple, much like Judge Cooper. For his magnificent use of native material the highest praise his country and the rest of the world could give him was to call him the American Scott, a tag that to us, and probably to Cooper in later life, seems at once to concede inferiority and bumptiously to assert equality. It contains, nevertheless, at least as applied to these two works, genuine and intelligent criticism of Cooper.

Like one of Scott's novels of border warfare, *The Spy* (1821) is set in the land between contending armies. This neutral ground in Westchester, where loyalties are uncertain, life not safe, property insecure, is not only fought over by the regular armies, with more or less civilized punctilio, but is at the mercy also of marauding partisans of each side, the American Skinners and the British Cowboys, who give to the fighting some of the brutal horror of Scott's caterans. As Scott, reconciled to England, manages to give an impression of fairness to both sides regardless of where his romantic sympathies fall, so Cooper does too, aided perhaps by the fact that his wife's family, the De Lanceys, were on the king's side in the war and one of them was even a Cowboy leader.

In *The Pioneers* (1823) Natty Bumppo, an old hunter known locally as Leather-Stocking, who had hunted on the site of Templeton long before the Judge came with his settlement that made game scarce, can not fit into the new world. Ironically, the hunter, the one man in the community never wasteful of animal life, is the only one arrested for violating the new game laws; he has killed out of season a deer that dogs were chasing and soon would themselves have killed. What explodes the story into greatness is a plot device of the sort Scott uses: Natty is a servant hiding his master, a former English officer, and like a feudal retainer, must resist the search of his hut. Natty's grand confrontation with the law of the settlement is brought on by his loyalty to an old tie; it leads in the end to his breaking all ties and to his going to the West, like so many Americans, to be forever free of the restraints of society and its laws.

Natty Bumppo, for whom there was no place in the settled world that Cooper knew, had entered deeply into Cooper's imagination. Cooper was to use Natty over the years in four more novels: *The Last of the Mohicans* and *The Prairie*, published in 1826 and 1827 at the height of Cooper's popularity, *The Pathfinder* and *The Deerslayer*, published in 1840 and 1841 in the midst of his quarrel with his neighbors and his bitter libel suits against the press. When the five *Leather-Stocking Tales*, to give them the name Cooper himself used, are read in the order of the events of Natty's life, the last written, *The Deerslayer*, is the first, *The Pioneers*, the fourth, and *The Prairie*, in which Natty dies, the last. But the most profitable way to follow Natty, it seems to me, is in terms not of his but of Cooper's life. From Natty's beginnings as a grumbling old man in *Pioneers*, a mixture of realism and Scott, to his chivalrous youth in *Deerslayer*, on his first warpath with his noble friend Chingachgook, the drunken old Indian of *Pioneers*, Natty has become in Cooper's hands one of the great mythic characters in American fiction, the embodiment of an American dream.

After *Pioneers*, which an English magazine called in praise a palpable though not a servile imitation of Scott, Cooper seems in his next two novels, *The Pilot* (1824) and *Lionel Lincoln* (1825), to be trying to free himself from his master. Cooper had undertaken *The Pilot*, he insisted, after a conversation in which he maintained that Scott's *Pirate* did not have the knowledge of seamanship its admirers found in it, and to show what a seaman could do with ships and the sea as a subject. He had spent five years as a common sailor in the merchant marine and as a midshipman in the navy, and through his real knowledge of the sea created with *The Pilot* a new genre, the sea tale, that he was to develop magnificently throughout his entire career. Cooper liked to dwell, with simple pride and at times argumentatively, on the originality of *The Pilot*. If it is only the first step that counts, and not the later steps, *The Pilot* is Cooper's most original achievement. But perhaps this only shows how much Cooper and his contemporaries, and we ourselves too, overvalue originality. For *The Pioneers*, with its strange, beautiful scenes of daily activity, its unhurried account of the hurried building of a new world, the impassivity with which it regards the death of the degraded old Indian and the exile of the old hunter, is, it seems to me, a far finer, more serious book, for all its echoes of Scott, than the uniquely original and thrilling *Pilot*.

In *Lionel Lincoln* Cooper seems to be going back to the Waverley novels, in fact to Waverley itself. Lionel is an officer in the English army called on to serve in Massachusetts at the outbreak of the Revolution. It is refreshing to see Lexington and Concord—two splendid chapters—from the British point of view, to feel the shame of the retreating officers, harried, forced to dismount and march like common soldiers, fired on from behind barns and fences by farmers and shopkeepers who have the impudent courage to go back to Boston to sell provisions to the British at high prices but who will not, indeed can not, stand up in orderly ranks to fight like honest men. Lionel does not share the feelings of his fellow officers, for he is American-born and rejoices in his despised countrymen's valor if not in their cause. We are certain that ultimately, just as Waverley did, Lionel will join the rebels and fight on their side. Our reasonable expectation is suddenly and melodramatically frustrated. Lionel in the end is loyal to England. The wise old patriot whose fervent talk of liberty had influenced Lionel turns out to be Lionel's father and, more significantly, a dangerous, murderous madman whose notion of the greatest foe of liberty is his keeper and the greatest wrong ever done to liberty his detention in the madhouse from which he has escaped. Cooper's tale if written today might be taken to be a parable pointing out that political liberty is a pointless ideal when compared to the freedom of the individual, even that of a dangerously demented one. It could not have meant this to Cooper, at the time an apparently conventionally patriotic American; and yet it may have meant something close to it. He was always inclined to believe in the force of oaths and covenants; obeying them made for stability. If it was right for Lionel, as it was for the De Lanceys, to remain bound by an oath, perhaps it is madness to try to shake the loyalty of the oath-bound. Yet, whatever it means, *Lionel Lincoln*, whose hero fails to act like his counterpart in Scott, is Cooper's first setback in his career as a novelist.

In 1826, Cooper at the height of his fame went to Europe with his family and stayed there for seven years. His work took on a romantic intensity of patriotism that only distance from home can give. *Notions of the Americans: Picked up by a Travelling Bachelor* (1828), a non-fiction work about America inspired by a request of Lafayette, is sober in its facts. American life, Cooper admits, tends to create uniformity and mediocrity, but somehow it is all made to sound like a golden idyll. An enchantment is given to pre-Revolutionary American pirates in *The Red Rover* (1827) and to pre-Revolutionary American smugglers in *The Water-Witch* (1830). His truest American achievement in Europe, he always maintained, lay in the three novels he wrote about European life, *The Bravo* (1831), *Heidenmauer* (1832), *The Headsman* (1833). In them he brought American opinion, as he put it, to bear on European facts. He examined aristocracy and found it to be a system benefiting only aristocrats.

Cooper's romantic European novel, *The Bravo*, is his

first successful novel of ideas. It is Cooper's theme that the republic of Venice with its great concern for public welfare and virtue was an elaborate mechanism to benefit only the few and that it succeeded because in large part even these few believed in its pretensions and did not realize what a narrow, vicious mechanism it actually was.

Cooper, a careless slovenly writer like other great novelists of his time, apparently rarely taking time to rewrite, was nevertheless a craftsman working steadily at the problems of his craft—whether aware that it is a craft or that it has problems, we are not quite sure. He is often struggling in one novel after another with the same idea or device or turn of plot, using it sometimes awkwardly sometimes cheaply, until he finds a work in which it fits perfectly as the embodiment of his meaning.

The Bravo is one of the first of these perfect solutions. From *Precaution* on, there is often in a Cooper novel a character engaged apparently in wicked conduct who yet retains our sympathy and interest. Our question as readers is, why has the novelist attracted us to people who commit unattractive acts? The novelist's answer is evasive. Judge Temple in *The Pioneers*, who has bought up his Loyalist partner's land on a confiscation sale and selfishly kept it for himself, explains at the end that he has held it on a secret trust for his partner's family, the Effinghams, and has not revealed it to them in order not to interfere with their chance of recoupment from the British government. The charming young man who has turned pirate under the Rover is actually a naval officer who has been sent to capture him. The dashing smuggler in *The Water-Witch* with whom the heroine has run off turns out to be a girl, the heroine's cousin. The sad, attractive bravo, by reputation Venice's worst assassin, has not committed the atrocious murder of his poor friend of which he has been convicted; he has in fact never killed anyone. We are certain that the bravo will be pardoned and at as late a moment as possible. But the signal that comes from the palace while he is on the block is for his execution; the heroine who has come forward to throw herself into her lover's arms is met by his head rolling toward her on the stones. Cooper's use of the device of apparent wickedness and absolute goodness is this time not an evasion but the very moral of his tale: the good man must appear to be wicked so that the wicked state may appear to be good. Having found the perfect use for his device, and having successfully stood his story on its head to make its meaning clear as he had once stood it on its head, in *Lionel Lincoln*, only to muddy it, Cooper, I believe, never used this device again.

With *The Bravo*, for which he received £1,300 for its publication in Great Britain, Cooper was at the top of his worldly success. In the course of the next decade he succeeded in making himself one of the most unpopular men in America. The steps by which he came to be mocked and vilified by the most powerful American newspapers are many—some praiseworthy, such as his taking Lafayette's side in a political controversy over the relative cost of the French and American governments; some foolish, as in his unfounded but persistent belief that an unfriendly review of *The Bravo* in a New York newspaper was a translation from the French, a hidden attack instigated by the French government because of his taking Lafayette's side; some an astounding mixture of the silliest folly and profound wisdom, as in *A Letter to His Countrymen* (1834) in which he discusses the unfortunate American tendency to defer to European opinion, his prime examples being his own supposed mistreatment and American reliance on false political analogies from abroad. To give but one instance of this unwise reliance: because English aristocrats obtained control of their government by stressing always the dangers of the Executive, the monarchy, Americans foolishly believe that our Executive, the president, is to be feared, whereas in fact the danger of usurpation comes not from the president but from Congress; Cooper was not only making a fascinating and still interesting political analysis but, more narrowly, was also undermining the basis on which the new Whig party was attacking his fellow-Democrat, "King" Andrew Jackson. The *Letter* ends with a dignified farewell to writing; the very next year he resumed his career with *The Monikins* (1835), an over-ingenious, fatiguing animal satire dealing, as the *Letter* had, with the relations of England and America.

The prosperous, commercial, democratic America to which Cooper returned in 1833 may have changed from the America he had left seven years before, but perhaps there was an even greater change in Cooper, who had violated Jefferson's dictum that an American should not stay abroad more than five years. The tendency to uniformity and mediocrity so warmly remembered in Europe in *Notions* was hard to bear in fact. He found that he had been a freer man, could speak his mind more freely, in Bourbon France than in egalitarian America.

He had been troubled by Americans abroad because they did not assert their equality with English lords; back home in Cooperstown he was troubled because his fellow-Americans aggressively asserted their equality with him. The villagers would not even recognize that the pleasant, empty bit of land on Otsego Lake, three miles from Cooperstown, on which they had picnicked "from time immemorial" was Cooper family property but preferred to believe that it was somehow theirs. A grossly distorted, widely published version of this quarrel with his neighbors—which was not about the picnicking itself but whether Cooper, who had no intention of stopping it, had the right to—led to Cooper's first libel suits against the press and to his first novels about contemporary American manners, one, the attractive *Homeward Bound*, the other, its unattractive sequel, *Home as Found* (both 1838).

As the Templeton of *The Pioneers* was based on Cooperstown, it was inevitable that Cooper should use Templeton again and sound (as a matter of novel-writing) that he should use as characters the descendants of Judge Temple, the Effinghams (unaware apparently that the head of the family, the mild, handsome Edward Effingham, who lived in a house like Cooper's in a town like Cooperstown and had a quarrel like Cooper's with his neighbors, would be taken to be Cooper's portrait in praise of himself).

He had originally planned to write only one book, beginning with the Effinghams on shipboard at Sandy Hook, returning home from a long stay in Europe. As if unwilling to come ashore to face the unpleasantness of the American scene, he placed his beginning further back, to the commencement of the voyage, so that the novel-length *Homeward Bound* is wholly taken up with the journey home. With a sense of duty to his theme the problems of American life that were besetting him are brought aboard ship to the small various world of a transatlantic packet, a delightful setting for a comedy of manners, and a new use for the sea tale.

In *The Pioneers* the Judge, crowded together with his settlers in the one place of worship and in the only other meeting place, the tavern, managed somehow to keep his distance from them. On the packet the Effinghams are helpless before the snooping Steadfast Dodge, the editor of the *Active Inquirer* in Templeton. On behalf of active inquiry—something we still believe in or at least encourage—he pushes everywhere, into the large cabin that the Effinghams have hired for their privacy. To score against Dodge, and perhaps because the sea tale required adventure, Cooper has the packet wrecked and has the ship's company and the able male passengers, except the cowardly editor, fighting bravely against the Arabs. Cooper has married his comedy of manners and his adventure story a little awkwardly—he was to do it better later—but it is nevertheless a worthwhile union. The comicalness of things, the ordinary embarrassments of life, for the first time in his work, persist even amid the adventure and were to persist in some of the later sea tales.

The novelist's most skillful achievement in *Homeward Bound* is in having the events of the story proceed from the character of the packet's master, Captain Truck, who is entranced by questions of manners. It is a point of manners that causes the start of the chase of the packet by the British warship, and it is a point of manners that ends it, that resolves the grave question whether in the waters of New York Harbor the captain should surrender the English embezzler to the warship. Captain Truck is reluctant to give up the foolish young man who has fought the Arabs so well. Insulted by an English treasury official, Truck puts the official off the packet. Unfortunately for the young man, politeness now demands that, having won on this minor issue, the captain should gracefully concede the major one; his sense of propriety demands not only that he should surrender the embezzler to the warship but also that, since he has failed to perform his undertaking to carry him to New York as a passenger, he should first return to him his passage money.

Just as Dodge in *Homeward Bound* fawned on the embezzling clerk masquerading as a baronet, in *Home as Found* Americans in New York fawn on everything English. It is a fault of which the inhabitants of Templeton are free, and we ought to admire them for it. We cannot, for they are too unpleasant in their fierce egalitarianism and too smugly righteous in their active inquiry into the private life of the Effinghams. Cooper has given them no function except to grumble against Edward Effingham and his daughter, and yet the villagers are alive, if not in themselves, in the vividness of their speech, and Aristabulus Bragg, the pleasantly disingenuous lawyer who acts as a buffer between his employer, Edward Effingham, and his true masters, the people, is genuinely alive. It is Edward and Eve Effingham who are lifeless, above all in their stilted speech.

Cooper, our great novelist of adventure, has a curious ideal of inaction for his upper-class characters. In order not to soil themselves they recoil from life, a withdrawal much like those "confounded renunciations" that Philip Rahv finds so distasteful in James's heroes and heroines. Edward Effingham does not renounce his property rights to the Point; nominally he preserves them, but his supineness in the face of the villagers' tyranny contributes to making *Home as Found* a remarkably unpleasant book.

This ideal of inaction was to find its triumphant use in Cooper. In his very next novel, *The Pathfinder*, the British commander, so easygoing that he has a dangerous traitor in his post whom he never bothers to find, comes off better in our minds than his opposite number, the efficient, active French officer who employs the traitor.

"Traitor" was one of the terms, "base-born caitiff" another, that editors used of Cooper in writing of *Home as Found*; unlike Edward Effingham, he responded vigorously. He brought a new series of libel suits and was for years involved in them. They ruined his standing with the press and to some extent with the public. They should also, we would predict, have ruined his work as well. But his output was as abundant as ever and during the years of his most intense litigation, on the whole, better than ever.

One of his most famous books, *The Deerslayer*, comes from this period. After *Lionel Lincoln*, it seems to me Cooper's most ambiguous novel. On the surface it is a story of adventure that relies on brilliant contrasts. Natty Bumppo, the young deerslayer, fights Indians chivalrously, the other two white men fight treacherously, scalping women and children for the bounty the Colony offers. The two white women of the story are sisters: Hetty virtuous and half-witted, Judith wicked and intelligent (using virtuous and wicked in the Victorian sense). Natty carries his notions of chivalry—or as he would put it his "white gifts"—so far that, released by the Indians to carry a message, an offer to free him if Judith will become a squaw, after delivering the message he returns to the Indians, even though this leaves the two women unprotected. The fantastically inner-directed Natty is keeping faith with a tribe, one of whose warriors a few days before had offered him friendship and then fired on him when Natty ashamed of his distrust had imprudently dropped his guard for a moment. Yet Natty is as certain as Lord Jim that honor demands that he keep his word to the savages. It is one of the ambiguities of the story that Cooper shows none of the doubts that Conrad has about the conduct of his hero. (Later, in *Satanstoe*, an honorable man breaks off a parley and starts firing rather than return to a captivity that meant the certain death of the Negro slave who was with him.)

Before he goes back to be tortured, Natty, to show his skill with his new rifle, shoots an eagle, a waste of life he regrets a little too piously. It is these childish idle shots that save him, for they bring on the Redcoats who massacre the Indians and rescue him.

We have the feeling of being in the midst of a fairy tale where failing to help others or performing trivial, meaningless acts—and here we have both—is the right way to overcome dangers. In a way, Cooper's resort to magic is unobjectionable, for this last-written book about Natty is the first in terms of his life—he cannot die. We might understand the story better if it were more frankly mythic throughout; it has generally, instead of the suggestion of magic, a tone of great seriousness, which the occasional magical means do not diminish. We are left, as in Kafka, on the verge of a great enlightenment, bewildered yet not dissatisfied that it does not come.

As well as becoming a novelist of ideas, as in the *Home* novels, Cooper was turning into a novelist of crotchets, inventing crotchety characters to express his extravagant views and also to express his very sane views extravagantly. Jack Effingham, Edward's sharp-tongued cousin, speaks for the crotchety side of Cooper in the *Home* novels. But Jack is at times too argumentative, too sneering in his comments, and we are not sure then that it is Cooper's views that we are hearing.

Cooper discovered that the way to make himself clear was not to curb his spokesmen but daringly to give them their head. In *Afloat and Ashore* and *Miles Wallingford* (both 1844), two halves of a double-length "I was born" novel supposedly written in the narrator's middle sixties, the first person form permits the author to be willfully self-indulgent. Cooper has abandoned the relatively disciplined but restricting dialogues of the *Home* novels for the luxuriant anarchy of the monologue. One would expect catastrophe (and it was to come in *The Redskins*) but *Miles Wallingford*, to use the hero's name as the title of both parts, is a remarkable success. Miles interrupts his adventures at their most exciting moments to air his views —correcting current opinion on questions of international law, scoffing at the current Greek Revival houses. He so obviously is enjoying himself, is so high-spiritedly happy in his complaints, which are so much like Cooper's, that he carries off the tour de force of an impossibly long adventure story, which, however, is usually better on sea than on land.

When we go forward in Cooper's work we find that extravagant views of Jack Effingham's, which we had taken to be dramatic devices, the excess of argument, are actually Cooper's. Jack, arguing with a cultivated Englishman aboard the packet, maintains that after the Stuarts were deposed and the House of Hanover substituted, with the powers of the monarch curbed and those of the Whig aristocrats increased, Parliament so constituted could no longer make laws for the American colonies, even apparently seventy-five years after the Stuarts' overthrow. This seems a fanciful notion by a conservative consoling himself that there never was a rebellion by America. Its essential part, that the Hanoverians were not lawful kings,

shows up next in Cooper's nonfiction, in a review of
Lockhart's *Life of Scott* (a work naturally disappointing
to Cooper, for the references to him quoted from Scott's
journals are brief and slighting and give no idea of the
extent of their acquaintance in Europe or of Cooper's
effort to help the financially troubled Scott to obtain
American copyright for his work). In his review Cooper
is outraged that Scott could speak of George IV as his
king *de jure*, even though this was more than a century
and a quarter after the Glorious Revolution of 1688
and at a time when there was no serious Stuart Pretender.

What is serious for us is not the quirky oddness of his
views on the House of Hanover but the splendid use to
which Cooper put them in one of his best sea tales, *The
Two Admirals* (1842), which like *Richard II* and *Major
Barbara* is concerned with the mystery of legitimacy and
succession. An English law baron has such respect for the
laws of property that he does not want his own bastard
son to be left his brother's great estate. A stranger from
over the water in Virginia is the true heir and despite the
bastard's opposition makes good his claim to the estate
and is welcomed back to his inheritance. The very men
who welcome him oppose the other stranger from over
the water, their true prince, the Young Pretender, who
has just landed in Scotland. Only the thoughtful Admiral
Bluewater and a Papist see the analogy between the two
claimants. All of the others, including Bluewater's close
friend and superior, the commander-in-chief of the fleet,
accept without question and without thought the Hano-
verian George as their king. The captains of Bluewater's
division, on the eve of fighting the French who support
the Pretender, know nothing and care nothing about the
reasons for the war in which they are to engage. ("Pray
what is the rumpus all about? . . . They're an uneasy
set ashore . . .") Bluewater hopes to keep them out of
the battle through their unreasoning obedience to him as
their immediate superior in the chain of command, but

he himself is the victim of unreason, of friendship; he cannot abandon his superior who against odds has thrown his ships into battle. Bluewater comes to his friend's rescue to win and to die in a battle that according to his rational principles should be lost. His blind friendship, the others' unthinking professionalism, have triumphed over the claims of legitimacy. But what we as readers are made to see—whether Cooper wanted us to or not it is still his achievement—is that the new arrangements men have made, no matter how doubtful in their origins, have their legitimacy if they last, that the present, the world we live in, has its right to be free of the claims of the past.

The right to be free of the past is most easily won by being indifferent to it. The fleet, which we would think would cherish ancient traditions, is interested in the present. We see it in its many aspects as a living tissue of complicated interrelations. The midshipman who is called "My lord" because he is the son of a duke has to carry out orders that are usually given to a servant. It is above all the sheer professionalism, the lack of pretension to patriotic motives, the frank interest in pay, rations, prize money, promotions, the concerns of everyday life, that fascinate Cooper and delight us. Cooper in his next novel of the sea, *The Wing-and-Wing* (1842), so holds our interest in the professional life of the British navy that he actually makes us see from an English officer's point of view the complexity of the problems that arise from impressing as an Englishman a sailor so American that he is called by his fellow seamen "The Yank" and treating him as a deserter when he naturally tries to escape.

Cooper often has in his novels a character, usually a minor one, who has a single dominating trait, a humor, as it used to be called, that governs most of his conduct. It is often a tiresome device. In *The Two Admirals* he uses it prodigally. The captains are little more than humors; if one is domestic and has his wife decorate his cabin, another will not let his wife aboard ship. Our feeling that we are seeing in all of its rich variety the life of a whole fleet comes in part from the number of mechanically contradictory humors Cooper has used. Once again we see that the novelist in handling his technical problems has discovered that too much of a bad thing can make it good.

The Wing-and-Wing is the only novel of Cooper in which the hero dies (I mean in his young manhood in the course of the tale and not in an after note describing his later years). Death was a technical device frequently used by nineteenth-century novelists to solve a problem, and it may be useful, if a trifle grisly, to look briefly at some of Cooper's deaths.

The most famous are Uncas's and Cora's in *The Last of the Mohicans*. Uncas's is necessary for his father, Chingachgook, to be left the childless last of his race, Cora's in order that she and Uncas, who have been attracted to each other, can be united in "the blessed hunting-grounds of the Lenape" in the funeral chant of the Indian maidens. The sentimental union hereafter avoids the unpleasant question of the intermarriage of the two races here on earth, which is prohibited by a taboo so strong that its violation, as we see in Conanchet and Ruth in *The Wept of Wish Ton-Wish* (1829), must be punished by death.

In *Wing-and-Wing* the devout Catholic heroine, although she loves him, has refused to marry the romantic atheistic Frenchman who is filled with enthusiasm for his country's Revolution and hatred of priests. Her refusal is in part the cause of his reckless death that suggests not only punishment but also, with some skill, how hopeless their marriage would have been. Dying, Raoul's genuine tenderness can take the form of Revolutionary cant: "Poor Ghita! Well, thine is not the only innocent mind by millions that hath been trammelled by priests." After Raoul is dead, lying on the ground with his eyes still open, and Ghita is alone "she bent over the body, gazing long and wistfully into those windows of the soul that had so often beamed on her in manly tenderness, and she felt like a miser with his hoarded gold, unwilling to share it with any other." Amid the now stale genteel rhetoric the sudden freshness of the metaphor of the miser carries with it a hint of triumph, of the long happiness the bereft woman will have in living with the memory of the dead lover who alive could only have made her unhappy.

Long sentimental death scenes were fashionable, and Cooper has his in *Miles Wallingford* just a few years after the death of Little Nell. Miles's sister, Grace, dying leaves her money to a young man whom she loves but who loves another. Henry James in *The Wings of the Dove* has avoided Cooper's sentimentality by avoiding Milly Theale's death scene entirely, but in the end it is Cooper who has been more realistic about the dying woman's gift: unlike Merton Densher, Grace's young man accepts the money and marries the woman for whom he has jilted Grace.

After *The Deerslayer* Cooper's work in setting and tone is generally closer to ordinary life and often hostile to romantic attitudes. He seems even to repent of earlier romances, or at least to feel the need to treat the same themes again to bring out this time the ugliness in them, so that the glamorous smuggling of *The Water-Witch* and the elegant piracy of *The Red Rover* become shabby mean trades in *Autobiography of a Pocket Handkerchief* (1843) and *Jack Tier* (1848). The seamy underside of the American Revolution, which had been a small if significant part of *The Spy*, becomes in *Wyandotte* (1843) almost the whole story, and we are left with the impression that the struggle for freedom was an effort of demagogues to confiscate the property of their betters. This darkest of Cooper's treatments of the Revolution is much more than a gloomy political tract. The confused vagueness of the fighting, the treacherous murders, like the murders at the climax of *Jack Tier*, seem to point to some deep uncertainty about the goodness of life, an uncertainty that the last few pages of each book try to cover up. The murders in *Jack Tier* are the more horrible because they are the work of a commonplace villain and the most appalling of them is of a silly commonplace woman who at the moment of death is talking foolishly with her murderer. That in her misuse of nautical speech she is copied from the admiral's widow in *The Red Rover* is not, I believe, a failure of invention on Cooper's part but a deliberate signal to the reader to be aware of the relation between the two works, of the lush romantic wickedness of the early one that has withered into hideous banal horror. Lounsbury, writing in a perhaps more assured age than ours, found the climax of *Jack Tier* "merely grotesque and absurd"; for a modern reader, if we drop the "merely" it is a perfect description.

Cooper's five novels about Natty Bumppo, his greatest accomplishment, were not planned as a series but more or less accidentally took the shape of one in the course of being written over a period of nineteen years, and were not brought together as *The Leather-Stocking Tales* until 1850, the year before his death. The one grand opus he did plan is *The Littlepage Manuscripts* (1845–46), a trilogy about three generations of great New York landlords and their relations with their tenants, inspired by that rowdy jacquerie which because of its considerable violence and occasional bloodshed is known in New York history as the Anti-Rent War.

The first in this series of first person narratives, *Satanstoe*, is one of Cooper's sunniest and most charming books. He uses the first person form brilliantly about a person not like himself and not even like himself in his ideas, a young colonial in the 1750s, open to life and adventure, happy in every relation, seeing in domestic slavery, and in his personal slave, only ties of loyalty and affection, and equally happy looking upward, so certain

of the superiority of the England he looks on as home
that he pleasantly takes for granted the condescension of
well-bred Englishmen to him. This certainty of English
superiority helps him win the charming wealthy heroine;
for she is sure that her other suitor, the heir to a baron-
etcy, cannot truly love her but has been driven to love
by a long tour of duty in the colonies.

The second *Littlepage Manuscript*, *The Chainbearer*,
set in the disturbed American world at the end of the
Revolution, is a more powerful but less successful work,
perhaps because its narrator, Mordaunt Littlepage, unlike
his father comes to grips with his subject, the relations
of large-scale landlords with their tenants. Cooper tries
manfully to uphold the rights of property, but *The Chainbearer* succeeds most as a novel when it puts the propa-
ganda to flight. We are on Mordaunt's side, when for a
moment the tight-minded young man, forgetting his purpose, admits, "The earth is very beautiful in itself; but it
is most beautiful in the eye of those who have the largest
stake in it, I fear." But such an admission helps open our
eyes to how pathetically small is the stake the tenants
seek, how touchingly ineffectual their efforts to give
legality to their claim of title, as when they buy from a
squatter, trading an old saddle for his "betterments."

The Redskins is, I believe, universally considered a
novelistic catastrophe. Yet it has buried in it one of the
clearest statements of one of Cooper's greatest themes
that has been struggling since *The Pioneers*, since Chingachgook's death and Natty's exile, for full expression: life
and history are seen as an unending series of dispossessions.
In *The Redskins* an old Indian proclaims that now the
great white men who dispossessed the Indians are themselves being dispossessed. To Cooper, as to the Indian, the
defeat of the great landowners would be the passing of
the great race.

The first person narrative, which Cooper had been
using almost exclusively for several years, was abandoned

after the disaster of *The Redskins*. In the remaining five years of his career he wrote five novels, *The Crater* (1847), *Jack Tier, The Oak Openings* (1848), *The Sea Lions* (1849) and *The Ways of the Hour* (1850), no one of them truly distinguished by itself but, taken together, striking in the variety and freshness of their approach to new and old themes. Cooper's increasing interest in questions of religion leads to the conversion to Christianity of a murderous Indian in the forests of *The Oak Openings*, and of a rational Unitarian in the long antarctic winter of *The Sea Lions*. *Jack Tier* may have been for Cooper another aspect of religious faith—the horror of life without it. In both *The Crater* and *The Ways of the Hour* he is concerned with the problems of the society around him, showing in the one how a Utopian colony in the South Seas—Utopian because it is ruled by a benevolent despot—is ruined by demagogues, and in the other using the exciting theatre of a murder trial to demonstrate the absurdity of deferring to popular opinion, of counting noses to determine matters of fact that should be decided not by the rules of democracy but by the methods of science.

After *Ways of the Hour* Cooper decided to give up novel writing; it was becoming unprofitable. It is a decision that we possibly take too seriously because *Ways of the Hour* happens to be his last novel. He was after all only sixty-one, intellectually as alive as ever; had health and life not failed him, he might have resumed novel writing, as he had once before after saying farewell to it forever.

In the half century after Cooper's death in 1851 his literary reputation in America was at a low point. To a cultivated American, like Henry James in the mid-1870s, it was embarrassing that "the acutest critic the world has seen," Sainte-Beuve, should have admired *Red Rover* or that there should be "ardent allusions" to Cooper in such writers as Balzac and George Sand. One is struck above all by how much of Cooper's work seems to have quickly disappeared from view. James was probably unaware that the then daring notion of his *An International Episode*, that an American girl might refuse to marry an English lord, had been anticipated by Eve Effingham's refusal of the baronet in *Home as Found*. James's friend, Cooper's grandniece Constance Fenimore Woolson, was surprised a few years later to find in Florence that her great-uncle had written a charming book on Italy, surely a striking instance of the impermanence, the discontinuity, of American life that Cooper had so often described (". . . an American 'always' means eighteen months, and . . . 'time immemorial' is only since the last general crisis in the money market!").

Cooper was remembered almost solely as the author of *The Leather-Stocking Tales*, which were ruined literarily by Mark Twain in "Fenimore Cooper's Literary Offenses," a brilliant assault on Cooper's more or less serious faults in grammar and more or less trivial impossibilities in plot. Mark Twain's schoolma'am approach has long been a blight on Cooper. When interest in Cooper revived around forty years ago, it was possibly for this reason that it was chiefly in his nonfiction; his interesting political, social treatise, *The American Democrat*, and his travel books were reprinted for the first time since their original issue. His interest in the structure of society, or as he would put it, the question of station, is much like our own; we have come to realize that he is still close to our problems when he uses terms so stiff and old-fashioned, even in his own day, as *caste* and *master*, for he knew that the egalitarians' way of destroying the social inequality he was defending was to soften, and ultimately to suppress, the terms that accurately expressed it.

Interesting as Cooper is in his nonfiction, it is after all as a novelist that he should concern us, if we are to concern ourselves with his greatness. He is most accessible to us, most easily the subject of our concern, it seems to me, in those novels that like his nonfiction deal successfully with the structure and manners of a large segment of society. They are the novels also in which, if he is not a master of his form, he is at least an apt student of it. Any selection among them must be idiosyncratic; mine would be *The Pioneers, Homeward Bound, The Two Admirals, Satanstoe*. No work of Cooper's can be free of bad writing, but these—is it merely that the themes hold us more closely?—seem to me freer than most. But to limit ourselves to works that as a whole deal successfully with society in terms that we understand is to deprive ourselves of his great fragments, as Yvor Winters has called them, that abound even in his most imperfect work. It is also to deprive ourselves of what many have considered to be his masterpiece, *The Deerslayer*, which of all of Cooper's books is the furthest from the world we live in but, like our dreams, nearest to ourselves.

Stephen Crane
in Our Time

MARSTON LAFRANCE

In his preface to a twenty-year-old book about Stephen Crane, the late John Berryman warned scholars that "no one will ever be able to work casually at Crane and be certain of anything. So many people have been wrong about him so often." [1] And two subsequent decades of Crane scholarship suggest that serious work is in itself no guarantee that anyone, present company included, will be right about him either. The critical dice—which Berryman handled with great gusto and a certain success—are still loaded; real gamblers are obliged to stake their professional reputations; and anyone who has survived a few passes with even the clothes on his back has felt the immense odds against his breaking the bank and thereby closing this particular game. All of this is as it should be, certainly, for such conditions make the Crane corner of American literature an exciting place. The serious player can only do his homework with care, keep Berryman's warning firmly in mind, and then commit himself according to whatever light he has. My view of Crane, then, is very like that of Max R. Westbrook, James B. Colvert, Will C. Jumper, and Jean Whitehead Lang; [2] but these excellent scholars are not to be blamed if, during the next twenty years, my name should be added to Berryman's list.

The essential Stephen Crane, as I see him, is in no way dated: although he wrote during the 1890s what he has to say seems as current as if it had been written yesterday. Neither is he satisfactorily explained by any of the various critical labels which have been forced upon him—a whole shovelful of tags which Edwin H. Cady brought together ten years ago: "realist, romantic, naturalist, imagist, existentialist, symbolist, impressionist, expressionist, and *pointilliste* (I may have overlooked some)." [3] Crane is indeed a realist, but his is a psychological realism; and the qualifying adjective is necessary because he nowhere shows much interest in external reality for its own sake, at least not enough to present it without distortion (otherwise, of course, he would hardly have been called an imagist, impressionist, expressionist, or *pointilliste*). Morally, despite his "romantic" individualism, he seems to me about as hard and unromantic as it is humanly possible to become. He is not, and at no time ever was, a card-carrying naturalist or symbolist insofar as I seem able to understand these terms. What he has to say can reasonably be called existential in character—just as *Heart of Darkness, Billy Budd,* or the final chapter in *Letters from an American Farmer* can—but a knowledge of existentialism will in itself no more explicate "The Blue Hotel" than it will explain why Kurtz dies unhappily; and there is no reason to suppose that Crane thought he was writing specifically existentialist fiction. Crane, to me, is preeminently the ironist who wrote *The Red Badge of Courage, Maggie, George's Mother,* a few superb short stories and sketches, and two slim volumes of fascinating poems. And Crane's irony, as these writings should imply even at a first reading, is the stuff with which the dice are loaded: irony refuses to be caged by the literary historian's equations of race, place, time, and prior reading; it is not really necessary to symbolic fiction; irony of the caliber Crane commands is anathema to literary naturalism; and it is not particularly vulnerable to the erosions of time.

Time washes over Crane's work and touches only the material counters which his irony uses as playthings. Jimmie Johnson would now drive a different kind of truck in New York, among Fidsey Corcoran's professional paupers heroin would now claim precedence of alcohol, modern methods of killing one's own species are vastly more efficient than those Henry Fleming had to learn, and Alek Williams today might live in an integrated housing project. But the superficiality of all such changes borders upon the comic; in fact, like the surface scratches on a block of granite, they in themselves merely emphasize the permanence of what lies beneath. An illusory view of reality, for example—such as Maggie's blockheaded notion that Pete is a gentleman—still frustrates whoever acts upon it. Countless people, who are far better than Jimmie, conduct themselves with a deliberate hypocrisy to remain socially acceptable, to avoid facing up to their own indulgences. Everyone at some time has to cope with the problem confronting George Kelcey, who "was perfectly willing to be virtuous if somebody would come and make it easy for him." The only battles of any importance in *The Red Badge* are those which are fought within Henry's mind, and by winning them he conquers the psychological no-man's-land between boyhood and manhood. That mob-meanness which Crane uncovered in Whilomville remains a root evil of democracy, as omnipresent and vicious, as contemptible as ever. The current alarm over ecological problems implies a greater need than ever for aware "interpreters" of man's relations with external nature.

This timeless quality of Crane's work is most obvious in his poetry, for most of his best poems are extremely condensed ironic parables which float freely in a psychological landscape devoid of datable properties. External nature usually is generalized into a single image—the sea, mountains, a desert, "the universe"—either the protagonist or the observer is Everyman, and the action, explicit or implicit, is impersonal, universal to mankind. A comparatively simple example of this technique would be the following poem from *War Is Kind:*

> The wayfarer,
> Perceiving the pathway to truth,
> Was struck with astonishment.
> It was thickly grown with weeds.
> "Ha," he said,

"I see that none has passed here
In a long time."
Later he saw that each weed
Was a singular knife.
"Well," he mumbled at last,
"Doubtless there are other roads." [4]

The pathway to truth has to be a moral route. If it were not obscure and difficult to travel all men would take it, and they would thus honestly know truth instead of having to be hypocrites who merely pretend they know it. The impeding weeds suggest the external difficulties which beset any man's striving after truth, which insure that this path will be neglected; and if they appear to become insurmountable knives—as they do for the "way-farer"—the moral weaknesses of the traveler have reinforced the external hazards so heavily that all progress stops. The ironic barb in this poem, confirmed by many others, is the implication that most men soon give over and rejoin the "huddled procession" of those who, also aware that they have given up, live easy lives by communally defined values and public "truths"—all those who travel a superhighway, well-marked and easily traversed, which leads nowhere. Because they dare not leave this through-route they carry on until they drop, and meanwhile they cordially hate anyone who would again urge them off into the lacerating difficulties of the search for truth. The point, at the moment, is that such a poem applies to any man, anywhere, in any age. Crane's best fiction and sketches, once one gets beyond the surface properties, offer the same relevance. As man's entire packet of moral possibilities is likely to endure so long as man does, and as these moral qualities inevitably are the center of Crane's interest, the relevance of what he has to say partakes of the same permanence.

To read him in such fashion is, of course, to deny that what he has to say is literary naturalism. And anyone who denies naturalism in Crane opposes a critical doctrine of some thirty years' standing affirmed by such reputable scholars as Malcolm Cowley, Winifred Lynskey, Charles Child Walcutt, and Donald Pizer. All attempts to defend one's refusal to join this bandwagon immediately run head on into a critical maze of definitions, for *naturalism* is one of the most Protean terms in the critic's handbook; and the only way of emerging from this maze is, I believe, to ask oneself not what naturalism theoretically *may* be, but what it *has* to be if it is to function as a useful tool in the hands of anyone faced with the practical demands of critically analyzing a specific text. With this rather commonsense end in view, and a text written by Crane, naturalism, in either theory or critical practice, does not present insuperable difficulties. Lars Åhnebrink defined it, twenty years ago, as

a manner and method of composition by which the author portrays life *as it is in accordance with the philosophic theory of determinism* (exemplified in Zola's *L'Assommoir*). In contrast to a realist, a naturalist believes that man is fundamentally an animal without free will. To a naturalist man can be explained in terms of the forces, usually heredity and environment, which operate upon him.[5]

This definition essentially agrees with Parrington's—that in spite of the usual presence of objectivity, frankness, an amoral attitude on the part of the author toward his material, and a bias toward pessimism, philosophic determinism is absolutely "vital" to naturalism.[6] And in 1939, midway between Parrington and Åhnebrink, Charles Child Walcutt stated firmly that the occasional characteristics of naturalism—such as Parrington listed—can all be present in a work that is not naturalistic, that "a novel in which they appear will be naturalistic only when the philosophy of materialistic monism is somehow applied to its conception or execution."[7] By 1950, therefore, Proteus seemed securely trapped in critical nets unavailable to Howells, who used *naturalism* and *realism* interchangeably, or Norris, who considered naturalism an amalgamation of the best qualities of realism and romanticism.[8]

But then, in 1956, Walcutt attempted to surround naturalism by listing all its various hallmarks,[9] and as a result the definitive philosophic determinism became effectively buried among a double-handful of occasional characteristics all clamoring at once for precedence. Such an approach made the ground rules of naturalistic criticism so amorphous that anyone could play: all one had to do was find any combination of these characteristics in a given text and file such findings to claim the acreage for naturalism. Crane's works, already thus classified by literary historians (who seem to have ignored the poems and nearly everything written after *The Red Badge*), became a happy hunting ground because, quite obviously, the occasional characteristics of naturalism are everywhere present in them.

The environments in which Crane's stories and poems are set—the sea, a desert, the slums, the half-civilized West amidst a terrible blizzard, a shooting war—are certainly as bleak and unwholesome as those of *Moll Flanders*, *The Beggar's Opera*, or *Oliver Twist*. Crane's work reveals an effective use of both animal imagery, just as *Richard III* and *The Duchess of Malfi* do, and mechanistic imagery such as can be found in Capek's *R.U.R.* Except for Dr. Trescott, Crane's characters are common enough: like the rank and file one encounters in the Old Testament, they are from the middle and lower classes, not wealthy, not preeminently virtuous and just, not even overly intelligent. They suffer conspicuously from vanity, selfishness, fear, laziness, a whining self-pity, faulty perception—the human failings which beset all men. None can very enthusiastically be called heroic, for their limitations tend to constitute the essence of their reality.[10] The external world with which they have to cope is inevitably godless, mechanistic, amoral, "flatly indifferent" to man's moral and emotional life, and the separation between man and external nature is absolute; readers who do not care for Crane's style can examine the same external world, complete with the same separation from the moral world of man, in the poetry of Matthew Arnold. Crane's work, like most memorable literature from the Song of Deborah to the Snopes trilogy, contains plenty of violence; and survival is a real value so far as his characters are concerned, just as it is to Odysseus and Telemachus. Also, Crane is frank enough to call a spade a bloody shovel: although the "shocking" aspects of his work seem oversold, his dealings with taboo materials being rather small-business operations, to an age which vibrated over *Little Lord Fauntleroy* he may well have seemed frightful.

Thus, most of naturalism's traits are readily available: unwholesome environments, animal and mechanistic imagery, undistinguished characters from the lower classes, an amoral and mechanistic universe ultimately beyond man's control, violence, survival, taboo materials. But all of these qualities taken together do not make Crane a naturalist: all are means of saying what he wants to say, and the end—what is said—is not determinism. All of the above characteristics can be found in Steinbeck's *Grapes of Wrath*, for example, and in addition—insofar as neither the dust bowl nor the mess the Joads encounter in California is their fault—there is a good bit of environmental and economic determinism thrown in. But no one, presumably, would call this novel naturalism. The physical conditions of the dust bowl may be beyond man's control, but the novel specifically and angrily affixes the responsibility for human suffering upon human greed, fear, brutality, hypocrisy—upon precisely those human failings which are exposed with deadly efficiency in Crane's work. Hence, Åhnebrink's definition has to be accepted, I believe, if "naturalism" is to be a useful critical tool distinct from "romanticism" on the one hand and "realism" on the other. At least one post-Walcutt scholar has reaffirmed it in a tone of desperation: naturalism is "no more than an emphatic and explicit philosophical position taken by some realists," specifically a "pessimistic materialistic determinism." [11]

Naturalistic readings of Crane always seem apologetic in manner. The method used is that of Berryman's Freudian approach to Crane's life: instead of beginning with the text and finding out what the author has to say, the critic begins with an external body of dogma which tells him what he ought to find in the text. My quarrel with this apologetic criticism has three obvious fronts: it inevitably places undue emphasis upon Crane's earlier work; it inevitably (and sometimes hilariously) misreads the text in order to affirm the doctrine—or to show how Crane "failed" to measure up to its demands; and it is inevitably wasteful of Crane, that is, one always seems to end a naturalistic reading of a Crane work with enough unused parts left over to constitute a new story in themselves— all Crane's irony, all freedom and responsibility in the characters, all affirmations of moral realities, all force of conscience. Malcolm Cowley has argued, for example, that Henry Fleming "makes himself a hero by running away," [12] although the text clearly shows that he makes himself miserable by running away, so miserable, in fact, that after he returns he chooses to stay and risk death rather than run again into that awful forest. Winifred Lynskey claims that Henry's "moral victory" is "irrational and subhuman," [13] and thus she misses a couple of human results which Henry's comrades probably did not miss—that Henry, after perceiving (rationally, so far as I can determine) that "the great death" was, after all, "but the great death," simply shuts his loud mouth and accepts his position in the regiment; and this is the full extent of his "heroism." Walcutt has poor Henry running about an "equilateral triangle" of "instinct, ideals, and circumstance"; [14] and as this notion barely distinguishes him from the squirrel he sees in the forest, one hardly smiles when Walcutt has him run right past the tattered man without ever seeing him and desert Jim Conklin.

A much more regrettable sort of error concludes a fine essay on *Maggie* by Donald Pizer,[15] easily the best naturalistic critic of them all. This essay, which neither distorts the text nor is obviously wasteful of Crane, examines *Maggie*'s "characteristics which clash with its neat categorization as naturalistic fiction. For one thing [he observes immediately], Crane's technique of irony is foreign to the naturalistic vision; for another, Maggie herself, though she becomes a prostitute, is strangely untouched by her physical environment." And these remarks introduce some of the most intelligent criticism this novel has received. *Maggie*, he concludes, "is thus a novel primarily about the falsity and destructiveness of certain moral codes. . . . Crane's ironic technique suggests that his primary goal was not to show the effects of environment but to distinguish between moral appearance and reality, to attack the sanctimonious self-deception and sentimental emotional gratification of moral poses." So far so good—and very good indeed—but then, apparently as an afterthought, he tries to reclaim the book for naturalism and thereby falls off the wagon: Crane "was less concerned with dramatizing a deterministic philosophy than in assailing those who apply a middle-class morality to victims of amoral, uncontrollable forces in man and society. *Maggie* is therefore very much like such early Dreiser novels as *Sister Carrie* and *Jennie Gerhardt*." And this has to be nonsense because it contradicts all that Pizer himself has said superbly in this very essay. The forces which destroy Maggie are never amoral: they are always immoral—the cruelty, dishonesty, selfishness, sentimentalism, hypocrisy, and irresponsibility deliberately practiced by Pete, Mrs. Johnson, and (after chapter 13) Jimmie—and as such, assuredly, they never are uncontrollable by the human beings who willfully indulge them.

That aspect of Crane's work which lesser naturalistic

critics most often ignore, or run afoul of, is his irony—never more strident and overwhelming than it is in the early Bowery stories and sketches. Mrs. Johnson, Pete, George Kelcey, Charlie Jones, Bleecker, Fidsey Corcoran, the "assassin" of "An Experiment in Misery," the drunken father in "A Dark-Brown Dog," the "professional strays" in the crowd before the lodging-house door in "The Men in the Storm" are all treated with a contempt which is leashed by Crane's irony. When this leash is slipped, as it is in an angry letter to a woman who could not understand *Maggie*, the truth is delivered without ambiguity. All such people suffer from a conceit which is necessary to mask their moral cowardice: "A person who thinks himself superior to the rest of us because he has no job and no pride and no clean clothes is as badly conceited as Lillian Russell." And what follows is plainer still: "the root of Bowery life is a sort of cowardice . . . a lack of ambition or to willingly be knocked flat and accept the licking." [16] Although this letter has been quoted again and again, its obvious implication concerning Crane's fiction still seems to be missed: that if man's life is determined by external forces beyond his control then all such ironic lashings are gratuitous, and therefore either Crane must be a remarkably sloppy craftsman or these early works must not be naturalism.

A stylistic corollary of this critical impasse, by no means so obvious, is the fact that the techniques for exploiting irony are inimical to those which successfully handle naturalism, and the root cause of this hostility is the objectivity of the author toward his materials. Naturalistic writing, at least in theory, seeks to obliterate the personality of the author; thus the "scientific" objectivity of the naturalist emulates that of Stephen Dedalus's withdrawn god absently paring his fingernails. Detachment is just as important to ironic writing as it is to determinism, and when Crane's ironic objectivity wavers—as it does in the stories in *Wounds in the Rain*—the result is not first-rate fiction. But all ironic writing necessarily implies the moral and aesthetic preferences of the author. The objectivity of the ironist is only that which is necessary to sustain the tension between the antitheses he perceives, and thus he is implicitly present as the constant authority behind the specific ironies revealed in the work; otherwise there would be no great reason to read such a work ironically. Hence "the disappearance of irony as a prevailing tone is worth attention as a difference between Realism (Howells, Fuller) and Naturalism (Norris, Dreiser). It is a change in which the felt presence of the author's taste and reservations about human nature is succeeded, with an accompanying loss of incisiveness, by a truly faceless impersonality which is uncritical." [17] The distinction between these two kinds of objectivity can be felt by anyone who will read the artistic tour de force of Fleming's journey through the forest and then try *An American Tragedy*, an exchange which is a bit like laying aside a razor for a sandbag: although the latter instrument certainly is effective, it eventually becomes apparent—say after five hundred pages—that a sandbag lacks even a blunt edge.

Irony is not actively hostile to symbolic writing, but neither is it necessary. And if one asks which is the more important to Crane's work, irony or symbolism, the answer has to be irony, for reasons which seem to me unassailable. The mere existence and identification of any symbolic action or image utterly depends upon its context, and the context in every important Crane work is provided by a patterned progression of action which may as well be called a plot. This plot inevitably is the conceptual basis for the story; and as it recurs from story to story, and thus survives loss or gain of particular incidents and imagery, Crane's excellent emblematic images have to be a craftsman's embellishment of a preconceived structure. Thus, they function to reinforce the conceptual plot, and they cannot legitimately be extracted from their context and arranged into patterns expressive of meanings contrary to the implications of the plot which defines their function. Crane's imagery is all that anyone could wish—memorable, functional, original, conspicuously effective—but such a capacity no more makes him a symbolist than his poking about the slums of New York makes him a naturalist. That which makes Crane what he is, is his ironic mind.

The ironic mind is not easily described because it is a mental house divided against itself which obstinately refuses to fall. Sometimes it wavers, as Evelyn Waugh's apparently did prior to *The Ordeal of Gilbert Pinfold;* sometimes the tensions necessary to sustain the division become destructive, as may have happened with Swift; or the ironist can simply stop expressing himself, as Melville did for twenty years; or the tensions can relax toward a wry humor, as occurs in most of Mark Twain's work and in several of Crane's less important "Midnight Sketches"; or, apparently, irony can sour into mere vituperation such as one finds in *Generation of Vipers* or the later Mark Twain's fulminations against "the damned human race." But irony at its best produces intensely compacted prose of great energy in which every rift is overloaded with ore: *A Modest Proposal,* "Bartleby," *The Loved One,* "A Clean, Well-Lighted Place," *Miss Lonelyhearts, The Red Badge of Courage.* All the authors alluded to command, though unequally, the ironic mind which naturally, unavoidably, perceives in terms of a double vision. These paired antithetical perceptions can be described however one wishes—the illusory versus the real, what ought to be versus what is, the internal ethical standard of the perceiver versus the external socially-approved practice—but the point is that the ironic mind naturally perceives, simultaneously and separately, both aspects of such contradictions. This approach to Crane is justified for at least two good reasons. One is that rarest of all things in Crane criticism, agreement: everyone, no matter what critical label he hopes to affix, grants that Crane is an ironist. The other is that the two antithetical points of view, first embodied in the "little man" and the "quiet man" of *The Sullivan County Sketches,* are everywhere present in Crane's work: both "the involved, self-deluded character and the detached ironic narrator" [18] are found in every important Crane story from these early sketches to "The Upturned Face."

Given a mind which perceives in terms of such antitheses, there will be, of course, at least two possible emphases in its expression: in Crane's work the poles are generally the detached, ironic presentation of external fact and event, and the intense awareness of what takes place within a mind laboring under emotional stress, usually of fear. As Crane admitted to young Willa Cather, "he led a double literary life; writing in the first place the matter that pleased himself, and doing it very slowly; and in the second place, any sort of stuff that would sell." [19] And one infallible method of distinguishing between first and second-rate Crane is by means of the two emphases deriving from his perception: in "the matter that pleased himself" the emphasis is always upon what happens within the mind, man's moral world; and in all that "stuff" written to sell, the emphasis falls upon an ironic presentation of external fact and event. This alignment will hold, I believe, despite the fact that in his work the externalities are superbly presented. One can read "An Experiment in Misery," for example, or "The Men in the Storm," or "War Memories," thoroughly enjoy the external facts and events in themselves, and never feel any need to look beneath them for anything more; yet in all three of these sketches Crane's attention is focused primarily upon what occurs within a mind—specifically that of the young man who conducts the experiment, that of the decent men in the crowd before the lodging house, and that of Vernall the war correspondent—and the factual externalities are the means by which the mental or moral reality is implicitly communicated to the reader. The implications of this alignment seem fairly obvious: reality, or truth, for Crane is moral, that which the poems describe as "a breath, a wind,/A shadow, a phantom"; and the world external to man—amoral, mechanistic, and indifferent to his very existence—is merely the setting in which man's moral life has to be lived. As such, this external world cannot offer much dramatic possibility to a writer. As Crane states in "The Blue Hotel," "there can be little of dramatic import in environment. Any room can present a tragic front; any room can be comic." Thus, Crane is always more interested on the human beings in the external "room" than he is in whatever physical reality surrounds them.

But this critical alignment and the implications it offers are reinforced by additional formal evidence. Irony can perform a great many functions, but by itself it seems incapable of providing the plot for a story. Once given a plot, irony can go to work on it by piercing the comfortable illusions and pretenses which make life bearable for most people, by tracing parallel actions or effects in a manner uncomplimentary to the protagonists, by exposing hypocrisy and stupidity—Crane performs all such feats in his earliest news-writing, for the antics he observed at the Jersey shore provided the "plot" for his irony to work upon—but the plot itself, an ordered structure of progressive action, seems aesthetically distinct from the irony which may inform every part of it in the finished story. Crane obviously needed a plot which would take full advantage of his ironic perception, and he conceived it even before he published his first fiction. This plot traces the protagonist's progression to an awareness of a hitherto unknown reality. Its concealed irony, bitter enough for any protagonist, lies in the fact that the unknown which he comes to understand is new only to himself, not new, not unknown, to others: hence, the protagonist endures all his struggles and discomforts merely to perceive correctly a specific reality which has been fully present and available to him before his progression to the awareness of it even began. The progression begins when the character confronts this unknown—an imminent experience, situation, condition, always something which he has not yet experienced. A normal apprehension about this unknown which he realizes he will soon have to experience sets his imagination working, and the imagination immediately conceives all sorts of illusions about the coming experience. Once this process begins, the character's uneasiness quickly increases to real fear simply because his attention shifts from the unknown itself to the lurid images produced by the imagination. Thus, given a mind as active as Henry Fleming's is, it is no wonder that these illusions should cause great fear; and when Henry panics and runs away, Crane states precisely what he is trying to run away from: "On his face was all the horror of those things which he imagined." The imagination is, of course, spurred to greater activity by the increase in fear; and both illusions and fear continue to mount until the unknown is actually experienced. This climactic moment is always an ironic deflation because mere reality never can measure up to the images evoked by an overheated imagination. Hence, the fact of experience does away with fear because the unknown thereby becomes the known; and the comparatively prosaic nature of the experienced reality reveals the illusory notions of the imagination for what they are. But the character, after the fact of experience, is left with the memory of both his fears and his illusions; and such recollections, if a man has any sense, should make him feel ashamed of himself.

The latter steps in this plot, those which follow the fact of experience, are embodied for the first time in Henry Fleming; but the rest of it can be found in the Sullivan County stories—perhaps most obviously in "Four Men in a Cave" and "The Mesmeric Mountain"—and, with the single exception of *George's Mother*, some version of this plot provides the essential structure for every important story Crane wrote thereafter.[20] It also helps one understand three of his best sketches, "An Experiment in Misery," "The Pace of Youth," and "War Memories," because in each the protagonist progresses to the awareness of a moral reality and has to overcome his own illusory notions in the process: the youth of the experiment comes to know the "point of view" of the professional pauper; Stimson in "Youth" learns that young love in others is beyond his power of control; and Vernall becomes aware of what, to him, "the real thing" of war actually is. Crane's use of this same plot structure again and again should prove the truth of another statement he made to Willa Cather, that "his limitations were absolutely impassable. 'What I can't do, I can't do at all, and I can't acquire it. I only hold one trump.' "[21] This plot clearly traces action within the mind, and thus it provides the conceptual basis for Crane's best work, the stories "that pleased himself" because their emphasis is on his primary interest. It is conspicuously absent from the rest of his prose.

Crane's poetry does not fit the critical alignment to which his prose works conform; it represents a distinct class—a third emphasis of the ironic mind—in itself. Given the mind which perceives in terms of paired antitheses giving rise to the above two emphases in its expression, common sense suggests that such a mind must have at least one further capacity: the ironist must be able to transcend, and thus be the master of, his own irony, must be able to sustain the clarity of the antitheses he perceives; otherwise the contradictions will blur toward ambiguity and ironic expression will become impossible. This personal orientation of the ironist, by means of which he controls his own irony, has to be the authoritative norm behind the ironic expression—those values implicit in "the felt presence of the author's taste and reservations about human nature" which informs ironic prose. And if it is the implicit norm behind Crane's use of his "one trump" plot, then one should not expect to find this norm explicitly set forth in the stories based on this plot. One finds a comparatively direct expression of it in the poems —and in certain letters such as those to Nellie Crouse and John Northern Hilliard [22]—for the poems, considered together as a unit in themselves, are Crane's only major work in which he is free of the structural demands of his plot. Unfortunately, the poems seem more difficult to cope with than his prose; but at least one of them spells out, almost in didactic fashion, some of the principal values of Crane's norm. The first of these is compassion for man's plight as a moral orphan in an amoral universe. And any man who sincerely feels such compassion will

> Teach the gold of patience,
> Cry gospel of gentle hands,
> Cry a brotherhood of hearts,[23]

and will practice all of these virtues for their own sake, without thought of other reward here or hereafter, merely because the world is as it is and he is a man. Thus, the poems cannot be ignored by anyone who hopes to "be sure about anything" concerning Crane's prose.

The plot of Crane's best stories clearly catches the protagonist at a climactic moment in his moral life; and the progression to awareness therefore implies an end greater than the specific unknown presented in the individual story, for the shame which the protagonist ideally feels after his ironic deflation has to imply an increased knowledge of the self—its strengths, weaknesses, limitations, its place in the amoral external world full of other fallible human beings—otherwise there would be no reason for the protagonist to feel ashamed of his own past conduct. And to conduct oneself as a man in Crane's world requires more than an awareness that reality is, after all, but reality. The values of Crane's norm presented in the poems—acceptance of the moral desert in which one has to live, compassion for one's fellowman, teaching, patience, gentleness, brotherhood, love, unremitting labor —comprise the moral context in which the important prose works have to be placed in order to understand fully what Crane has to say in them. Thus, it seems reasonable to argue that any treatment of Crane's fiction which either ignores or contradicts what is said in the poems is quite apt to be wrong. In fact, if I were to rank Crane's works in the order of what seems to me their relative importance, the poems would come first; and "The Open Boat," in which Crane makes his plot open outwardly away from the immediate situation to imply most clearly the greater context, the world view set forth in his poems, would come next before *The Red Badge*.

This world view is not Christian, so far as I can determine, although the virtues mentioned above are common to decent men of all faiths and were conspicuously practiced by Crane's father, the Reverend Jonathan Townley Crane, D.D. Crane nowhere belabors the point, and one has to look as closely at what he affirms as at what he rejects. What he certainly rejects is all orthodoxy, all codified, communally certified religion: the organized church is to Crane pretty much what it is to George Kelcey, a spiritually defunct institution of pointless formalism, "dreary blackness arranged in solemn rows . . . made by people who tilted their heads at a prescribed angle of devotion." What he affirms is best set forth in the poems, which offer two opposed concepts of "God," two opposed concepts of truth, and two opposed voices that Westbrook calls the voice of perspective and the voice of arrogance.

The voice of perspective draws Crane's deepest sympathy; it is

characterized by humility, kindness, a quiet determination, and by a consistent belief in a truth which is symbolic, elusive, but always real. The voice of arrogance—representing the values Crane attacked in his prose and fiction as well as in his poetry—is characterized by pride, dogmatism, often by an aggressive manner, and by a stubborn insistence on a literal truth.[24]

The quiet voice of perspective and the elusive moral truth are equated with a private god of a man's "inner thoughts"; and the arrogant voice which insists upon a literal truth—arrogance in Crane's work being an infallible sign that the offender is suffering from some sort of illusion—is equated with an external god which remarkably resembles both the wrathful god of fundamentalist protestantism and one of Crane's own Bowery louts with unlimited power. The individual's "god of the inner thoughts," which Crane affirms, "whispers in the heart" and is described as "those eyes of my soul"; also, this god is confined strictly to the individual:

> PERCHANCE, FRIEND, HE IS NOT YOUR GOD;
> IF SO, SPIT UPON HIM.
> BY IT YOU WILL DO NO PROFANITY.[25]

And the whispered commands of this god have to be obeyed if the individual is to remain true to himself.

Crane's individual god of the inner thoughts seems to me the conscience, not the New Testament God of love. Crane's god offers pity and understanding, not love: pity for man's position in an amoral universe, understanding of action in accordance with a private moral standard when such actions all too often are misunderstood by society. This unsleeping inner eye which watches the moral health of the soul offers no hint of future rewards or punishments as inducements to right conduct, no assurance of prosperity in this world, or even of social acceptance. Yet Crane's characters are judged, by his irony, in terms of their obedience of what this god commands. Those who obey are "personally honest": [26] they act morally in terms of whatever values they are able to perceive. And such personal honesty, the luxury of a healthy, affirmed conscience, is inevitably its own reward. Maggie, for example, misjudges Pete's character, and thus honestly makes a wrong choice; but because she acts honestly in accordance with what she is able to perceive she goes to her death morally untouched by all the nastiness of her mother, lover, and brother. Jimmie, however, is personally dishonest: he willfully damns his sister to avoid a moral truth which he does perceive—that "what is wrong for Pete cannot be right for him." [27] Will C. Jumper was the first critic to call Crane a stoic humanist; this seems to me as good a descriptive tag as can be had, and critically it is more relevant than assuming he was a Christian is apt to be.

Crane is more stoic than humanist in his early work, and as he does not seem to get all that he wants to say straightened out in his own mind before *The Black Riders* and *The Red Badge*—both of which had been written by September 1894 [28]—one has to be careful with the works written earlier. Because his humanism had to wait until he created Henry Fleming there is a certain ironic pessimism in the Sullivan County tales, and in *Maggie*, which is not present in his later work. His four campers learn nothing from experience because they are not allowed sufficient awareness even to be ashamed of their own weaknesses. Thus, their adventures at best end with the ironic deflation, and as the latter part of Crane's plot is omitted they never develop as characters from story to story. Crane himself later spoke of his "clever Rudyard-Kipling style" and of his "eight little grotesque tales of the woods which I wrote when I was clever" (*Letters*, pp. 32, 59). The world of *Maggie* is a moral slaughterhouse; but the external environment, either physical or economic, is in no way responsible for this moral mess. Except for Maggie herself this world contains essentially two sorts of people: those who look upon human misery and do nothing but enjoy it—such as the audience at the street fight in the first chapter and the audience gathered about

Mrs. Johnson in the final chapter—and the hypocrites such as Mrs. Johnson, Pete, and (after his deliberate dishonesty in chapter 13) Jimmie, who are always actively vicious. Given a world where the active people act only to destroy, where the others do nothing to interfere because they enjoy watching the destruction, where innocence can therefore only hasten one's ruin, there would not seem to be much hope for it, no matter what its external environment was. Assuming that Crane's ironic presentation of the hypocrites is not merely wasted effort, external improvements—better parks, inside plumbing, unlimited grocery money—are not going to launder the moral nastiness of this world because the cause-effect relation runs the other way. The human beings create their environment. And the obvious evidence for such a claim lies in the antics of Mrs. Johnson: no matter how bad her environment, either moral or external, may be at any given point in the story, Mrs. Johnson inevitably acts to make it worse.

Critically, the trouble with Maggie's world is much the same as that which makes the campers' world "grotesque": the pattern of selections, rejections, and emphases chosen by an extremely young author trying hard to find himself does not present what Howells would have called a true perspective of reality.[29] Maggie herself, as a character, best implies such oversimplification: she is a victim whose level of awareness is so low that she cannot even perceive correctly the reality of Pete until after she has been seduced by him; and as this position necessarily fixes her awareness well below even that of her mother, Pete, and Jimmie, she is hardly believable as a character. Likewise, it is unreasonable to suppose that none of the campers ever learns anything from the adventures they share, that even Mrs. Johnson never has a good moment in an entire lifetime. Young Crane doth protest too much; but young Crane was very little older before he became aware of it—apparently late in the summer of 1892—and set about changing it. A copy of the 1896 printing of *The*

Red Badge is inscribed to Howells, specifically "as a token of the veneration and gratitude of Stephen Crane for many things he has learned of the common man and, above all, for a certain re-adjustment of his point of view victoriously concluded sometime in 1892." [30] Although Howells was not fond of *The Red Badge* Crane chose the right book for his inscription, for this was the first work written after his readjustment.

The Red Badge reveals important differences from the earlier works, all of them in the general direction of Howells's compassionate view of mankind. This novel is more humanistic than Crane's previous stories because Henry Fleming is a more completely human protagonist. Henry is endowed with both sufficient awareness for him to gain a reasonably tenable view of himself, the external world, and his place in it, and a conscience which demands that he accept this position once he perceives it—and as such perception and honest acceptance are the only salvation Crane ever offers his characters there is nothing very pessimistic about his work from this novel forward. Maggie has the healthy conscience but lacks awareness; George Kelcey—whose tale apparently was begun before *The Red Badge* and finished after it—is well-aware of his own progressive degeneration, but his conscience succumbs to the lures of vanity and laziness. Because Henry has both qualities Crane's plot is completely set forth for the first time: once the hideous dragon of war is deflated to merely the great death, and Henry realizes it is but the great death, his chagrin at his past actions—running into the forest, deserting the tattered man, dreaming of romantically heroic gestures—implies that Henry is well on the way to conquering Henry; and such a moral victory, for anyone of Henry's age caught up in a shooting war, is neither irrational nor subhuman. The final steps in Crane's plot, those which occur after the climactic deflation by experience, necessarily imply a world in which moral winning is at least possible; but nobody wins in *Maggie* or

George's Mother, and the Sullivan County campers remain static characters. Crane hoped that "in truth, this change in my life should prove of some value to me, for, ye gods, I have paid a price for it" (*Letters,* p. 33). The evidence suggests that Crane accomplished his readjustment of point of view—technically, from the omniscient narration of *Maggie* to the third-person limited narration of *The Red Badge*—by forcing himself to humanize his *use* of his own irony; and if so, then certainly Crane had to conquer Crane as much as Henry ever conquers Henry. A fine passage from a letter to Nellie Crouse implies as much:

The final wall of the wise man's thought however is Human Kindness of course. If the road of disappointment, grief, pessimism, is followed far enough, it will arrive there. Pessimism itself is only a little, little way, and moreover it is ridiculously cheap. The cynical mind is an uneducated thing. (*Letters,* p. 99)

And this letter, appropriately enough, was written in January, 1896, the month in which *The Red Badge* became a best seller and the world at large first heard of Stephen Crane.

This readjustment was permanent. After *The Black Riders* and *The Red Badge* Crane simply accepts the amoral externality for what it is—merely an unavoidable premise, a given condition of man's life—and concentrates his attention and skill upon man's conduct, that which is not a fixed or determined condition, in this situation. Four men in an open boat adrift on an amoral sea presumably have had the conditions of their immediate situation given them by forces beyond their control; but what those four men *do* in this situation, how they conduct themselves within the boat, is up to the men themselves. If they are to behave as men should, they must perceive correctly the externality surrounding them and their own strengths and weaknesses, and then they must act honestly in accordance with the values they perceive. Thus, all of Crane's protagonists—from the little man of Sullivan County to Timothy Lean of "The Upturned Face"—travel a painful journey to awareness of both the physical reality confronting them and their own moral flaws. Those capable of shame for their own failings acquire a certain quiet humility and, with it, a stoic acceptance of man's moral responsibility in an amoral universe which, because of its flat indifference to human life, implicitly mocks the very values it is man's duty to uphold. Death is certain. The ungrieved conscience is sustained for its own sake. But in a world full of poltroons, moral cowards, hypocrites, and conceited fools, one personally honest man immediately recognizes and respects another; and thus there exists that silent, unacknowledged brotherhood among decent men which "The Open Boat" defines as "the best experience of life." [31]

Stephen Crane in our time begins his second century, and for anyone who does not wish to work casually at him some extremely tempting opportunities are available. His poetry, for example, despite one book and some four or five good essays, has not begun to receive the critical attention awarded his prose—even though the excellent edition by Joseph Katz has been at hand since 1966. And what happened to Crane in Havana when he disappeared there briefly in the autumn of 1898? This period obviously marks a crisis in Crane's life, but it is a complete blank. Or how is one to explain the "Intrigue" poems? These are possibly the sorriest sequence of poems ever written in English. Why were they written? Perhaps even more interesting: what was Crane's reason for publishing them? Again, no one knows the answers. Also, no one has really made much of an attempt to analyze Crane's distinctive style—its intensity, the specific ironic devices used, his odd responsiveness to color. Also, "Death and the Child" and "War Memories," two works which seem to me first-rate Crane, have been virtually ignored by critics, and strangely little has been done with *George's Mother*. Also, there are some forty-five sketches Crane wrote during his New York years, which seem quite important to an understanding of his development; yet all but about a half dozen of these pieces have been ignored. Such a listing of gray areas in Crane scholarship can easily be extended.

Berryman's warning still holds; and the dangers and difficulties he had in mind explain why serious Crane scholars in our time still have plenty of important work to do. But the casual reader can at least be certain that what Crane has to say will remain as valuable as ever it was, that the way in which he says it will remain unforgettable, that the study of his best work will always return full value for whatever effort one may wish to invest.

The Relevance of John Dewey's Thought

SIDNEY HOOK

The abuse of the term *relevance* by radical extremists in educational institutions might justifiably have set up an allergic reaction in the minds of critical readers to its use. Nonetheless, if we recall that *relevance* is a relational term, the question, "Relevant to what?" is one whose legitimacy cannot reasonably be disputed. To the extent that the demands for relevance by educational revolutionaries was intelligible in recent stormy years, it referred to the bearing of studies on the acute social and political issues of the day—a bearing that was foolishly elevated to the sole criterion of an educational curriculum appropriate for modern man, and then degraded by tying it to the "happenings" of the passing scene.

When I speak of the relevance of John Dewey's thought I refer not to its bearing on the contemporary crisis situations but to its bearing on the condition of man, his problems and predicaments in war *and* peace, good times *and* bad, whenever he reflectively examines alternatives of action in the course of choosing a desirable way of life. John Dewey wrote millions of words on the topical issues that arose during the three quarters of a century that spanned his adult life. But it is not for that reason that his ideas have relevance today. They are relevant to areas of thought and action in which our basic intellectual and practical interests are still involved—education and ethics, culture and politics, social philosophy in the broadest sense. In some of these areas his views are emerging once more; in others, events and institutional change are giving an *actualité* to positions that seemed Utopian if not unrealistic at the time he enunciated them.

As one familiar with the whole corpus of Dewey's writings would have expected, the basic educational ideas and ideals that pervade them have been foremost among the rediscoveries of his thought. Addressing the American Association for the Advancement of Science in 1909, Dewey affirmed the central importance of science in the curriculum of the schools long before his post-Sputnik critics sought to reconstruct the American school system to overtake Soviet technological achievements and developments. But by the study of science Dewey does not mean the acquisition of a miscellaneous store of information of facts, laws, theories and interesting correlations that constitute the subject matter of so much of the science curriculum of the schools. He means the understanding of what it is that confers scientific validity upon a particular conclusion or "the knowledge of the ways by which anything is entitled to be called knowledge instead of being mere opinion or guesswork or dogma." It is this kind of knowledge which for him is of most worth. Long before the critics of "scientism" appeared on the scene Dewey warned against the view that any specific method in the particular sciences—whether it was physics, biology, or psychology—could define the pattern of rationality. When Dewey criticized the traditional humanistic education of his days, his analysis was directed against the formal study of languages and literature that gave a narrow training in certain techniques that constricted the imagination and emotions instead of liberating and humanizing them. For him the humanities were not merely subjects to be taught, they were the means of affecting liberal and humane minds, what he sometimes called "the production of a social and socialized sense." They were preeminently the field in which the qualities of value were revealed and their interrelations explored. A half century before Snow's superficial book on *The Two Cultures* appeared, Dewey had defined the problem facing reflective citizens concerned with education as "how we are to effect in this country a combination of a scientific and a humanistic education."

Dewey's conception of this combination was profound not superficial because he was aware of a third culture—the social or cultural—that embraced the "two cultures" and without reference to which humanistic training was in danger of becoming precious, if not snobbish, and scientific training harnessed to barbaric goals. The very distinction between the humanistic and scientific disciplines presupposes an overarching cultural or social dimension expressed in institutions, basic habits and some hierarchy of value choices that make up the quality of life or the distinctive character of civilization at any given time. An education that seeks to make its students imaginatively aware of those dynamic forces in society that ultimately affect the direction of both scientific and humanistic activity must stress the understanding of its basic social and economic structure, the problems and conflicts of the encompassing cultural milieu, and the alternatives of development or retrogression always open to it. This is required particularly in a democratic society where every adult citizen theoretically counts as much as any other in determining the ultimate direction of its policy. That is why the abstract celebration of moral values—dignity, integrity, happiness, serenity—is insufficient to tell us what changes in social institutions are required to give them a concrete embodiment in the life of most human beings. Similarly, without the assessment of the effects of science and technology upon our social life and upon the quality of the resulting experience, we run the risk of adapting our ideals to the unplanned and unintended consequences of the applications of science rather than organizing its resources in the responsible service of man. Neither humanistic nor scientific education traditionally conceived, because of their failure to understand the encompassing third culture of social, economic, political, and historical studies, can tell us when to produce, what to produce, and why.

This suggests an even more fundamental area of thought

in which Dewey, albeit much misunderstood, anticipated some very recent intellectual developments, namely, in the very conception of philosophy itself. Many have been the conceptions of philosophy that have prevailed in different societies: and these differences are present within our own. Dewey continuing the Greek tradition has maintained that philosophy is a quest for wisdom but as distinct from ancient, medieval, and almost all other modern thinkers, he has rejected the attempt to identify or ground wisdom with or on some metaphysical or transcendental (ultimately religious) insight or with the purely descriptive knowledge of the natural sciences. Wisdom for Dewey is a moral term "and like every moral term refers not to the constitution of things already in existence, not even if that constitution be magnified into eternity and absoluteness. As a moral term it refers to a choice about something to be done, a preference for living this sort of life rather than that. It refers not to accomplished reality but to a desired future which our desires, when translated into articulate conviction, may help bring into existence." [1]

This makes a philosophy a *normative analysis* of the basic value conflicts of the culture of which it is a part. It is a conception of philosophy which is both an historical interpretation of what philosophy has been and a proposal of what it should be and do. It makes the philosopher a moralist but not a moralizer or social reformer. It faces certain difficulties which I have attempted to meet elsewhere.[2] But what is significant for present purposes is that this conception, derided or ignored for many years by most American philosophers who have regarded philosophy either as a quest for a reality beyond the reach of scientific methods, or as an analytic explication of scientific methods or as a linguistic analysis of basic concepts whose ordinary and peculiar uses, when not properly distinguished, gave rise to intellectual confusion, has now strongly emerged on the philosophical scene and is moving more and more to the center of current philosophical concern. Unfortunately not all who are now concerned with normative analysis of values in their social bearing have understood Dewey's conception of the vocation of the professional philosopher as distinct from the activity of the citizen. They seek to politicalize philosophy by harnessing it to some specific controversial political program rather than to the analytic functions of clarifying the alternatives of social action and their consequences.

To some readers this will suggest that Dewey's thought has been an anticipation of the certain themes in later-day existentialism. This would be more false than true. The existentialists have been concerned like Dewey with moral choice, its phenomenology and psychology. But their irrationalism, their contention that no grounds can be given for our basic choices, that they are all on the same level, would raise doubts on Dewey's view whether they have a right to any theory of *moral* judgment. For the existentialists a moral choice is a passion. For Dewey it is more than a passion, it is a conviction for which rational grounds can be given, that is, it is "a passion that would exhibit itself as a reasonable persuasion." A persuasion can be reasonable even if it is not logically entailed by the facts of the problematic situation in which the judgment is made. For Dewey the usual objection to the view that values or ends can be rationally determined, namely, that rationality is a quality of *means* that are adapted to achieve specific ends but that the ends themselves are a matter of arbitrary choice, does not hold. For he denies that there are any ultimate ends and contends that there is a plural means-end continuum in all problematic situations of moral choice. We never confront bare facts with pure ideals. The factual situation already includes some value commitments, not questioned in that particular context, and the pure ideal presupposes some assumption about the factual causal circumstances out of which it arose and the factual consequences to which it leads. That

The Relevance of John Dewey's Thought [5 9

is why Dewey holds that "if ever we are to be governed by intelligence, not by things and by words, science must have something to say about *what* we do, and not merely about *how* we may do it most easily and economically." [3] The typical response of some philosophical intuitionistic critics to Dewey's view that moral virtue is intelligence is that this makes the economical use of means to the achievement of *any* given end moral (for example, "then the person"—it is said—"who discovers that cyanide is the cheapest and quickest way of destroying the victims of a genocide program would be the most moral"!). But Dewey's point is that he is prepared to show that the choice of that given end in the determinate historical situation is unreasonable or unintelligent. Despite the denial by emotivists and existentialists that ends and goals are beyond rational evaluation, that it is unintelligible to speak of them as being "rational" or "irrational," "foolish" or "wise," the facts of ordinary experience, as well as of ordinary language, give this position the lie. We are continually discussing the reasonableness or unreasonableness of pursuing specific goals, ends, objectives, or ideals.

It is not enough to vindicate the cognitive validity of value judgments today. More important than the acceptance of beliefs about the good and the better is the way in which the beliefs are held. Despite widely held opinions to the contrary, it is not from ethical skepticism or even from subjectivistic relativism we suffer most. For at their worst they make for an indifferentism that the exigencies of practical choice often reveals as merely a conventional pose. And at their best they make for an initial tolerance toward expressions of difference that may broaden the spectrum of choice. The major threats to democratic political and social life stem not from relativism or skepticism but from fanaticism. We live in an age of true believers whose self-righteous absolutisms brook neither contradiction nor delay in bringing about the promised land of their faith. Disagreement is automatically attributed either to immeasurable stupidity or to unmitigated venality. Some of these fanaticisms are on the side of the angels, like absolute pacifism whose consequences often embolden aggressors like Hitler to believe that they can make armed moves, and ultimately, war with impunity. The fanatical social revolutionist equally with the fanatical reactionary or standpatter holds his beliefs in such a way that nothing that occurs can disconfirm them. The less fruitful and effective those beliefs are, the greater his impatience, the more intense his conviction of their truth. Only too often he ends up proclaiming that the evil system that defeats his demands— demands so clear, so obvious, so eminently reasonable —must be destroyed "by peaceful means if possible, by any means if necessary." In a few short strides the Utopian idealist becomes a bomb-throwing guerrilla warrior, an arsonist or an assassin—still self-righteous and full of moral indignation and completely unaware of the way in which the means he has used have corrupted both his ideals and his character.

In practice the fear of failure may curb fanaticisms except of the messianic varieties that border on the psychotic. But Dewey is interested not in the techniques of frustration or repression but in an intellectual approach that would prevent or at least hinder the emergence of fanaticism. To this end he believes that the cultivation of an historical sense is essential. Whether it is peace or justice or freedom or welfare that we have made the end-all and be-all of our social or political program, "the gist of rationality" in striving for them is "temporal perspective," for in human affairs, in contrast with pure logic and mathematics, our decisions are based on judgments of "more or less" rather than on judgments of "either-or."

This historical perspective on human affairs is wedded to a lively sense of the pluralism of values exhibited in such affairs. It is not that Dewey denies the validity of a moral stance that at some point stakes one's life, honor, and fortune on a position and digs in behind the declaration: "Hier stehe Ich. Ich kann nicht anders" (Here I stand. I can do no other). The question is: on what am I standing? On my conscience or on a platform of reason? For Dewey, conscience has no moral authority unless it is the result of a rational conscientiousness. And if it has moral authority, it necessarily requires taking note of the plural values of experience and their interrelatedness, and of rationally assessing the consequences of one's stand upon them. Especially today when "conscience" is often and sincerely invoked as an organ of ultimate and superior insight into one's moral duty—and not only as an easy pretext of avoidance of one's duty and responsibility, for betrayal of cause and country—it becomes necessary to point out that those who with a righteous pride affirm that they are prepared to take some action "in complete disregard of consequences," are immoral fanatics. For morality is always an affair of consequences. If we are prepared to say "let justice prevail though the heavens fall" well and good—provided we understand that the fall of heaven also means the death of love, the loss of freedom, the end of happiness, and the euthanasia of all other human values. And if these are rationally grasped as the true consequences of pursuing or realizing absolute justice, of what use or good would such justice be? We can ask the same questions of any other single value-term substituted for *justice*. The interrelatedness of values and the consequences of the means used to achieve one value or the constellation of values of which it is a part, makes the sharp disjunction between "merely" instrumental values and "pure" intrinsic values untenable.

Occasionally it is asserted that survival is the truly ultimate value which in cases of moral conflict always has an overriding validity. Reflective human behavior does not always square with the assertion. Sometimes the worst thing we can know of a human being is that he survived under the conditions laid down for survival—that he torture and destroy the innocent, betray friends, family, cause and country.

For Dewey each situation has its own unique good discovered by intelligent analysis of the factual situation and of the competing value claims. No formula can guide our resolution. Sometimes we must give heed to the overriding imperatives of justice; sometimes we must subordinate the claims of justice to the overriding need of human welfare; sometimes both justice and welfare may temporarily be sacrificed to the requirements of security and survival. "This is opportunism," jeers the absolutist. To which one can legitimately retort that if opportunism means "the seeking of immediate advantage with little regard for principles or ultimate consequences," this is decidedly not opportunism, since regard for consequences is of the very essence of this approach. On the other hand, an absolutism that disregards fruits and consequences is the very quintessence of fanaticism, and often leaves no alternative where absolutes conflict except war, so that in the end sheer might determines what prevails in human affairs.

There is another generic sense of opportunism which stresses the intelligent application of principles to new occasions. In this sense, the social philosophy of Dewey is as opportunistic as scientific medicine. Those who issue the same prescription for all medical affairs are quacks. Social absolutism can be regarded as a kind of quackery in human affairs despite the high-mindedness and personal sincerity of its exponents. Sincerity is always a desirable trait in politics but unless accompanied by intellectual humility, by a consciousness that one may be wrong in an area in which claims to certainty reveal a severe limitation of intelligence, it can express itself in monstrous form. Hitler did not lack sincerity.

Long before the misleading slogan of "participatory democracy" was sounded by the spokesmen of the so-called New Left, Dewey had developed the idea, expressed in germ in Jefferson's later writings, that democracy was not only a political form of government but a way of life, that it "must begin at home, and its home is the neighborly community." [4] The nature of community requires more than mere physical contiguity. It involves face-to-face relations and direct communication among citizens so that joint undertakings can be initiated. Individuals sharing ideas and emotions lose the feeling of being dwarfed by social forces moving behind their backs, of the impersonality of the political process and the anonymity of large numbers and organizations with their inescapable bureaucracies. This explains why Dewey welcomed grass-roots movements and was quite critical of the functioning of purely formal mechanisms of political rule.

How then does Dewey differ from the gurus of the New Left who would justifiably repudiate any suggestion that he has inspired their thought? First by his acceptance of the principle of majority rule. For him this is a necessary but not sufficient condition of democratic community decisions. The New Left is contemptuous of majorities if they do not agree with the program of the leadership of the moment. Despite its rhetoric, it is elitist in conception and character. Second, Dewey's conception of participation does not entail the view that all individuals are capable of doing everything, that all political functions are interchangeable, and that responsible leadership is incompatible with democratic accountability and control. The New Left professes that all leadership other than its own must end in a cult of leadership. In an attempt to conceal the character of its actual elite control of organizations, meetings, and assemblies that flaunt the slogans of participatory democracy, it becomes manipulative. Every group that shouts "All Power to the People" not only has no mandate from the people to speak in its name but is at the same time engaged, under the skillful direction of its ideologues and managers, in frustrating the decisions of the larger majority of the people among whom it is agitating whenever the popular judgment runs counter to the predetermined goals of the shouters. Thirdly, for Dewey the survival and expansion of democracy depends upon its use of scientific method or creative intelligence to solve its problems. For the New Left and its congeners, "science" and "reason" are suspect tools of the Establishment used to fashion rationalizations in behalf of the *status quo*. This is a kind of primitive Marxism that mocks the genuine insights of Marx himself.

We must now confront a profound difficulty in Dewey's political philosophy which to the extent that he solves it requires the introduction of a faith that in the eyes of some may seem to transcend his commitment to the scientific attitude. The difficulty arises from the conjunction of a series of positions each of which appears to be well-grounded. Dewey believes that our reflective behavior as well as the conclusions of analysis commits us to a cognitive theory of ethics according to which judgments of good and bad, right and wrong can legitimately be called valid or invalid, true or false. He also is aware of the growth and complexity of government and that most of the tasks of government are administrative, requiring specialized and expert knowledge in the manifold technologies of the industrial arts and sciences. Why then, one asks, does not Dewey draw the conclusion that the likelihood of good government depends upon entrusting political rule to those who have the expert knowledge? Scientific judgment and truths do not depend upon the vote of majorities or even upon the participation of individual citizens in the scientific process. If scientific knowledge, as Dewey believes, is the only reliable method of reaching conclusions in human as well as in natural affairs, why not entrust the political destiny of the community to those who possess this scientific knowledge? And if we do, how can we still be loyal to the spirit and letter of democracy?

This is another way of asking Plato's question: if we do not elect the pilot of a ship to whom we entrust our lives and goods, why should we elect the pilot of the ship of state whose decisions may determine our collective lives and estates? We cannot make the easy answer of the emotivist: we elect pilots on the basis of their knowledge and craftsmanship to take us to our destinations but the pilots have no authority to determine what our destination should be; for a choice is expressive of an attitude or wish or preference and not dependent upon any knowledge, scientific or other. Dewey cannot make that answer, for, as we have seen, he believes that the relevant scientific knowledge can help "form the social and moral ideas for the sake of which it is used," and that "science must have something to say about *what* we do [and *where* to go], and not merely about *how* we may do it [and *how* to get there] most easily and economically."

Dewey is quite aware of the objections that can be made to the Platonic view, shared by Santayana and other honest totalitarians, that knowledge and knowledge only gives incontrovertible authority to rule. And in writings spanning his entire life he has voiced these objections incisively and vigorously—that history shows that the dictatorship of the wise becomes corrupted by its monopoly of power into the rule of vested interest, that it is not necessary to be an expert to judge or evaluate the recommendations of experts, that those who actually wear the shoes know best where they pinch and therefore have the right to change their political shoes in the light of their political experience.

But these rejoinders of Dewey are not enough to justify the democracy of a *self-governing* community. For they could be accepted by an elite to justify a nonparticipating democracy in which the electorate passively registers its approval or disapproval of executive or legislative decisions but does not engage in the multifarious activities of joint association that Dewey regards as the *sine qua non* of democratic health and vitality. Intelligent decisions in a democracy require extensive participation by the citizenry on all levels. Has the common man the capacity as well as the willingness to make intelligent decisions? And if he does not possess them now, can he be educated to acquire them? If his education isn't sufficient to enable him to acquire political sophistication and some expertise, has he the wit and gumption to learn from experience? Dewey answers all of these questions affirmatively, despite his awareness of the fact that the powerful mass media of press, radio, and television are hardly geared to the educational needs of an enlightened commonwealth. On what then do his beliefs rest? On the same faith that underlay Jefferson's faith in the success of the American experiment, namely, that most human beings who have access to relevant information can learn from their own experience, including their mistakes and defeats, and can discover what they really want, what they must do to achieve it, and what price must be paid for its achievement. They can learn this better than exalted rulers or leaders who claim to have superior knowledge of what is really good for those whom they rule or lead. It is a double-barreled faith—they *can* learn it, and they *will*.

It is interesting to observe that something like this faith was held by Marx, too, not about the people as an undifferentiated mass but about the idealized working class. At a time when democratic political institutions had not yet been introduced into Western Europe, when, since peaceful reforms were seemingly impossible, revolutionary action seemed necessary to those who experienced conditions as morally unendurable, Marx sought to assess the prospects of ultimate victory for the working class in the aftermath of a series of shattering defeats.

The proletarian revolutions . . . criticize themselves constantly, interrupt themselves continually in their own cause, come back to the apparently accomplished in order to begin it afresh, deride with unmerciful thoroughness the inadequacies, weaknesses and paltrinesses of their first attempts, seem to throw down their adversary only in order that he may draw new strength from the earth and rise again, more gigantic, before them, recoil forever and anon from the indefinite prodigiousness of their aims, until a situation has been created which makes all turning back impossible, and the conditions themselves cry out: *Hic Rhodus, hic salta.*[5]

What is this but a colorful account of how the working class presumably learns from experience, suffused with an expectation and hope that it will eventually triumph? Dewey writes with much greater sobriety than Marx, not about the workers but about the public or organized citizenry, faced not by one task or challenge that is finally mastered but by a succession of them, working not under conditions of illegality and despotism but within an accepted tradition of change. Yet despite all these differences he, too, expresses the same faith in man and his ability to learn from experience that animated Marx's faith in the working class. Marx's faith turned out to be mistaken, for the workers in the Western world never espoused the cause of revolution, and the workers elsewhere supported at best revolutions from above engineered by a small group of professional revolutionists. The workers of the Western world did learn from experience, however, but it was a lesson that Marx did not altogether anticipate, namely, that they could realize their demands for bread and freedom more effectively and in a less costly way by working within the democratic political process, and using the tax system and welfare state to redistribute wealth more nicely and justly, than they could by guillotine and firing squad.

Has Dewey any better reason for his faith that the masses will find their way to a participating democracy, a commonwealth in which institutions function to be helpful to all individuals seeking to achieve their maximum growth as persons—through "methods of consultation, persuasion, negotiation, communication, co-operative intelligence"?[6] This faith has been sorely tried by events in the United States since Dewey died, and by the growth and partial success of movements in many areas of public life that have relied not on the methods Dewey stressed as essential to a participating democracy but on force and violence or the threat of force and violence. It is true enough that it is very dubious that the genuine gains in civil rights, social welfare, education, and health are attributable to this violence, and a good case can be made for the contention that force and violence in behalf of good causes, by developing reactions and backlashes, have hindered them rather than helped further them.[7] It may even be true that if the democratic methods Dewey enumerates are not employed in the political process, the ideal of a self-governing participating democracy will remain a chimera. Nonetheless it remains true that despite these considerations Dewey has a right to hold this faith. Its invalidity has not been established. Like all faith it involves risk and gamble even if it be more reasonable than any other. It is a risk and gamble not only because it assumes that where fundamental interests collide men will use their intelligence to find the shared interests on the basis of which their differences can be composed, but because it also assumes that those who have the creative intelligence to discover ways of building on shared interests will have the moral courage to propound and defend them in the face of violent opposition. The behavior in recent years of the faculties of institutions of higher learning, not only in the United States but in most countries of the world, in meeting violent disruptions of the academic process show lamentably that intelligence and moral courage do not go hand in hand, that they seem to be two independent variables in the life of the mind.

Among other reasons this is why it is still an open question whether Dewey's faith in intelligence will be vindicated. Or to put it in another and more paradoxical way, it is still an open question whether events will not make it more reasonable and intelligent, given existing human propensities and their institutional contexts, to use methods of social action that Dewey himself eschewed and condemned. Despite hysteria-mongers and apologists for one or another variety of totalitarianism, the history of politically democratic societies shows that more has been won by the methods of intelligence, of peaceful negotiation, persuasion and reasonable compromise than by any other method. But the future in this respect is more problematic than the past.

It remains briefly to discuss the relevance of some of Dewey's more technical philosophical ideas to the contemporary scene. This may be briefly summarized by the statement that Dewey's ideas are highly relevant to some of the present philosophical concerns of contemporary professional philosophers but that the latter are unembarrassedly unaware of it. Many of Dewey's positions are widely accepted but not in the form in which he developed them. Although a leading protagonist of a naturalistic and functional theory of mind and an arch-foe of psychophysical dualism, today a more materialistic or physicalistic theory largely prevails. This is a family of doctrines that accepts some version of the identity-thesis that "mental processes are purely physical processes in the central nervous system," to use the language of one of its systematic exponents. Those who have developed this theory have done so independently of any perceptible influence of Dewey. To the extent that they believe that the true relation between the mind and the brain depends upon the findings of science, Dewey would endorse their position. He would, however, contest their apparent isolation of the mental from the social and cultural, and maintain that the categories of the physical and mental are neither exclusive nor exhaustive. He would also assert that the dimension of the social, although it has necessary physical and biological correlates, is not reducible without remainder to them.

More surprising is the seeming evanescence of the philosophy of naturalism which received one of its most significant expressions in Dewey's *Experience and Nature*. To some, naturalism is a philosophy based upon the question-begging assumption that the methods of science are the only valid ways of acquiring knowledge and that, aside from commonsense knowledge which is continuous with science, there is no reliable knowledge except scientific knowledge. This conclusion has brought naturalism not only into conflict with all varieties of supernaturalism but also with those who believe in the existence of ontological or metaphysical truths (that are neither scientific nor logical) and more recently with those who on the basis of their introspective experience of intention and choice assert the existence of a freedom of action for man that scientific method cannot establish. The Kantian dualism has been reasserting itself according to which human life, especially man's moral life, cannot be accounted for in terms of scientific explanation. The doctrines of all of these newer tendencies are incompatible with Dewey's clear-cut rejection of psychophysical dualism.

Dewey was unsympathetic to the doctrines of logical positivism or logical empiricism that flourished in the last two decades of his own lifetime not because of its absorption in the language and methodology of the natural sciences but because of its suspected atomism, its slighting of normative ethical and social propositions, and its emotive interpretation of their meaning. When this movement was eclipsed by the ordinary language analysis inspired by Wittgenstein, Dewey's initial neutrality turned to hostility on the ground that although it was true that *some* philosophical problems arose from errors in logical grammar, most of them arose from genuine *problems* in the extension of scientific categories from one domain to another. There is a haunting similarity between some pages of Wittgenstein and some pages of Dewey. Long before Wittgenstein, Dewey had established, by linguistic analysis of the way in which the question was posed, that the so-called problem of the external world was not a genuine problem and that the very use of mental or sensory predicates, without which the question could not be asked, already presupposed the world of physics and the environment of everyday things. Nonetheless, for most philosophical problems Dewey would deny that because they cannot be coherently stated in their own terms that therefore they are no more than mistakes in a logical grammar or false moves in a language game. He would maintain that they arise out of unclearly formulated scientific problems, and that philosophical analysis should go on to attempt to state the problem in such a way that we can see what would constitute relevant scientific and commonsense empirical evidence for its resolution.

Since Dewey believed that central to philosophic activity should be the normative analysis of value judgments, he is far from agreeing with Wittgenstein that philosophy leaves the world pretty much the same after it is through with its philosophizing. For Dewey all genuine knowledge is an implicit judgment of practice whose truth is established by some experimental activity that literally transforms part of the world. If there is genuine scientific knowledge of what is morally true or false then philosophy, for better or worse, does not leave the world unaltered. This explains why for Dewey the social responsibility of science is not a problem which has emerged only in consequence of modern technology. For him all knowledge involves possible control, and when achieved, some actual change in the world.

Dewey himself set great store by his last great work: *Logic: The Theory of Inquiry*. This is a book not in formal logic but primarily in the methodology and philosophy of scientific investigation. As far as present day logicians are concerned, it might as well not have been written; and few are the philosophers of science who are familiar with it. Ernest Nagel who studied with Dewey is the only outstanding philosopher of science who reflects his influence.

Although predictions in intellectual history are hazardous there is some reason to believe that in the future Dewey's purely technical philosophical work will be rediscovered, reassessed, and developed. If his educational and social views are taken seriously by professional philosophers, they will go on to explore the epistemological and logical views that Dewey thought was bound up with them. Although they may reject a great deal, they will also find that Dewey's philosophical writings are chockfull of fruitful insights, and that although they do not constitute a finished system, they hang together in a coherent way.

Probably Dewey's philosophy will remain in temporary eclipse until the present phase of irrationalism and anti-intellectualism in American life runs its course, and reflective Americans once more seek a philosophic outlook consonant with an age in which a more adequate science of human nature serves the ideals and goals of an enlightened morality. The original inspiration of Dewey's philosophy was to find a rational basis of authority in morals comparable to the method by which claims and counterclaims in the natural sciences could be settled. This emphatically does not involve "the assimilation of human science to physical science" which represents only another insensitive form of absolutism, for it "might conceivably only multiply the agencies by which some human beings manipulate other human beings for their own advantage." This is the historical upshot of allegedly scientific Marxism in the Soviet Union and elsewhere that has betrayed both the spirit of scientific inquiry and the humanistic ideals of a responsible freedom. To the last Dewey remained true to his original inspiration. His legacy to our age is a philosophy that would extend the area of desirable human freedoms by the arts of intelligence. Its most important corollary in social and political affairs is the interrelatedness and continuity of ends and means, of process and product.

Taken seriously this approach to human affairs puts us on guard against shortcuts and panaceas, empty revolutionary rhetoric, and the "reasons" of the heart, blood, or passion that have resulted in intellectual absurdities and often culminated in atrocities. At the same time it does not justify, out of fear of substituting new and greater evils for the old and familiar ones, a defense or glorification of the social *status quo*. For, according to Dewey, the cumulative effect of human knowledge and the consequences of human decisions make it impossible to preserve the *status quo*. Our choices, and even our refusal to choose on basic issues, make matters either better or worse. We must take our problems one at a time, admitting that some are related to others, and that some are larger than others, and therefore require large steps that in perspective may appear revolutionary. The health of society can be achieved like the health of the individual with which in many ways it is interrelated. As Dewey himself has put it:

The human ideal is indeed comprehensive. As a standpoint from which to view existing conditions and judge the direction change should take, it cannot be too inclusive. But the problem of production of change is one of infinite attention to means; and means can be determined only by definite analysis of the conditions of each problem as it presents itself. Health is a comprehensive, a "sweeping" ideal. But progress toward it has been made in the degree in which recourse to panaceas has been abandoned and inquiry has been directed to determinate disturbances and means for dealing with them.[8]

This invites a program of unending social improvement inspired by visions of excellence. It is a program in which the political and cultural freedoms, essential to a humane and democratic society, and on which other desirable social and economic freedoms must be built, come first. These freedoms can never be taken for granted. They can always be lost when men lose their nerve and intelligence.

To a willful romanticism that focuses only on goals, Dewey's melioristic outlook will seem prosaic. To a near-sighted realism that immerses itself only in efforts to preserve the familiar and customary, Dewey's vision of the consummatory experience that guides and tests institutional change will appear Utopian, if not fanciful, too optimistic in its estimate of human potentialities. But like William James, John Dewey would have defended his right to believe in the fruitful marriage of freedom and science as warranted by the nature of man and history.

Mr. Emerson—
of Boston

ELEANOR M. TILTON

Puzzling and provocative to his contemporaries, the object of derision and idolatry, Emerson has been so variously explicated and evaluated that from one commentator to another we can scarcely believe they are writing of the same man. Who is Emerson that he can be associated with opposites so extreme that it scarcely matters whether they derive from history or fiction—with Horatio Alger and Baudelaire, Pollyanna and Nietzsche, Norman Vincent Peale and Paul Tillich? His contemporaries could not decide whether he was diamond or glass, infidel or saint. Contemporaries of our own would persuade us that a tragic vision lies below the surfaces of the crystal, but those closer to him in time insist upon his adamantine cheer. For Hawthorne he is the amorphous successor of Bunyan's papist and pagan. For Melville he is the fair traveler who orders ice water in a steamboat saloon. It is apparently required that he be associated with someone else: a Plotinus-Montaigne, a Franklin with wings, a new-model Jonathan Edwards.

Screening Emerson from our view is the label Transcendentalist, not a name he chose for himself but one attached to him, to his friends, and to anyone else whose eccentricity one wished to reproach. As a popular pejorative term, it implied a visionary indifference to the reasonable requirements of the world, or a presumptuous claim to know what could not be known, or just what Unitarians deserved. From that distance that made Boston, Cambridge, and Concord indistinguishable, it might be simply the Boston religion. In time transcendentalism, whatever it was, turned out to be not so fearful as a few indignant clergymen might declare. After all, even students at Andover Theological Seminary could find Coleridge in their bookstore.[1] *Aids to Reflection* was not, it is true, written to give comfort to Unitarians, but it scarcely provided grounds for infidelity. Emerson was one of many responsive readers of Coleridge, Carlyle, and Goethe. What he made of his reading was not a formal theology, a metaphysical system, or a creed.[2] As he knew, he was ill-prepared by training and ill-equipped by temperament for such labors.

Emerson's metaphysics have been explored to distraction—to distraction from what is central to his purpose, that purpose being to rouse young men to discover for themselves their faith, their calling, and their moral life. He had certainly the hope of freeing them from any creed that looked backward for its authority and forward for its rewards, ingeniously evading the present moment; but he did not suppose that freedom was to be obtained by the reformation of institutions. Nor was a reformed theology Emerson's object as it was Theodore Parker's. Emerson was not eager to have much of Parker in *The Dial*[3] intended for the untried young, engaged in self-exploration. The periodical was meant for expression, not for debate. Emerson's reputation is not enhanced by assigning to him a role in the promulgation of a native philosophy. He did not suppose himself to be addressing the nation. Writing to Carlyle, he temperately describes the furor over his Divinity School address as the "storm in our washbowl,"[4] aware that his address might be unsettling to the parish of Harvard College, but not at all to the world.

Claiming as his parish young men uncertain of their beliefs and their vocations, Emerson spoke to them from his own experience. He found irresistible, invitations to address college students; he thought of the audiences for his private courses in terms of the young men he saw before him; and he welcomed opportunities to talk with them in small groups and reciprocated by inviting them to Concord. Always his object was to prompt them to say for themselves: " 'There is a better way than this indolent learning of another. Leave me alone; do not teach me out of Leibnitz or Schelling, and I shall find it all out my-self.' " [5] Every sentence of the paragraph that closes with this imaginary utterance is designed to cut the leading strings, including the most recent. The young are not to bind themselves even to the transcendental triumvirate of Kant, Fichte, and Schelling. To the end that there should be no sacred texts, new or old, he turned away disciples, and like Channing whom he emulated, he refused to stand *in loco parentis*. He warned the young men whom he met informally for dinner at the Albion that he took them as contemporaries, though he was twice their age.[6]

He had found out for himself that a vocation is indeed a "calling," and that the caller is within. What he had learned he taught but not as rule or example,[7] for precept foils discovery. Neither future rewards nor past examples would serve. No external model of father, uncle, or ancestor would do; nor were the counsels of place and class to be trusted. Himself of the class for whom the professions of the minister, the lawyer, the doctor (the last resort) were subtly dictated, he had accepted the rule and followed the painful procedure of self-assessment recommended to young men on the verge of decision. The ledger showed as assets: ambition, eloquence, and a love of true virtue; as liabilities: social ineptitude, no talent for logic, and a faith without ground. His very application of the rational method of the countinghouse testifies to his conformity to the Boston method for answering the questions: "What shall I do? How shall I live?" And the clinching reply might be in the manner of William Paley derived from considerations of duty and expediency.

From every quarter witnesses (e.g., James and Santayana) to Massachusetts rationality can be summoned. Let an irritated English traveler testify. Thomas Hamilton in 1833 observed that Boston "is the metropolis of Unitarianism" and accounted for the fact by the character of the New Englander, a "being of reason" not of "impulse." "A Unitarian will take nothing for granted but the absolute and plenary efficacy of his own reason."[8] After all, the winner in the long-age debate between John Cotton and Peter Bulkeley had not been the "enthusiast" Cotton but Emerson's rational ancestor. Emerson supposed himself to have affinities with the successive rebels against the tradition Peter Bulkeley helped to establish. He could find a few "new lights" in his own family and was willing to take the label to himself,[9] although it could entail the less welcome tag of antinomian. If he had known local history better than he did, he might have found humor in the fact that Boston, always reasonable, had dismissed the charges against the most inflammatory of the itinerants of the Great Awakening—James Davenport—on the grounds that he was *non compos mentis*.[10] Assailed by the high-flown charges of Andrews Norton, Emerson would find Unitarians similarly reasonable.

In the context of Boston "reason," Emerson's uncritical appropriation of the transcendental terms *Reason* and *Understanding* begins to look like irony—to us if not to Emerson. Of the limits of reason in Boston's sense he had learned in his youth from David Hume, but Hume's language gave him no satisfying rhetorical instrument;[11] he had to wait for Coleridge to find that. That there were questions Boston reason could not answer warranted its demotion to "mere" Understanding, but the word *Reason*, with its accretion of associated respect might be made to deserve its value. What better way to unsettle parishioners than by using the sacred word in texts that cannot be precisely interpreted by recourse to local tradition, the latest textbook, or imported cant? Emerson himself was unwilling to abandon mind to the fallible heart, and he stood aside from contemporary sentimentalists.

The terms are from Coleridge, but Emerson takes them out of their context because they satisfy what has long been his thought—thought discoverable in his early journals and letters, if from all the respectful concessions to authority an uncertain young man is bound to make we separate out the signs of the direction he will take. Apparently as slow and hesitant in thought as he was in speech, Emerson scarcely answers to the modern requirements for the reckless radical. When finally in 1836 he came before the public in his own person to speak in his own language, he drew upon the interest of long-accumulated capital. What he had borrowed he paid back.

Among his creditors is David Hume. Not enough attention has been given to Emerson's reading of Hume; it has been taken for granted that his reading of Hume is a minor fact of his youth possibly because no one of his continuing ideas has been traced to Hume. But I hope to show that it is from Hume that Emerson derived the idea of "compensation." Although Emerson would have encountered the notion of compensation in animal life in William Paley's *Natural Theology*, Paley is not a likely source for this "watchword" of Emerson's "spiritual world." [12] Emerson's borrowings are from writers who evoked his respect for their seeming originality, their demonstration of the act of thinking, and their style. Paley's well-organized and lucid compilation of bare facts does not answer Emerson's requirements, and I can not believe that he was so solemn a youth as not to see that Paley's lucidity is the sort that verges on the ludicrous. Paley invites us to consider, for example, the compensating "guts" of the "sea-fox" and the "desperate" case of the lobster; his contented aphids we will meet again later. Paley had perhaps also the disadvantage of being required reading; the dangerous Hume was not so handicapped.

Before introducing the relevant passage from Hume, we need to examine the record of Emerson's response to his reading of this feared and fearful doubter. First the Emerson family mentors were not so fearful that they had not read Hume. It was safe enough, Uncle Samuel Ripley thought in 1818, to give Charles Emerson the history to read; he was too young to be infected with whatever poisons Hume the historian might distill. [13] Not discouraged

from exploring dangerous ground, Emerson may have
read something of Hume before 1821 when he drew upon
Hume for the second of his two Bowdoin Prize essays.
The first quotation from Hume entered in his journal is
from "Of the Delicacy of Taste and Passion," [14] and it is
to this passage Emerson alludes in his prize essay. Since
nothing else he says of Hume needed a primary source,
Emerson probably did not venture far in 1821. What is
suggestive is his equivocal evaluation of Hume.[15] Hume's
theory of happiness "discovers great philosophical sagac-
ity," but the "gloomy uncertainty with which he would
envelop all knowledge" is an "outrage upon the feelings of
human nature." Nevertheless, commonsense philosophy
has not so convincingly answered Hume "as to remove the
terror" attached to his name. Emerson closes this portion
of his essay with praise of Hume and reproof of his critics.

It has lately become prevalent to speak slightingly of this
great man, either lest the ignorant should suspect him to be an
overmatch for the orthodox philosophers, or in order to re-
taliate upon infidelity that irresistible weapon, a sneer. Such
a course of conduct is injudicious, for inquiry is not likely to
sleep in such an age, on such a subject; and if there be formi-
dable doubts to which no unanimous solution can be formed,
it is more philosophical, as well as more manly, to ascribe to
human short-sightedness its own necessary defects, for the end
of all human inquiry is confessedly ignorance.

Emerson was liable to inconsistencies, but he leaves us
with no doubt that Hume is one of his great men.

In his journal Emerson twice notes Hume's theory of
happiness, once by formal précis [16] and once by quotation.
Though in a recognizable Epicurean context, the thought
that "every wise man will endeavour to place his happiness
on such objects chiefly as depend upon himself" would
surely have pleased Emerson. And he could perhaps derive
comfort from: "When a man is possessed of that talent
[delicacy of sentiment], he is more happy by what pleases

his taste than by what gratifies his appetites, and receives more enjoyment from a poem or a piece of reasoning, than the most expensive luxury can afford." We cannot imagine that Emerson intuitively sensed in Hume's work the character of "le bon David," beloved of his friends for his serenity and courtesy, but there is no doubt that Emerson admired Hume's reasoning and the succinctness of his narrative.[17]

In 1821, Emerson is reading Hume only to get up his essay on a subject more acceptable than his essay on Socrates had been;[18] by the following year he is enamored. A note of bravado is detectable in his letter of 21 November 1822 to his friend William Withington as he announces that he is keeping dangerous company:

The next books in order upon my table are Hume, and Gibbon's Miscellanies. I shall be on the high road to ruin shortly with such companions, but I cannot help admiring the genius and novelty of the one, and the greater and profound learning of the other, maugre the scepticism and abominable sneers of both. If you read Hume, you have to *think;* and Gibbon wakes you up from slumber, to wish yourself a scholar and resolve to be one [Emerson's italics].[19]

This brace of exciting skeptics follows upon the recommendation of Dugald Stewart's *Second Dissertation* on the grounds that it will "save you a world of reading" because it is "an instructive abridgment of thousands of volumes of Locke, Leibnitz, Voltaire, Bayle, Kant, and the rest." Between the bland recommendation of Stewart as a labor-saving device and the praise of the genius of Hume who evokes thought there is a world of difference. In 1822 Stewart is among the approved protectors of youth,[20] but that he is no match for Hume, continued reading proves. An "idolator of Hume, save when he meddles with law & prophets," [21] Emerson appealing to his Aunt Mary (16 October 1823) finds nowhere another David equal to this "Scotch Goliath":

But where is the accomplished stripling who can cut off his most metaphysical head? Who is he that can stand up before him & prove the existence of the Universe & of its Founder? . . . The long & dull procession of Reasoners that have followed since, have challenged the awful shade to duel & struck the air with their puissant arguments. But as each new comer blazons "Mr. Hume's objections" on his pages, it is plain they are not satisfied the victory is gained. Now though every one is daily referred to his own feelings as a triumphant confutation of the glozed lies of this Deceiver, yet, it assuredly would make us feel safer & prouder, to have our victorious answer set down in impregnable propositions.[22]

He had been reading Hume's "Essay upon Necessary Connection," and his journal entry about it adds the same wish for controverting "impregnable propositions." [23]

In the same vein, within three weeks, he writes his aunt again, the reasonable foundations of his faith manifestly shaken; if all ideas are insecurely grounded, then "our firmest faith in intellectual & moral truths sometimes passes away like the morning cloud before the queries of the sceptic." [24] And "Humism" is also the burden of a lost letter of 1 February 1824.[25] Although in the letters of 23 October and 11 November the tone suggests an affected melancholy, I doubt that Emerson was as she hoped merely entertaining his aunt. In her reply to the letter of 11 November, she rightly recognizes the shadow of Hume and, as habitual to her, belittles her nephew's admiration. She is now reading Hume but "never was more disappointed—expected to find new mental excitement & many moments of inspired thought," [26] and she offers the cold comfort of the argument from design.

From Hume, Emerson had already learned that the argument from design was no argument at all, no argument for reason, that is, whatever it might be for sentiment, imagination, or feeling. To provide a ground for a continuing inner conviction required an avid and continuing accumulation of the "laws" of nature. Emerson's lifelong avidity is well-documented.[27] The argument from design, so favored by Boston Unitarians and Federalists,[28] is a permanent element in Emerson's thought, linked inextricably to the idea of compensation. It is in the context of the argument from design, advanced by Hume as a natural if not a necessary idea, that Emerson finds the "Law" of "Compensation." The final chapter of Hume's "The Natural History of Religion" reads in part:

A purpose, an intention, a design is evident in every thing; and when our comprehension is so far enlarged as to contemplate the first rise of this visible system, we must adopt, with the strongest conviction, the idea of some intelligent cause or author. . . . *Even the contrarieties of nature, by discovering themselves every where, become proofs of some consistent plan,* and establish one single purpose or intention, however inexplicable and incomprehensible.

Good and ill are universally intermingled and confounded; happiness and misery, wisdom and folly, virtue and vice. Nothing is pure and entirely of a piece. All advantages are attended with disadvantages. *An universal compensation prevails in all conditions of being and existence.* And it is not possible for us, by our most chimerical wishes, to form the idea of a station or situation altogether desirable. The draughts of life, according to the poet's fiction, are always mixed from the vessels on each hand of Jupiter: Or if any cup be presented altogether pure, it is drawn only, as the same poet tells us, from the left-handed vessel.

The more exquisite any good is, of which a small specimen is afforded us, the sharper is the evil allied to it; and *few exceptions are found to this uniform law of nature.* The most sprightly wit borders on madness; the highest effusions of joy produce the deepest melancholy; the most ravishing pleasures are attended with the most cruel lassitude and disgust; the most flattering hopes make way for the severest disappointments [italics mine].[29]

Emerson was certainly sharp enough to see that Hume has set this passage up in order to apply it ironically to his summation of his "Natural History"; however sublime the "universal propensity to believe in invisible, intelligent power," [30] the actual manifestations in all the religions of the world degrade the deity. Hume concludes by pointing the way of escape:

The whole is a riddle, an aenigma, an inexplicable mystery. Doubt, uncertainty, suspense of judgment, appear the only result of our most accurate scrutiny concerning this subject. But such is the frailty of human reason, and such the irresistible contagion of opinion, that even this deliberate doubt could scarcely be upheld; did we not enlarge our view, and, opposing one species of superstition to another, set them a quarrelling; while we ourselves, during their fury and contention, happily make our escape into the calm, though obscure, regions of philosophy.[31]

It is clearly with this essay in mind that Emerson writes his letter of 11 November 1823. And in it, in praise of the contemplative life, he offers Newton, idol of New England Federalists, as "a compensation to the race for many generations of darkness & [centuries] of barbarism." [32] Hume's "Natural History of Religion" had described for him the darkness and barbarism.   ,

Before his reading of Hume in 1822, there is no use of the word *compensation* in Emerson's letters or journals; and no passage that might be so titled by the reader. The first use of the term occurs in an essay on "Greatness," under the date 20 December 1822,[33] within a month of his letter to Withington. On the sound Unitarian principle that "the world is a school for the education of the mind" (cf. "Discipline," in *Nature*), Emerson can allow that doubt "exercises" the mind. "But, because of the stern principles of Justice & Retribution, which prevail in the Universe, a deeper sight [Hume's?] than ours might discern a dreadful compensation taking place." In Wide World 10 and Wide World 11 (both of 1823) we find stillborn essays on the theme of "compensation," [34] and in the second essay it is called "Nature's Law." And by January 1826, recovering the use of his eyes, he can begin a new essay: "Compensation has been woven to want, loss to gain, good to evil, & good to good, with the same in-

dustry, & the same concealment of an intelligent Cause." [35]
And, finally, for the draft essay on the "Unity of God"
(of March 1825), he had drawn heavily on Hume's "Natural History of Religion," renewing his familiarity with
this work, and showing indirectly his continuing respect
for the still undefeated "Scotch Goliath." [36]

Emerson is still haunted by Humean doubts. Hume had
taught him that reason provides no evidence for unity of
consciousness; there can be no "imperial self." [37] No more
than Coleridge could Emerson bear to be reduced to a
loose aggregation of changing sensations, "the natural
alien" of the "negative eye." [38] Preserving somehow from
first to last the faith of his fathers in mind, rarely tempted
by the sentimentalist's elevation of heart over head, and
in a Limbo of doubt from which there was no immediate
egress, Emerson entered the ministry with the hope that
his own improving and improved eloquence would serve
at least his own need. His fourth sermon is on compensation: "All things are double one against the other." [39]

He had, meanwhile, Channing, Bishop of the New, to
incite him to find for himself the way out of Limbo. Channing certainly taught self-reliance in the ordinary sense,
but so did New England fathers—and aunts and mothers,
for the fatherless Emerson boys were self-reliant in that
sense. It was indeed a matter of pride among Unitarians
that sons should be independent of fathers. It was a sign
of modern liberalism that fathers should not have exclusive
control over their sons' lives.[40] Again a number of witnesses
might be summoned, but the testimony of the father of
Emerson's young friend, Samuel Gray Ward, will serve.
Referring to his son's abandonment of business and bank-
ing for farming and painting, Thomas Wren Ward is un-
disturbed. He writes his business partner: "He has to live
for himself, and I am not so confident of what is best for
myself, much less for him, as to induce me to urge him
to any course against his judgment." [41]

Unitarians taught also, out of Bishop Butler, that human

life was probationary; and for Emerson, the ministry was certainly a period of probation. In a letter to his aunt (10–13 December 1829) he laments that he is not ready "to explore & explain the way of the star-led wizards— Am looking for the same truth they sought on quite another side & in novel relations." Yet for his Christmas sermon, he "must do (what seems so proper & reasonable) conform to the occasion." A comparison of his journal entries and sermons shows plainly that he can "say only what is trite," [42] and will continually struggle to conform his thought to the conventional language of his uneasy office. That the agent of change was Coleridge is too well documented to need iteration. The bulk of the letter here cited is given to a defense of Coleridge. Emerson is answering his aunt's withering scorn of Coleridge's "little egotisms"—"Coleridge, the blockhead," as she would call him, with his pretensions of intellect matching that of Milton and Plato.[43] Conceding a little to his aunt, Emerson piles up points to Coleridge's credit, among them "His theol. Speculations are at least *God viewed from one position* & no wise man wd. neglect yt one element in concentrating ye rays of human thot to a true & comprehensive conclusion" (Emerson's italics). Emerson affixes his copy of this letter so that it forms the first pages of Blotting Book Y, its front cover adorned with mottoes and notes from Coleridge.[44]

Even before his serious reading of Coleridge, Emerson had given clumsy expression to an idea of his own in his sermon of 11 July 1829:

The idea of existing in immediate connexion with the Deity is the most grand that can influence the actions of a human being. The very fact that so stupendous a faith can enter naturally into the soul & become a principle of action is of itself a mighty argument for the truth of Religion.[45]

Not the limp diction alone, but the concession that argument is needed betrays his difficulty. His ideas lie scattered, unrelated; and he has no assurance. Coleridge will not give him a new thought so much as help him toward confidence in his intuition that "God is in every man." With no learning to support him long in a profession that defeated heroic aspirations, bound in principle to be accommodating, and still unsure of the new relations he was beginning to make out, he continued to suffer the pains of his ill-fitting profession.

As the shipboard meditations of 1833 reveal, moral excellence, not easily reached, if ever, by a single man or by the human race, was yet for Emerson the very ground for living. He had once written his aunt that to be a good man was perhaps his sole vocation; [46] he might leave intellectual achievement out of it. Her scoffing reply may have driven him on, but I doubt it. Through all Humean skepticism, the love of "moral perfection" remained; and I think with it the belief that he had something to say, if no certainty that he had the means to say it. In 1833 he would write:

The definition of Moral Nature must be the slow result of years, of lives, of states perhaps of being. . . . I propound definitions with more than the reserve of the feeling above-named—with more because my own conceptions are so dim & vague. But nevertheless nothing darkens, nothing shakes, nothing diminishes my constant conviction of the eternal concord of those laws which are perfect music & of which every high sentiment & every great action is only a new statement & therefore & insomuch speaks aloud to the whole race of man. . . . Not easy are they to be enumerated but he has some idea of them who considers such propositions as St. Bernard's, Nobody can harm me but myself, or who developes the doctrine in his own experience that nothing can be given or taken without an equivalent[.] [47]

Self-reliance and compensation are finding new relations here; and the shadows of both Hume and Coleridge lie upon the passage, but central is Emerson's own revelation. He had already, waiting in Liverpool to board ship, decided that within the church, any church, the moral life was constricted and deflected, reduced either to obeying trivial precepts or continually postponed by promises of reward in a mythical future life. During his own "week of moral excitement," [48] he had struggled seriously with the nice ethical question of whether his distaste warranted his refusal to perform an office his parishioners wanted, aware that he might fall into that state of excessive scrupulosity in which others are sacrificed to one's own virtue.[49]

Even after the week of "moral excitement" and the trip to Europe, he moved with characteristic caution as if waiting for another inner light. Carlyle and Goethe and the discovery that his heroes were not flawless completed his education for freedom, preparing for his new parish should he find it, but he had first to try the Boston way. The subjects of his earliest lectures—science, travel, literature (including ethical writers)—are all "proper & reasonable," but discrete borrowings from Coleridge are numerous. For example, in "The Naturalist" Emerson offers an abstract of the sixth of Coleridge's "Essays on the Principles of Method" and uses it to rescue the argument from design from the microscopic view of William Paley,[50] whom his audience would surely recognize in the "happy Aphides."

In the lecture "Modern Aspects of Letters," Coleridge is singled out for revealing praise.[51] *Aids to Reflection* is dismissed as the "least valuable" of Coleridge's work and parts of the *Statesman's Manual* may well be skipped. The reader of the *Biographia* will find everywhere beauty:

> Pitching her tents before us as we walk
> An hourly neighbor, . . .

Wordsworth helping him to describe his pleasure in Coleridge the critic. Praised as a critic, Coleridge is to be admired for his definitions, so nicely discriminated. The distinction between Reason and Understanding is "all-important," but more to the point: "Out of every one of his distinctions come life and heat. . . . They fill the mind with emotions of awe and delight at the *perception of its own depth*" (italics mine).

The limits of reason, that is Understanding, had been clearly demonstrated by Hume, but neither Hume nor his commonsense critics gave any grounds for confidence in an inexplicable and continuing belief, too weakly named the moral sense or sentiment. The miracles exploded by Hume, Paley's version of the argument from design reduced to trivia, and history, that tale of woes and wars—these feeble buttresses of Unitarian faith could be put in their place as contrivances of the Understanding. With Reason rescued from the disgrace Hume had thrown upon her, one could once again believe with one's fellows and one's ancestors and with their emphasis that "Man is a *rational* animal." Emerson could then write his brother Edward in 1834: "Beasts have some understanding but no Reason. Reason is potentially perfect in every man—Understanding in very different degrees of strength. The thoughts of youth, & 'first thoughts' are the revelations of Reason." [52] Giving the terms his own value and relation, Emerson could ultimately do without them, but while they remained usable and dear, he could deploy them in his letter of proposal to Lydia Jackson, assuring her that she satisfied both his Reason and his Understanding. [53]

As he told Miss Jackson, in all the important matters of his life he trusted more to his pen than to speech. Possibly *Nature* should be regarded from this point of view—a letter to his parish, prolegomenon for all that should follow. In 1836 with *Nature* to announce his way and an audience already exposed to Coleridge, Sampson Reed, Carlyle, and Goethe, Emerson was ready to meet his new parish with lectures that were the more provocative and unsettling because much that was already familiar would be irradiated by a new language, a new light. In no act impetuous, with no treasure prodigal, Emerson did not change ideas as if they were clothes. He thriftily stored ideas as he garnered them and awaited the moment they should find their right relations and their language. Recurring metaphors, not easily traced without a full Concordance, live faintly in the letters and journals until they find their use. House and lands and their appurtenances figure early (1823) as providing in spite of Hume a "tolerable confidence of the reality of existence," [54] and as belonging to the worldly as distinct from the contemplative life exemplified by Newton. They appear again in 1832 distinguishing those who occupy themselves with "secondary objects." [55] Brought under the stewardship of the Understanding (1834) to support our "animal life," [56] the house does not find its right and Emersonian relation until the lecture "Prudence" is revised for the first series of *Essays.*

One class live to the utility of the symbol; esteeming health and wealth a final good. Another class live above this mark to the beauty of the symbol; as the poet, and artist, and the naturalist, and man of science. A third class live above the beauty of the symbol to the beauty of the thing signified; these are wise men. The first class have common sense; the second, taste; and the third, spiritual perception. Once in a long time, a man traverses the whole scale, and sees and enjoys the symbol solidly; then also has a clear eye for its beauty, and lastly, whilst he pitches his tent on this sacred volcanic isle of nature, does not offer to build houses and barns thereon, reverencing the splendor of the God which he sees bursting through each chink and cranny.[57]

Though not his best by any means, this passage is a paradigm of his mature thought, form, and style. And it shows at once what belongs to Boston and what exclusively to Emerson.

There were men of common sense and of taste too in the Saturday Club; there was only one "wise man." That he himself had to bring the club into being suggests that even Emerson could not be always in communion with his elusive Celestial Self. He had always to deal—and in the way of Boston—with the daemonic self, with ambitions and limitations, with hostages to fortune and faith, with a history and a house. Assuredly a Bostonian, Emerson may well have been a saint.

Consistency
in the Mind and Work
of Hawthorne

ARLIN TURNER

Almost a century and a half of criticism has produced little disagreement as to the power of Hawthorne's major works or his mastery of fictional techniques. Except for those contemporaries in America who berated him for helping Franklin Pierce to the Presidency by writing his campaign biography and afterward for dedicating a book to him, and those readers in England who took offense at his treatment of the British in *Our Old Home* and in his *English Notebooks*, posthumously published—with these exceptions, avowals of respect and critical approval have been the rule since Elizabeth Palmer Peabody, later Hawthorne's sister-in-law, read his tales of the early 1830s and called at the Hawthorne residence, believing that a member of that household was the anonymous author.[1] Most of the American and English critics of his own time and later have evaluated his literary achievement and have given it high marks. Even those who have dwelt most on what they call Hawthorne's failures, or on "the death of the artist" in him, have proceeded from the assumption that he is a major author.

Within this consensus as to Hawthorne's worth, there has been surprising diversity, even antagonism, in determining the facts of his life, his thought, his beliefs, and the components of his literary work. There has been still greater diversity in interpreting and evaluating those facts. Hawthorne's habitual independence and the stubborn individuality he often displayed have been generally recognized. But since biographers and critics, in the nature of their undertakings, normally seek to fit their subjects into recognized categories, the traits of independence and individuality have not been put to much use by those writing on Hawthorne and have not seemed to lessen the diversity among them. The consequence is that we have not one

Consistency in the Mind and Work of Hawthorne [99

Hawthorne but many, and some among the many show little kinship to the others.

There can be no quarrel, surely, with any generation for creating its own Hawthorne. Every age, we say, is entitled —or even has an obligation—to rewrite history, including literary history, and thus to re-create its past. Literary criticism is subject to no less extreme swings of the pendulum than literature. Every age reads both current and earlier books through its own lenses, and judges them by its own standards. Revisionism is a continuing phenomenon. Nor can there be any quarrel with an individual reader for finding what he seeks for himself in Hawthorne's tales and romances. The understanding and the criticism special to an era or to an individual may reveal less about Hawthorne than about those interpreting him. And we often say that the greatness of a work—the Bible or *Hamlet* or *The Marble Faun*—is attested by the variety of interpretations and the range of applications it allows. The book Henry James wrote on Hawthorne (1879) says little about Hawthorne but much about James. It had no facts to offer beyond those taken from George Parsons Lathrop's *A Study of Hawthorne*, published three years earlier. The merits of Hawthorne's work are asserted in James's words and are further indicated by the fact that they prompted some of James's most characteristic critical pronouncements. The assurance with which psychological critics interpret Hawthorne's works, on one hand, and the equal certainty of moralist critics on the other, resulting in an extravagant controversy between them in recent years—in these conflicting interpretations is testimony that Hawthorne's work is, in a phrase adapted from Walt Whitman, large enough to contain diverse multitudes.

The uncertainties, inconsistencies, and incongruities, even contradictions, that exist among the many Hawthornes may derive largely from sources close to Hawthorne, including his own notebooks, letters, and literary writings. The temptation has been greater with Hawthorne than with most other authors to read him directly from his imaginative works, to identify him with the poet Coverdale in *The Blithedale Romance*, for example, or to assign to him the guilt and melancholy prominent in his fiction. It has been still more tempting to take at full value what Hawthorne wrote about himself in his prefaces, and most especially what he wrote in letters to Sophia during their engagement, and *to himself* in his notebooks. The difficulty here is to realize a clear context in which to place statements of Hawthorne's that may be in some degree autobiographical. That context was a span of history reaching from his earliest ancestor in Massachusetts to his own day, in which he liked to contrast the commanding figures among his ancestors with himself, a nonentity. In his habit of searching for a meaning everywhere and interpreting as a symbol every object, event, or person, including himself, he included two centuries of New England history as well as the current scene. This was the realm of his fiction. It was his habit in this realm to obliterate—no more than half-consciously, perhaps—demarcations between the factual and the imagined. Hence whatever he wrote about himself, current affairs, or historical matters must be read in this context, and any assessment, in fact any description, of his career and his mind based on his own revelation must be adjusted for the imaginative quality of his view.

Hawthorne's contemporaries—relatives, classmates, neighbors, associates, and "discoverers" such as Elizabeth Peabody and James T. Fields felt themselves to be—saw him against a matter-of-fact background each knew as his own. The Reverend Charles W. Upham, pastor of the First Church, which Hawthorne's forebears had attended for two centuries, delivered a series of lyceum lectures at Salem and surrounding towns and published them in 1831 with the title *Lectures on Witchcraft, Comprising a History of the Delusion in Salem in 1692*. In their recital of events and in their tone of moral condemnation, the lectures re-created the era of the witch hangings and reinforced the prevalent severity in judging the bigotry and the cruelty of the Puritans in early Massachusetts. Thus Hawthorne and the readers of his stories had the same knowledge and presumably the same view of colonial New England. His readers were prepared for the historical and the legendary elements in "The Gentle Boy," "The Maypole of Merry Mount," and "Young Goodman Brown," but hardly for the division of guilt between the Puritans and the Quakers in the first of these stories and between the Puritans and the Cavaliers in the second, or for the ambiguous view of witchcraft in the last.

Responding to the transcendental thought that surrounded Hawthorne at Salem and Brook Farm and Concord, his sister Elizabeth and the Peabody sisters were unabashed disciples of Emerson. Four years before she became Hawthorne's wife, Sophia Peabody wrote her sister Elizabeth, "I think Mr. Emerson is the greatest man that ever lived. . . . In all relations he is noble." He is "diviner than" Carlyle; he is "Pure Tone." [2] How unlikely Hawthorne was to share such opinions becomes clear in his satire on transcendentalism in "The Celestial Railroad" and in his denial of Emerson as a philosopher in "The Old Manse," and is suggested elsewhere in his writings. That others outside Hawthorne's family realized his impatience with apparently both Emerson and Emersonianism is suggested in a letter Ellery Channing sent him at West Newton late in 1852, inviting him to come for a visit in Concord and to look about for a house to purchase. Channing accented his invitation by adding, "Emerson is gone, and nobody here to bore you." [3] The difficulties that beset Emerson in judging Hawthorne are suggested in his complaint to Elizabeth Peabody "that there was no inside to" one of Hawthorne's sketches and in a journal entry of September 4, 1842: "Nathaniel Hawthorne's reputation as a writer is a very pleasant fact, because his writing is not good for anything, and this is a tribute to the man." Emerson would not have overlooked the considerable ground

Hawthorne occupied in common with the American Transcendentalists, but it is evident that he was trying to read the stories in a context not suited to them. A realization of his failure in this regard may have prompted Emerson to lament after Hawthorne's funeral that he had hoped he "might one day conquer a friendship" with his Concord neighbor, but had waited too long.[4]

In identifying Hawthorne with the Transcendentalists,[5] Edgar Allan Poe may have had in mind the transcendental elements of Hawthorne's thought; it is more likely, however, that Poe was not recording such a close observation but was simply using the occasion to strike one of his favorite targets, the New England Transcendentalists. However that may have been, Poe was another of Hawthorne's contemporaries who viewed him against a background only hazily defined.

When Hawthorne wrote of John Brown in 1862 that "nobody was ever more justly hanged" and showed himself uncertain as to the moral position of the Union in prosecuting the war,[6] he raised still higher the barrier of political difference between himself and many in his region that had stood since his biography of Pierce appeared ten years earlier. Emerson, who could read *Our Old Home* only after he had cut out the dedication to Pierce,[7] Frank Sanborn [8] and Moncure Conway,[9] who thought Hawthorne's loyalty to Pierce was an aberration equaled only by his questioning of the Abolitionists—such of his contemporaries as these had difficulties in judging Hawthorne apart from the immediacies of their time and region. They were too close to the current debate on political, social, philosophical, and religious matters—and often too much identified with specific positions—to read with equanimity, even in his fiction, his skeptical views on human and social perfectibility, for example, on the ubiquity of evil and the inevitable consequences of guilt, or on the social and personal responsibilities of the individual.

Readers of Hawthorne since his time have profited from

the distance and the perspective his contemporaries lacked for setting him in his time and place. Far more important, however, in the context requisite for an understanding of Hawthorne is his own mind: his knowledge, his attitudes, and his way of seeing things, including of course his way of seeing his background, current and past. With fuller definition and more precise delineation of his mind comes a better understanding of both the man and his literary work.

During the fifty years after Hawthorne's death, both his portrait and his canon were filled out. Notebooks, letters, and works left incomplete at his death were published, and his widow, two of his children, a son-in-law, and others published biographical accounts or reminiscences. Except for books by Henry James (1879) and George Edward Woodberry (1902), the literary comments were likely to be tributes rather than criticism or evaluation. There was a willingness to take such a view as Emerson recorded in his journal, that Hawthorne "was a greater man than any of his works" betrayed.[10]

In the 1920s Hawthorne attracted psychological biographers, as did Poe and Mark Twain. They found authority in Hawthorne's own statements in letters and notebooks for weighting his life with solitude and gloom. They took his word for it that he had only the slightest dealings with the world about him (ignoring, for one thing, his considerable career as a public official), and they went beyond his word to say that he knew little and thought less about the social and intellectual currents of his time.

Beginning about 1930, Randall Stewart and other scholars have vastly expanded the store of exact information on Hawthorne. Wishing to lessen the burden of gloom and morbidity on the Hawthorne of the recent biographies, Stewart returned him to a place in his world, but in the biography he published in 1948 he overcorrected the portrait, leaving Hawthorne so normal—if not commonplace—as to have no distinctive relations with his times.

F. O. Matthiessen discussed in *American Renaissance* (1941) imagery, symbolism, and other elements in Hawthorne's art more fully than anyone before him and led the way into the study of fictional technique that has been prominent in Hawthorne criticism during the last thirty years. He recognized the contribution of human psychology to the tragic vision in Hawthorne's fiction, alongside the concepts of innate depravity and spiritual conflict. Matthiessen employed psychological, moral, and formal criticism together to produce a Hawthorne worthy of respect for both his thought and his artistry. Successors of Matthiessen in analyzing Hawthorne's fiction have published scores of "new readings," growing from newly assembled patterns of images and owing allegiance, many of them, to little more than the analytical method. Those engaged in narrowly psychological reading have analyzed Hawthorne's characters, the author himself, and at times characters and author together, with only blurred lines separating the creator from his creations. Alongside the image patterns of psychological readings, and often clamorously opposed to them, have been the patterns supporting moral, Christian readings. These analyses, whether psychological, moral, or formal, have remained so strictly within the works, have held so closely to reading for image, symbol, and myth, that they have cast only occasional and casual glances, in the manner common from 1920 to 1940, at the author in relation to the world in which he lived. They have furnished insights into individual works or specific aspects of Hawthorne's fictional technique that only such close analytical reading can yield, but they have contributed less toward an understanding of the author or his work as a whole.

Hawthorne's tales and romances have proved to be richly suited for the exercise of critical connoisseurship, especially in analysis of technique and interpretation through aspects of style. Yet, Hawthorne's works are particularly interwoven with his experiences, his observations, and his attitudes, and through him are related to his times. Aside from the indebtedness of his fiction to the observations and speculations recorded in his notebooks, his debt was great also to the human, social, and literary questions being discussed around him. These questions are of a kind to meet in his readers at any time—or to provoke in them—varied and firm convictions.

Hawthorne's ancestry and the related history were known to many of his contemporaries in Salem. In fact many prominent Salemites had ancestors in common with him, and many others had ties to the early colony as direct as his. These were the readers for whom Hawthorne wrote his early tales. "The Hollow of the Three Hills," probably his earliest published tale, a witch story, was printed in the Salem *Gazette* November 12, 1830. Other tales and sketches were published locally, and only a few of his works were published farther away than Boston. It may have been significant that for several years his tales were published without his name. Hawthorne referred several times—and in signed pieces—to his "sable-cloaked, steeple-crowned" progenitors, and mentioned the rumor that a curse had been handed down from a remote ancestor of his.

It is not necessary to suppose that, however much he toyed with the idea, Hawthorne took upon himself any guilt from his distant ancestors, but the effect on his fiction may have been the same as if he had. He considered himself an author, apparently by the time he left Bowdoin College in 1825 and began his twelve years of apprenticeship to letters, spent in isolation of considerable depth and self-consciousness. He was so thoroughly an author and he so wholly incorporated himself and everything related to him and his family among his materials of composition that his imagination played as freely over those materials as any others. The history of his own family was rich in the elements of fiction: guilt and its consequences—consequences both immediate and remote and visited on both the guilty and the innocent—revenge through a curse mysteriously borne out, prominence and power abused and lost, greatness fading into insignificance. In his mother he saw dramatized at close hand beauty and love condemned to grief and isolation. In himself he could pretend to see ultimate deterioration from his prominent forebears; and as his literary works appeared, he could remark with a wry smile how far he had missed the fame he sought. When he said in 1851 that he had been "for a good many years, the obscurest man of letters in America" [11] (recently *The Scarlet Letter* had won genuine success), he was enlarging the web of fiction he had already spun about his family in America.

It is hardly adequate to say that the curse and the land claim in the family lore were no more in Hawthorne's mind than fabrications to be used in his fiction—in this instance particularly in *The House of the Seven Gables*. His sister Elizabeth wrote his daughter Una in the early 1870s, when Julian was publishing his first novels: "If Julian makes a mark, as perhaps he may, he will redeem the family from the curse that was nearly all its inheritance from its ancestors. But I am wicked to say that, when our forefathers bequeathed us an unblemished name, and the best brains in the world." [12] Elizabeth's first sentence came spontaneously, it would seem, from the peculiar consciousness which the Hawthornes of her generation had inherited and which her brother renewed through his creative imagination. Her second sentence records, as a correction, on further thought, her deliberate withdrawal from the half-real, half-imagined realm so congenial to Hawthorne.

The Hawthorne who wrote the tales and romances must be seen, then, as one who was alert to the affairs of his time, and during much of that time was active in his own special way, but who dwelt imaginatively in a past extending backward two centuries. The intimacy with which he knew the past, the vividness with which he experienced it, gave him a distinctive outlook and accounted for much of the special quality in his fiction we call "Hawthornesque."

The difficulties of seeing one Hawthorne instead of

many have been increased, as I have said, by equivocal statements of his own, in both fictional and nonfictional writings. He rarely answers the questions he raises, and where dogmatism or at least clear assertion is expected, he often is indefinite or ambiguous. Furthermore, he may compound perplexity by playful false leads or deliberate understatement or a feigned adversity—or perversity. But more important, his mind was complex; what at first seems a clear, direct view may prove to have double or multiple facets. Everywhere with Hawthorne, one has to watch for unexpected qualifications and reversals and ironic turns, on pain of serious misreading. The insight and warm humanity and applicability of his works amply justify the effort and invite exploration of the mind back of them.

The modesty habitual with Hawthorne, whether genuine or feigned, handicaps any attempt to see him in clear focus. He undervalued his own work and disparaged his abilities; and by extension, he drew his ancestors and his native region into his self-depreciation. He feared his readers would fall asleep over his pages, he said, or would find them written in invisible ink; if he encountered books like his written by someone else, he could not get through them. These were of course meant as conspicuous undervaluations, but they are compatible with other evidences of the way his mind worked.

To keep in mind Hawthorne's modesty and his avowed deference to the thought and writing of others is essential to a reading of anything he said about himself or his books, but it is a mistake to put this trait forward, as Edward Mather does in subtitling his biography of Hawthorne "A Modest Man" (1940), without putting alongside it Hawthorne's uncommon firmness and independence of mind. He might say that the devil got into his inkwell and could be removed only a penful at a time, but the determinism implied was only metaphorical. In declaring that he hoped to write a brighter romance after *The Scarlet Letter*, he meant only a relative change, and imitation of another author had no attraction for him. His refusal to change his plan for *The Marble Faun*, even when adding the concluding chapter demanded by his readers and publishers,[13] is testimony that his self-effacement had limits.

Complementary and corollary to his own modesty, was the value Hawthorne placed on modesty in others and his slight tolerance for unwarranted certainty, intolerance, arrogance, self-righteousness, and other manifestations of pride. Immoderate dedication even to a noble cause, as with Hollingsworth in *The Blithedale Romance*, brings distortion or destruction to the devotee and those attached to him. In recoiling from intellectual pride, Hawthorne embraced a broad skepticism, and accordingly he questioned everything he encountered and especially all extremes. Thus he normally chose the middle way, and hoped that a balancing of antagonisms would produce moderation and melioration. By temperament a humanitarian and a reformer, he nevertheless found little to endorse among the reform movements popular in his time, for they were often so beclouded by fanaticism as to cast doubt on either the goals intended or the chances that success would bring improvement. Thus Hawthorne found himself at odds with members of his family and his neighbors in a region where few stayed outside the reform agitation. In the tale "Earth's Holocaust" (1844) he called the roll of current reform movements and concluded that all were superficial and likely to be fruitless.

Although Hawthorne's disparagement of petty reformers could find only scant approval with his sister Elizabeth, his wife's family the Peabodys, and others who were in some degree millennialists, this quirk of his could be tolerated, but not his denial of the abolitionist position widely held around him. He knew that in writing the biography of Pierce he was assuming a political role and an alignment unpopular with men in his region. In a letter of August 28, 1852, to William D. Ticknor, his friend and the publisher of the biography, he displayed a firm independence and a degree of pleasure in the antagonism he knew that independence would provoke. He thought Ticknor should "blaze away a little harder" in advertising the book, using the author's name prominently. "Go it strong, at any rate," he added. "We are politicians now; and you must not expect to conduct yourself like a gentlemanly publisher." [14] With no less independence and firmness he dedicated *Our Old Home* to Pierce a decade later, even when he knew the dedication would lose him both book sales and friends. Another letter to Ticknor, January 19, 1855, gives further evidence that such independence of thought and action was based deep within him. He had made a friend a loan from his savings. Ticknor had warned him against lending money to others who might be unable to repay him. Hawthorne acknowledged the advice to be good, and continued, "But when the friend of half my lifetime asks me to assist him, and when I have perfect confidence in his honor, what is to be done? Shall I prove myself to be one of those persons who have every quality desirable in friendship, except that they invariably fail you in a pinch? I don't think I can do that." [15]

Hawthorne's reliance on his own against the prevailing judgment around him did not align him against all reform. In casting his lot (and his savings also) with the dreamers at Brook Farm, he not only overcame his inborn skepticism of extreme measures for social improvement but also went beyond speculation to action that required daring and willingness to take a risk. Although Coverdale, the narrator of *The Blithedale Romance*, is less the author than a character in the plot, he probably was speaking for Hawthorne when he declared he was proud to have felt sufficient pride and faith in humankind to give his best efforts to the idealistic scheme. To the question that seems to demand an answer, whether Emerson or Thoreau or Margaret Fuller or Elizabeth Peabody had comparable pride and faith and daring, it can be said that their main reasons for not joining the Brook Farm community may have been no more, in each separate instance, than lack of faith that the scheme was workable; and after a few months Hawthorne left the community for the same reason.

While he was Consul at Liverpool, Hawthorne's response to the injustice and misery that he learned was abundant in the merchant marine was the response of a reformer with no less drive than conviction. Recognizing a vast evil that he believed could be meliorated by procedures easily within reach, he spoke in unequivocal language to both friends and officials. To Charles Sumner he wrote on May 23, 1855, first remarking that three cases had come before him in which seamen had been "shot dead by their officers," and then adding,

the most perplexing part of the matter is, that all this bloodshed and cruelty seems to be strangely justifiable, and almost inevitable under the circumstances. It certainly is not the fault so much as it is the fate, of our ship-masters to do these abominable deeds. They are involved in a wrong system which renders it impossible for them to do right; and they themselves become morally deteriorated by it, and continually grow worse. As for the seamen, they are no better than pirates. . . . I should like to know what is to become of us, at sea, in case of a war—but *that* you don't care about.

If you will let slavery alone for a little while, and attend to this business (where much good may, and no harm can possibly, be done) I think you will be doing our country a vast service. The shipping-masters in the American ports seem to be at the bottom, or near the bottom, of the mischief. . . . These shipping-masters should be annihilated at once;—no slave drivers are so wicked as they, and there is nothing in slavery so bad as the system with which they are connected.[16]

There is much of Hawthorne in this letter to Sumner. His humanitarian concern prompts him to practical suggestions: Sumner would learn what he could in America about the system in which the merchant ships operated; he would himself gather information on atrocities reported to the Consulate. The solution might be an apprentice system, compulsory for every vessel, to provide trained American seamen. In proposing that Sumner "let slavery alone, for a little while" and undertake reform in the merchant marine, Hawthorne disclosed a directness and a sternness of purpose not usual with him. He continued to judge reform efforts on the proportion of good over ill they could be expected to produce. Most interesting of all, perhaps, the author of this letter is conspicuously the author of the tales and romances. On no point under scrutiny does he see a simple conclusion. The seamen are "no better than pirates," being only such "offscourings" from other nations as the shippers are able to "entrap." The shipping-masters, fated to be at or near the "bottom of the mischief," are no "worse than the system of manning their ships inevitably makes them." Though many of them have admirable qualities and wish to improve the conditions, "they are human, and therefore apt to become devilish, under evil influences." Here are the same inevitability, the same determinism, the same propensity for evil that dominate his fictional characters, but here are also the same partial accountability and close-reined free will permitted those characters.

That is to say that the consul who analyzed the seamen and the shipmasters in Liverpool was no different from the author who probed the mind and the heart of Hester Prynne and Hollingsworth and Rappaccini and Aylmer. Both consul and novelist turned primary attention to the human beings involved and secondarily analyzed their circumstances and sought a context in which to judge them. From the 1830s, when he began publishing stories with the qualities we recognize as distinctly his own, he remained steady afterward in the outlook and the technique of his fiction. Such emphasis on plot, adventure, and suspense as he had found in Scott and the Gothic romancers and had employed in *Fanshawe* no longer interested him. Instead, his purpose was best served by establishing a situation at the outset, most often assumed rather than developed, and observing one or more characters as they experienced the consequences. Most often the situation underlying a Hawthorne story involves a moral question growing from the assumptions and beliefs of the characters.

Hawthorne made no claim to being a theologian, a philosopher, a literary theorist, or a literary critic, though he was more of each than is normally thought. His notebooks, which served him mainly for recording ideas that might be developed into sketches or tales and for storing up scenic details he could put to use in his fiction, contain a minimum of the abstraction, generalization, and formulation that bulk large in the journals of Emerson, Thoreau, and Melville. Some of the descriptions in Hawthorne's notebooks resemble those characteristic of Thoreau's *Journals*, but they stop short of the application and speculation normal with Thoreau. In the hints for stories, Hawthorne's focus was most often on people in special situations; and even when an idea he recorded suggests a mind running to abstraction, it is apparent as a rule that the author had in mind a story, an essay, and that the idea or problem would gain its significance and its interest for him primarily through the effects it might have on the characters involved with it.

Herein lies an important guide for the reading of Hawthorne. What is given at the opening and in the background of a story includes a set of assumptions and beliefs postulated for the characters. Thereafter a Hawthorne story does less to support or deny the beliefs than to trace out their effects on characters who hold them, and often to show also reinforcement and development of the characters' beliefs. "Young Goodman Brown" does not argue whether Brown attends a witch meeting, whether witches exist, or whether all, including even Faith, are joined in a common bond of evil. The author says explicitly, "Be that as it may"; but there is no equivocation as to the effect on Brown, for he believes that the satanic kingdom exists and that guilt is universal. Hawthorne would probably say that a reader is welcome, if he wishes, to create on his own some specific sin for the Reverend Mr. Hooper in "The

Minister's Black Veil," and it may be that he purposely left the way open for a reader to join thus in the creation of the story; but what the story does primarily if not solely is to show what happens in a community which holds the beliefs that prevail in this one and is subjected to the symbol of Hooper's veil. In another story, "Roger Malvin's Burial," the reader observes the initial situation develop and is invited to determine for himself, rather than take the author's word for it, the extent of Reuben Bourne's guilt, if any, at the same time that he observes the tragic effects growing from Bourne's own belief in his guilt. Similarly the murder of the phantom in *The Marble Faun* takes place in the presence of the reader, so to speak, and he as a consequence can judge the nature and extent of the guilt chargeable to Miriam and Donatello; but the reader can only conjecture what were the earlier relations between Miriam and the phantom and hence cannot assess the guilt fully. Thus Hawthorne can again give his characters an awareness of guilt without defining it. His focus is on the response of Miriam and Donatello—and of Hilda and Kenyon as well—to a guilt they recognize.

Examples can be multiplied of ideas or abstractions that belong to the awareness or the assumptions of Hawthorne's characters—and of his readers also. They are not to be debated, and as a rule not even to be presented in full, but to be observed in their bearing on the events of the plot. The idea of confession in *The Marble Faun* may be cited, specifically as it is dramatized in Hilda's visit to the confessional at St. Peter's. In the romance and in earlier notebook entries as well, Hawthorne passes over the theological aspects of the confessional to focus on the psychological. The same can be said of the idea in *The House of the Seven Gables* that the past is a weight on the present. The stunted chickens, the poisoned well, and the curse, along with other metaphors, assert what is assumed about the idea, at the same time that it is being traced out in the lives of the characters. In *The Blithedale Romance* Hollingsworth's overpowering dedication to his scheme for humanitarian reform, on the one hand, and Coverdale's social and human inertness, on the other, are at least incipient, if not present, when the romance opens. They are revealed as the narrative progresses and as the consequences are shown to be inevitable.

It may be that the richness of *The Scarlet Letter* and the strength of its appeal to widely diverse readers can be attributed in large part to the author's skill in managing elements in the background as they determine the actions, thoughts, and interrelations of the characters. The community in which the action takes place has a remarkable consistency in its social, religious, political, and intellectual aspects, and the characters remain integrally oriented within this community. Hester flirts with free thought on woman's role and on those points at which her humanity conflicts with society. Thus Hawthorne broaches a topic of interest to him and his readers without violating the integrity of the historical background. The elements of that background, beliefs in immortality, for example, and the relations between the minister and his congregation, are not at issue; rather at issue are the human effects of the situation given, the effects which their own beliefs and assumptions and attitudes produce on the characters in the presence of various forces.

In the sketches and in some of the tales, the underlying ideas may remain abstract, when no characters are employed or the characters are mechanical rather than human. The veteran commander, the dark-visaged stranger, and the last toper in "Earth's Holocaust," for example, are less persons than parts of the narrative machinery, as is also the Wandering Jew in "A Virtuoso's Collection." In such pieces as "Sights from a Steeple" and "Sunday at Home," essays rather than tales, the presentation is in the first person, with the author presumably recording his own experiences and observations. But the author is not Hawthorne in a full sense; in each essay he has a distinct personality and his own outlook. Likewise the first-person narrators in tales such as "The New Adam and Eve," "Fancy's Show Box," and "The Threefold Destiny" are ostensibly the author, but they are not Hawthorne, strictly speaking. They are creations of his, characters within the stories they tell and subject to effects subtly produced by the stories. Alertness to such distinctions as these among the character-narrators and the various types of author-narrators is essential to a perceptive reading of Hawthorne, and an awareness that not all the omniscient authors in his works are in fact Hawthorne will help to clarify the image that often appears blurred in the works of biographers and critics.

We have learned that it was Hawthorne's habit to write —in fact to see and to think—in metaphor and symbol, and that in his letters and notebooks and prefaces we may encounter the kind of figurative language, understatement, indirection, and playful expression normal to his fiction. We have learned to be cautious in assuming that a character, such as Coverdale in *The Blithedale Romance*, is autobiographical to the extent that may first appear. We have come to realize that the narrators of two sketches or tales, though both are omniscient authors, are not necessarily the same person, and are not to be identified fully with Hawthorne.

As we have gained experience in reading Hawthorne and have learned more about the working of his mind, while adding greatly to the factual information available, we have gained assurance in both biography and interpretation. His contemporaries found him no less distinctive, no less individual in his personality and outlook than in his literary production. We find him no less distinctive than they did, but our knowledge and perspective enable us to clear up uncertainties and reconcile inconsistencies and to begin with one Hawthorne rather than many as we proceed to interpret him in the manner suited to us in our time.

William Dean Howells
Perception
and Ambivalence

CLAYTON L. EICHELBERGER

To subject the work of an artist and critic as prolific as William Dean Howells to limited reappraisal is to resort to generalizations, any one of which, by its very nature, demands reduction. Yet such generalizations may serve well as points of departure. Viewed chronologically, the general substantive trend in Howells's novels is from simplicity to complexity, from external reportorial observation to internal motivational analysis, from the relatively restricted boundaries of unconscious individuality, through awareness, to the breadth of social complicity and beyond to social judgment. Artistically the work progresses from skillful expository narration to the widely discussed "dramatic unfolding," from the discovery of ambivalence in art as in life to a studied dismissal of oversimplification demanded by an increasingly experienced and perceptive authorial eye. Such generalizations apply well, however, only to the ascendency of Howells and begin to lose value—begin almost to reverse direction—as Howells's interests in social and economic conditions widen his vision and simultaneously restrict penetration into human individuality.

A major propelling factor in Howells's development is his increasingly conscious desire to see—honestly, faithfully, truthfully. A novel, he one time said, is "a perspective made for the benefit of people who have no true use of their eyes."[1] Henry James, who elevated the infinitive *to see* to the highest plane of creative reality, often said very much the same thing. Both the business of the novelist and the art of the novelist consist of *seeing*, first for himself, and then for his reader; and seeing, in the best sense, is the ultimate comprehension of reality. Not many of us would argue that Howells saw as deeply or as profoundly as did James, that he came as close to ultimate understanding; but in the retreating past too many of Howells's critics have been even less tolerant and have implied, or openly charged, that Howells was unable to see at all—at least that he was unable to see beyond the surface manifestations of external actuality. Most of us know better now. Even though we recognize that Howells stood in awe of the unexplored "fastnesses" of the mind, uncertain as to how the journey into those fastnesses was to be effected creatively,[2] we are reassured by his awareness of their existence; and our confidence in his ability *to see* is comfortably expanded as we find him again and again, patiently but persistently, distinguishing between actuality and reality, dispelling illusions, correcting our vision of life in the direction of twenty-twenty honesty. Especially in the more excellent novels of his golden period, the 1880s.

Those excellent novels do not want attention. *A Modern Instance, The Rise of Silas Lapham*, and *A Hazard of New Fortunes* are perennially subjected to reappraisal. We still have a tendency, however, to shunt aside the earlier fictive attempts. No doubt overwhelming evidence can be marshalled to demonstrate that Howells did not hit his creative stride before *A Modern Instance* in 1882, and certainly not before *The Undiscovered Country* in 1880; but that is not to say his earlier works lack value. More specifically, no one would argue, I think, that his first two novels, *Their Wedding Journey* (1872) and *A Chance Acquaintance* (1874) are artistically superior (although much can be said for their artistic qualities); but they are more important than we sometimes concede because they were written during a crucial period in Howells's literary career—a period in which he was adapting to an editorial position and during which he was consciously attempting to define a critical attitude and to effect a transition from creative reporting, in the travel genre, to the writing of fiction. In *Their Wedding Journey* and *A Chance Acquaintance* Howells was not only engaged in learning to see, both creatively and critically, but also in providing perspective for those who had no sight; and in doing so he established the direction his fiction was to take during most of the next two decades.

In our continuing attempt to understand Howells and his work, it may be instructive to look again at his first two novels—to rediscover his developing awareness of the difference between actuality and reality and his attempt to make visible that difference creatively in the attitudes of his fictive characters and in his own authorial response to those attitudes. *Their Wedding Journey* and *A Chance Acquaintance* are not primarily about places and things, as has sometimes been assumed, but about people. Although he does not yet exhibit the strongly conscious thrust toward motivational analysis which comes forward in *A Modern Instance*, Howells is looking at people, *seeing* people. Outstanding in what he sees is the fact that they share a common blindness which is outwardly exhibited as pretension, an assumption of personal superiority which in an equalitarian and democratic society is illusory and which reflects, in a universal way, a common human failing—a natural resistance to expansion beyond the narrow limits of our own established self-esteem. This thematic consideration finds a substantive parallel in Howells's concurrent exploration of the role of romanticism in literature and in life.

In March 1871, when work was well underway on *Their Wedding Journey*, Howells wrote to James M. Comly, editor of the *Ohio State Journal*, about his current project, saying it was to focus on American life and scene and was to fuse fiction and the travel-sketch genre.[3] About the same time he wrote his father that he was "fairly launched upon the story of our last summer's travels, which I am giving the form of fiction so far as the characters are concerned."[4] He was not confident of his ability to write fiction, however, and in what amounts to an apology in the first paragraph of *Their Wedding Journey*, he confesses a distrust of his "fitness for a sustained or involved narration." Yet much later, according to a *Book Buyer* literary column, upon the flyleaves of the collected edition of his works which he was inscribing to a friend, he noted his opinion of several of his own books. Of *Their Wedding Journey* he wrote, "My first attempt to mingle fiction & travel—fiction got the best of it." [5]

To one who gives *Their Wedding Journey* only a cursory reading, Howells's casual evaluation of the success of his early literary experiment seems to give undue importance to the fictional element. In his previously published nonfiction prose pieces, Howells had been drawing directly, and effectively, from his personal observations of actuality. *Their Wedding Journey* appears to constitute no major departure from that pattern. It is quite frankly based on a trip to Niagara, down the St. Lawrence, and back to Boston which the Howellses had taken one year earlier. Faithful to that experience, *Their Wedding Journey* does map a journey establishing the fact of both time and place.[6] The author so frequently breaks narrative for scenic descriptions and vignettes, for catalogues of character and clusters of de-romanticizing detail, that one is tempted to deny so much as the presence of fiction in the work or to conclude that Howells, in an attempt to produce a truly American work, has stumbled into a late nineteenth-century version of the topographical fallacy. A closer reading, however, assures one that *Their Wedding Journey* has a sustaining level of meaning. Henry Adams was probably correct in judging in his early review that the preserving quality of the novel rests in its "faithful" and "pleasing" picture of American life; [7] but he did not add that the artistic vision which gives a value other than historical to the novel is less dependent upon the details of rail travel and fashion, of provincial cuisine and mannerisms, than it is upon the fictionalized attitudes of the Marches as they view and react to the American scene.

The common reality of American life which Howells effectively evokes in *Their Wedding Journey,* whether he initially intended this or not, the reality which is of the decade but which at the same time transcends it, relates to the role of illusion in the lives of ordinary Americans. It is in this area that authorial perception illuminates the commonplace.

There is evidence to suggest that Howells, if he did not directly plan this more meaningful dimension of *Their Wedding Journey,* at least recognized it before publication of the novel took place. The function of the narrator, as he projected it, is clearly stated in the introductory paragraph: "Fortunately for me, . . . I shall have nothing to do but to talk of some ordinary traits of American life as these appeared to them [the Marches], to speak a little of well-known and easily accessible places, to present now a bit of landscape and now a sketch of character." [8] In a manuscript passage which Howells canceled before publication, he had also written, "It is with what they saw, and where they went, rather than what they are, that we have to do." [9] The role of the narrator, as announced in the published version, seems modest, even less than adequate, and may have misled many readers by setting them to look for places and things and characters sketched along the way and so to fail to see that the more interesting and significant focus is on Basil and Isabel March, ordinary characters being singled out for scrutiny. If one will underscore the phrase *as these appeared to them* in the introductory paragraph, and if he will combine with this emphasis the fact that Howells canceled the line which denied interest in *what they are,* he has evidence to support the contention that Howells, even before publication of *Their Wedding Journey,* already recognized the contribution that artistic perspective, which we associate with the fictional mode, had made to his experimental novel. Interest in *who,* but even more in *what* the Marches are, as reflected by how things appear to them, may very well be a

major unifying factor without in any way eroding Howells's interest in the American and the ordinary, for the
Marches qualify on both counts. It is true that they are not
representative of the middle and lower-middle classes to
which the word *ordinary* is popularly ascribed, but in
their shared attitudes—in their sentimental irrationality, in
their basic self-interest and quiet vanity, in their tendency
to rationalize the validity of their preconceptions and illusions—they are in no way atypical. Clara Kirk was quite
correct in asserting in a larger context that Howells used
the Marches "to bridge the gulf between day-to-day actuality and the novelist's reality." [10] It is in exposure of
their restrictive vision that he makes his own perceptions
clear.

Although dramatic conflict as such is nonexistent in
Their Wedding Journey, Howells does achieve minimal
character opposition by using Basil as a means of penetrating the illusions of Isabel. The first lines of dialogue in
the novel are assigned to her and establish her eagerness to
conceal her bridal identity, even though the nonbridal pretense which is so dear to her is betrayed by her gestures of
endearment. Not only do the lines expose her game of pretense, but they also reveal her habit of rationalizing her
pretensions as she explains the postponement of their wedding trip so as to place the two of them in the best possible
light. Basil's bemused warning that her caresses might expose her as bride suggests that he will serve as the practical, rational center of the story; and artistic dimension is
added to the work on numerous occasions when Basil, sitting in judgment on Isabel and her opinions, pricks the
bubbles of her illusions or, in a quite paternal way, prag-
matically manoeuvers around her whims, at the same time
communicating to the reader his own occasional perception of a reality she fails to perceive. But the character
alignment, it turns out, is not quite so simple as it at first
seems; for the difference in perceptivity of the two is not
one of major degree. Although Basil March is Bostonian

by adoption only, he has, through that adoption, been conditioned to share with Isabel many attitudes toward life. Soon one finds him not simply tolerating the games which Isabel plays by the rules of her own preconceptions, but actually joining with her in sentimentalized flights of fantasy.

The more consistent way in which Howells uses the Marches in exposing their common pretense is by placing their action in ironic contrast to their stated intentions. From the beginning they profess to be searching for an American experience, an experience of the commonplace; but they hold themselves apart from the very thing they seek. They were "in it, but not of it, as they fancied," Howells explains. They deliberately choose passage in "an ordinary carful of human beings," but shift to a drawing-room car the next day, having failed to achieve "the most American manner" in the common-passenger car. In the comfort and luxury of their new accomodations they are exultant, and they rationalize their decision. One is scarcely justified in describing the Marches as snobbish— they are such pleasingly gentle people—but they consistently think very well of themselves; they are always conscious of, if they do not display, their superiority— although they sometimes, as when they walk jesting through "a pomp of unoccupied porters and call-boys," do display themselves somewhat vulgarly. As Bostonians who have traveled abroad, they measure Western life as they observe it against superior Bostonian and European standards. In commonplace surroundings, engaged in a commonplace journey, they are impressed by their own cultural exposure and, in their private conversation, refer to it. They judge people by the fashion of their clothes and by the presence or absence of what they consider to be civilized proprieties in their behavior. They are quite taken by ordinary types who flatter their self-esteem by adopting subservient roles, and they are irritated by servants of the public, especially clerks such as the haughty, "castellated baron" of the ticket office, who deal in a lordly manner with those who subscribe to their services. They recognize Boston as "a place of the greatest natural advantages, as well as all acquirable merits," and they are not above dropping the name of that cultural center to win respect for themselves. Isabel stands aloof from "rude, silly folks" wherever she finds them and generally imposes a distance between herself and her fellow travelers, except when she condescends to make a fleeting, charitable gesture—a smile to the wife of a stricken man, a few quick words to an invalid in a wheelchair. Her only sustained effort to reach out takes place when she encounters the Ellisons, whom she recognizes as of her class.

Frequently in *Their Wedding Journey* the perception of reality is conveyed by a juxtaposition of contrasting passages. After an extensive poetic description of Niagara Falls (the type of sentimentalized passage in which Howells seems to burlesque rather than embrace romantic effectism), one is returned to the commonplace clutter of luggage and newsstand activity on the hotel portico. The romantic, allusive description of scene Westward from Albany is broken as the author-narrator loiters "in fancy" through a barnyard, detailing the commonplace. For an entire evening Basil and Isabel sentimentalize over Rochester. In this "vale of Arcady," Isabel rhapsodizes over the Genesee Falls. Basil points toward objectivity by contrasting the story of Sam Patch with that of Leander, but ends by quoting a lengthy, pensive ballad. The passage immediately following begins a new paragraph and focuses on the shabby griminess of the coach and the "squalid and loathsome company" in which the Marches find themselves, and the sentimentality which clouded vision the night before is dispelled. Repeatedly, in direct phrase and by implication, the narrator complains that the Marches "cast an absurd poetry over the landscape" and generally finds them "absurdly sentimental people." But he indicates understanding rather than censure when he adds, "whom yet I cannot find it in my heart to blame for their folly, though I could name ever so many reasons for rebuking it."

Their Wedding Journey incorporates a gentle awakening to reality, a recognition of common pretense born and nurtured by man's failure *to see*. What purports itself to be a narrative of observations of people and places gradually, but consistently, penetrates the surface of appearance to reveal an attitude of assumed superiority that is widely shared. While inconspicuously holding themselves apart, isolated from other human beings except those of their own kind, the Marches, without seeing their own commonness, look on the commonplace with a lively interest and tolerance which rarely becomes anything deeper than just that because it lacks understanding. The authorial conception of the work as a whole is ironic in that the wedding journeyers, wrapped warmly in their own interests as are all the other wedding journeyers they encounter, go forth to see but can see only superficially as they are accustomed to seeing. If there is any more than ordinary depth to their vision, it ordinarily should be attributed to their broader, more socially acceptable experience, especially in the form of foreign travel and residence in Boston; but what that broader experience has contributed to them in depth of vision is clearly negligible. The author, who perceives their pretense, shares it with the reader as a part of his vision of reality. At one point early in *Their Wedding Journey*, Basil summarizes an experience by observing, "Nothing is so hard as to understand that there are human beings in this world besides one's self and one's set" (p. 35), and the simple directness of the statement underscores its importance.

Chronologically, thematically, and artistically *A Chance Acquaintance* is a continuation of and an extension beyond *Their Wedding Journey*. Substantively it is both sequential and supplemental; artistically it reflects growth. In *A*

Chance Acquaintance, authorial awareness of human narrowness breaks forth in an imaginatively conceived and forcefully executed drama which verifies the text of Basil's observation; for the self-endorsed superiority of Miles Arbuton, the single most documented actuality in the novel, is directly attributed to his basic limitation: "he had always shrunk from knowledge of things outside of a very narrow world," and "he had not a ready imagination."

The contrast between the two leading characters in *A Chance Acquaintance* is so sharp that it verges on the simplistic; the surface impression is that the roles are Melvillian in the division of traits and that they are artistically structured rather than honest. The attitudes of both Kitty Ellison and Miles Arbuton seem stylized and exaggerated to the degree that characterization comes dangerously close to stereotyping. This is especially true of Arbuton. In the hands of the author the deck is consistently stacked against his vanity, which is symptomatic of his moral irresponsibility. One's antipathy toward him is roused the moment he is introduced with the ironic recognition of his right, since he has the appearance of an Englishman, to delay the Saguenay boat; and it is nourished from that point on. His haughtiness is immediately evidenced by his "cold dismissal" of the English players aboard the vessel and, tentatively, of the Ellison party, who dress with less "scrupulosity" than he finds requisite. "Guarding his distance as usual," he goes ashore at Tadoussac, surprised by his "concession to the popular impulse." He wishes for "someone qualified by the proper associations and traditions" to share his experience. He is "exclusive by training and instinct" and finds himself "hopelessly superior" to his fellow passengers. As an Europeanized American, he is an unnatural man, and he emerges as a contemptible snob. His "sentiment of superiority" is documented dramatically or expositorily on almost every page of the novel.

Dramatically Kitty Ellison represents the counter position. Her wide, clear eyes framed by long lashes bespeak the innocence of the natural child; and it is her naturalness and her sense of democracy which repeatedly oppose Arbuton's pretension and factitious aristocracy. In Arbuton she finds verification of her Uncle Jack's derogatory concept of a gentleman: "at the best, it was a poor excuse for not being just honest and just brave and just kind, and a false pretense of being something more." [11] When Arbuton exhibits aloof indifference to the environment, she expresses her deep interest in the "humble drama" unveiled to her. She finds natural grandeur in views which he slights, and she expresses simple delight in artifacts which he views as vulgar. Her "natural simplicity" and self-reliance, mingled with "an innocent trust of others" and "an ignorance of the world," contrast with his suspicion and arrogance. Her responses are honest and unrehearsed, often motivated by uninhibited sentiment, but sometimes revealing "decided opinion"; she had been trained to think, and, free from convention, "she thought and felt whatever she liked."

By establishing strong character opposition in *A Chance Acquaintance*, Howells created a dramatic situation which enabled him to expose more clearly and more imaginatively than in *Their Wedding Journey* the vanity and the concomitant illusions which he had come to see in American life. In its simplest form the conflict is social in nature, quite in keeping with Howells's developing social awareness. The many-faceted divergencies of American culture may be specified variously but are most commonly lumped together in Howellsian criticism as the unconventional (Western) vs. the conventional (Proper Bostonian).[12] It will be more fruitful for our purposes, however, and ultimately it may be more Howellsian, to phrase the overriding conflict as that between the natural (Western) and the unnatural (Bostonian); but in doing so we effect a curious reversal in that the *unconventional*, a negative term, assumes the affirmative qualities associated with *natural;* and the negative implications of *unnatural* are transferred to the traditionally affirmative *conventional*. This is appropriate, for Howells thought of himself as being on the side of both the new and the natural. Without doubt, it is the natural (the simple, the honest, the democratic) vs. the unnatural (the pretentious, the traditional, the artificial) that *A Chance Acquaintance*, on one level, is all about. And if we will add to this the recognition that the natural is not narrowly committed to a set pattern but that it may be self-contradictory, that it is large and may contain multitudinous diversities, we have an appropriate basis for understanding and accepting the meaningful ambivalence in the character of Kitty Ellison.

The reality of the situation is less simple than the sharp character and social contrasts suggest, and revelation of that reality is indicative of Howells's deepening perception. Neither Kitty nor Arbuton is cast in a pure mold. Occasionally beneath the artificial and polished externalities of Arbuton—when he impulsively throws a rock against the cliff, when he gives alms, when he steps between Kitty and the attacking dog—one glimpses momentarily a potentially appealing, but habitually restrained, natural man. Kitty, while remaining securely in the fold of Western democracy, is less rigidly structured than Arbuton. Because of her uninhibited and open nature, one is made to feel that she has sufficient largeness of character to conceivably embrace points of view other than her own. She consistently exhibits a sensitivity to Boston superiority and an innocent acceptance of the Easterner's wider horizons, especially in his knowledge of foreign travel and the accoutrements of culture; but her sensitivity is never allowed to diminish her democratic orientation.

Kitty is a much more complex creation than mere surface opposition to Arbuton suggests. Not only does she, like Isabel March before her, indulge in games of fantasy, but occasionally, as in her unwillingness to explore the lane opening into the Sault au Matelot because of its barnyard texture of feathers and chopped straw, she holds herself apart from the commonplace. She seems unconsciously to adopt, perhaps simply to accept because of the higher ranks of Western society to which she is accustomed, a position midway between that of the superior Bostonian and the humble natives of Quebec; but she is neither condescending nor openly subservient. Her basic tolerance has an ambivalent value representative of her Western heritage. It is important to note that the counterpart to the mythic proportions of Bostonian superiority in mid-nineteenth-century America was the myth of idyllic rusticity and provincialism of the West, of the Erie Creeks of the nation. No matter how one phrases the mythic contrast, it is sustained by the complicity of both Eastern and Western pretense. Positions of superiority, real or illusory, are not simply imposed; they are also tolerated. The "sentiment of superiority" which has become a behavioral pattern for the Bostonian is preserved, not only by the Bostonian, but also by the democratic Westerner who accepts it. In other words, the dramatic situation in which Kitty and Arbuton find themselves results from a mutuality of attitudes which involves pretense and illusion on both sides. This is not to say that Kitty accepts Arbuton's superiority without protest; indeed, she sometimes sharply and outspokenly challenges it. But her position is compromised by a Western attitude; she is not able to dispel Uncle Jack's idealized image of Boston which has become a part of her own orientation and draws her to the East. Although she resents the attitudes of Arbuton most of the time, she submits to them, as if his were a greater right, a greater nobility than hers; and in this acceptance, pretense undergoes an ironic reversal. "There's such a thing as being proud of not being proud," Kitty observes; and she gives evidence of this reverse pride when she insists on putting off Aunt Fanny's garments of pretense in exchange for her own less artful dress. Her wardrobe deceit and her acceptance of Fanny's matchmaking games are only symbolic of a deeper complicity.

William Dean Howells [1 3 1

Kitty represents the ambivalence of the Westerner, an ambivalence which, as we shall see later, relates to an equally mixed attitude toward romanticism on the part of the realist. It is in the portrayal of Kitty that Howells is most sensitive and perceptive, that he sees most clearly and most deeply in *A Chance Acquaintance*, a fact in part attributable to his own democratic affinities as nurtured by his own experiences in life. In the absence of cultural advantage enjoyed by older, established American societies, the Westerner, made conscious (from both within and without) of his own lack, rationalized, and often proved, his own self-sufficiency while he continued to yearn for social elevation and sophistication. Nostalgically remembering and often reminded of richness left behind, he was, because of his more complex needs, more tolerant than his Eastern brother who was self-consciously committed to the tradition-validated superiority of his social position. During Arbuton's period of infatuation and the time in which his proposal is being weighed by Kitty, it is apparent that he is not thinking in terms of accepting her as she is—he lacks that tolerance—but of molding her to fit his own standards; and although she insists on his introduction to Erie Creek as a matter of honesty, it is equally apparent that she is aware her marriage to a Bostonian would lift her above Erie Creek. The possibility that her "violent democracy" is subject to concession, that it is idealistic rather than real and so shares with the Bostonian's air of superiority an element of pretension, is in itself an ironic observation. Fulfillment of that possibility would satisfy the romantic reader in that, principle quite aside, the common heroine would be elevated to the rank of princess. But Howells rejects that possibility. Kitty's ultimate renunciation of Arbuton does not so much suggest Western democracy rising superior to a humbled Eastern aristocracy (such poetic justice also has a romantic flavor) as it is a denial of romantic oversimplification. Kitty is attracted to the East, but she is of the West. Her withdrawal from decision in the form of a counter decision is verification of her essential ambivalence which through the novel has both urged her toward and restrained her from love for Arbuton. That ambivalence is the source of Kitty's vitality; it is also her reality. Through it the obvious external conflict in the novel is transposed into a more deeply perceived internal one which remains, quite unromantically, unresolved. Once one perceives the ambivalence which pervades complex social reality and the way it is reflected in the conditioning of individuals, it becomes increasingly difficult to map the boundaries of conflicting attitudes or simply, without dishonesty, to resolve those conflicts which often continue without resolution in life. Although the external affair with Arbuton is canceled in the denouement of *A Chance Acquaintance*, the more subtle internal conflict perceived in the reality of Kitty is held in suspension, and it is on this level that the simplyfying processes of romanticism are denied.

Early in *A Chance Acquaintance*, Howells's awareness of the variance between appearance and reality, his desire to see through one to the other, and something of his impatience with those who choose to ignore the distinction between the two, thus avoiding the difficulty of handling that distinction fictively, are subtly parabled in a moment of low-keyed drama which takes place on the Saguenay excursion. Mrs. Ellison has injured her ankle and is sitting in a deck chair idly reading a guidebook as the vessel nears Cape Trinity, informing herself by report rather than direct observation.

"It says here that the water of the Saguenay is as black as ink. Do *you* think it is, Richard?"
"It looks so."
"Well, but if you took some up in your hand?"
"Perhaps it wouldn't be as black as the best Maynard and Noyes, but it would be black enough for all practical purposes."

"Maybe," suggested Kitty, "the guide-book means the kind that is light blue at first, but 'becomes a deep black on exposure to the air,' as the label says."

"What do you think, Mr. Arbuton?" asked Mrs. Ellison with unabated anxiety.

"Well, really, I don't know," said Mr. Arbuton, who thought it a very trivial kind of talk, "I can't say, indeed. I haven't taken any of it up in my hand."

"That's true," said Mrs. Ellison gravely, with an accent of reproval for the others who had not thought of so simple a solution to the problem, "very true." (Pp. 41–42)

Dissatisfied with Richard's initial response that the water appears black, Fanny prods him into the further suggestion that appearance and reality might differ in degree but that the variance has no pragmatic significance. Then, through Kitty's innocent observation that the water, like a certain widely advertised ink, may be blue in the depths but black on the surface where exposure to air changes its appearance, Howells notes the unreliability of superficial appearances which may only obstruct vision and conceal reality. That Arbuton has never expended the effort to distinguish between appearance and reality and that he feels no need to do so now are clear indicators of his narrow margins. If one holds himself apart from life and finds superficial appearance satisfactory to his purposes, he need not be perceptive. Arbuton's response is in character with his romantic conformation, and Fanny's quick acceptance of the easy answer is what one would expect of a person who plays matchmaking games, who amuses herself by trifling with the flounces and ribbons of life rather than attempting to understand and respect the deep emotions which are central to meaningful human experience. Howells, already committed to an attempt to penetrate the surface and to see clearly and honestly has little patience with the writer who embroiders mere surface designs. To praise Howells, as many of his contemporaries did, for his exacting reports of the commonplace is to seriously underestimate his artistry.

One finds evidence in both *Their Wedding Journey* and *A Chance Acquaintance*, and especially in the latter, of a critical consciousness working for clarification and for the creative manifestation of a critical position. In both novels Howells demonstrated his desire *to see* and experimented with methods of penetrating the commonplace surface of American life. But equally important to him was an understanding of the critical disassociation of traditional romanticism and the new realism, a disassociation which conflicted with their curious affinity for each other. It would be comfortable if one could say that the dividing line between the romantic and the realistic is not only clearly marked but that it runs precisely parallel to the line which divides the unnatural from the natural, the dishonest from the honest, and that all a budding realist such as Howells need do is denounce the one, cleave to the other, and demonstrate the choice in thematic selection. The suggested parallel is not without value, but the truth for which Howells reaches is less clearly defined and much less simple. Edwin Cady recently wrote, "Perhaps the real secret of the realist lay in the ambivalence of his sensibility with regard to romance. He was fierce and contemptuous in rejection because he yearned in his heart to have it." [13] Although the fierce and contemptuous rejection is not here apparent, it is this paradoxical sensibility which contributes in part to the fascinating ambivalence of Kitty Ellison; for she, in a further way not suggested earlier, is two persons in one. Her responses to situations in which she finds herself and to the attitudes of others are alternately and somewhat ambiguously motivated by "fancy" and, more perceptively, by "heart," reflecting what in a general sense may be labeled as romantic and realistic tendencies. [14] In this fluctuating duality of Kitty's portrayal one glimpses Howells the critic pondering the fusion of the romantic and the real in both literature and life.

That Howells is attracted to a more honest view of life is apparent in these early novels. The sentimentality of traditional romantic literature which clouds the surface and so restricts vision repeatedly elicits his mildly satiric response. Too often the Marches are foolishly sentimental people, and the narrator, in part by toying ironically with their sentimentality, shows them as they are. Each time he tightens the reins to draw them back to the world of actuality from their flights of fantasy, a satiric implication is rendered. Moving from the first novel to the second, one finds progression. The romantic effectism, ironically intended, that washes through so many descriptive passages in *Their Wedding Journey* is greatly subdued in the second novel, and the conventional use of poetic quotation has been stripped away. The essentially romantic flights of fantasy in which the Marches indulged as a means of escaping from monotony have continuance in Kitty Ellison's imaginings, but hers are less worn and more organic in that they add substance to the historical texture which stands as background to the contemporary love plot. More important, her fantasies tend to be flights into rather than away from, and repeatedly they grapple with the relationship between literature and life and between romantic and realistic perspectives. Conditioned by a rich literary experience, Kitty executes a turnabout: instead of finding in literature characters and situations suggestive of life, she finds about her, as she looks from a window or walks through the streets, characters and situations in life reminiscent of those she has encountered in literature. And both the literary and the real-life experiences provide pleasure. Since Kitty's reading has been abundantly romantic, the implication seems to be that real life may indeed be incorporated in romantic literature, that realism may indeed embrace essentially romantic experience, that the romantic and the real may fuse in a common vision of reality. This in no way erodes Howells's conviction that literature, if it is to be viable, must be written out of life rather than out of literature. In realism, it is the personal and direct involvement with life which renders apprehension of truth possible; and in saying that, one does not stand far removed from a romantic named Emerson, except that he relied on intuition rather than objective scrutiny, which is itself a telling distinction. The fundamental difference between romanticism and realism relates not so much to what one sees as it does to the way in which he sees, and in the shifting patterns of objectivity and sentimental idealism which characterize Kitty's response to experience one detects an ambivalence which parallels the thematic value of her role.

In this general context, a closer look at the garden of the Ursuline Convent in *A Chance Acquaintance* and at the nuns who walk there may be instructive, for they are the means by which Howells dramatizes both the divergence and convergence of opposing concepts as they are filtered through Kitty's ambivalent sensibilities. Kitty is surprised to find two gardens visible from her Quebec boarding-house window: one is a family backyard, a simple setting for domestic activity; the other is the convent garden of carefully patterned landscaped walkways. Both are walled, separated from the world at large, and in this sense restrictive. But while the first walls *in* a private, secluded—and natural—extension of life, the second walls *out* life and, like the carefully planned walkways, is regimented by traditional idealistic concepts in such a way as to suggest both artificiality and the romantic mystery of ritual. Kitty sees and henceforth ignores the family yard which "the great extent of the convent grounds" had left "scarce breathing space" (so romanticism has smothered real life); but she is attracted repeatedly to the garden of the nuns, and to two nuns—one tall and pensive, the other short and jolly—who sit and walk in the garden. "Black-robed, with black veils falling over their shoulders, and their white faces lost in the white linen that draped them from breast to crown," they are "maskers" who had sacrificed their individuality and are no longer real. "They were but figures in a beautiful picture of something old and poetical;

but she loved them, and pitied them, and was most happy in them, the same as if they had been real" (p. 56).

In her letter home, Kitty gives the two nuns contrasting value.

I have adopted two nuns for my own: one is tall and slender and pallid, and you can see at a glance that she broke the heart of a mortal lover, and knew it, when she became the bride of heaven; and the other is short and plain and plump, and looks as comfortable and commonplace as life-after-dinner. When the world is bright I revel in the statue-like sadness of the beautiful nun, who never laughs or plays with the little girl pupils; and when the world is dark—as the best of worlds will be at times for a minute or two—I take to the fat nun, and go in for a clumsy romp with the children; and then I fancy that I am wiser if not better than the fair slim Ursuline. But whichever I am, for the time being, I am vexed with the other; yet they always are together, as if they were counterparts. (Pp. 76–77)

From this impressionistic statement, which may be read as an expression of the duality of Kitty's own character and as an exemplification of the role of mood in conditioning vision, Kitty shifts abruptly to an almost shockingly casual discussion of the actual history of the garden, in which Montcalm was buried, how his skull has been preserved and decorated in the chaplain's room, and how some English officers recently "were horrible enough to pull out some of the teeth." She concludes, "Tell Uncle Jack the head is very broad above the ears, but the forehead is small" (p. 76).

The Ursuline Garden is a romantic garden. Withdrawn and isolated from the mainstream of life, dedicated to ideality (although the black cross at its center connotes the physical severity of the battle), regimented by the tradition of centuries, unreal, yet withal real in its unreality, it is the backdrop against which Kitty contemplates her mixed feelings for Arbuton. Captured by the spell of its moonlight enchantment, she puts aside her justified uneasiness and concludes that she is being a goose in clinging to her reservations about her very proper suitor; and Howells need not tell us that at that moment of irrationality the influence of the holy garden is an ironically unholy one. In Kitty's letter, the sharp juxtaposition of romantic sensibility and bold, verifiable fact is underscored by the image of the mutilated skull decorated and softened by an embroidered veil; and together the juxtaposition and the image make a dramatic statement of the gulf fixed between romanticism and realism, a statement which conflicts with the apparently intimate relationship of the dissimilar nuns. In a final reference to the two nuns in the concluding "Afterwards," we see the Ursuline Garden swept by "a fine, cold rain" and "the slender nun and the stout nun"— the pensive, remote one and the jolly, practical one—sitting side by side and holding hands. The diverging and converging lines have crossed to join an ambiguous web. Critically and creatively Howells's own lingering ambivalence toward opposing literary tempers has been recorded but not yet resolved.

Howells's first two novels may most aptly be described as exploratory. They reach beneath the commonplace to touch reality, and they look outward for definition and direction. In both penetration and outreach, rather than arriving at predetermined destinations, they uncover complexity and ambivalence which, if one is interested in seeing honestly, will not yield to simplification. Complexity and ambivalence are after all the nature of life, even common life; and discovery of that fact alone is a significant step forward for one destined to contribute in a major way to the emancipation of fiction from restrictive convention. The best of Howells's subsequent work builds on the foundation established by *Their Wedding Journey* and *A Chance Acquaintance*. After the portrayal of Kitty Ellison, Howells's interest in psychological understanding of individuality intensified and stimulated both perception and imagination in the memorable creation of highly particularized characters—Don Ippolito, Egeria Boynton, Marcia Hubbard, Silas Lapham, to name a few—each caught in the web of his own distinctive ambivalence which swings suspended between the towers of social difference, each finding himself the testing ground in the conflict of the conventional and the unconventional, the unnatural and the natural, the rationally pragmatic and the morally ideal—and none yielding to romantic simplification.

It was in the late 1880s, when Howells became entangled in sociological considerations, that his vision was diffused and that his fiction, no matter how interesting it may be from a socioeconomic orientation, began to ring less true. Howells always found it difficult to keep himself out of his novels. Both his inhibitions and his interests were too strong, or he was too weak, to allow for a consistently dispassionate view. In *A Hazard of New Fortunes* and after, his work is enriched with social criticism; but to the greater breadth of concern he sacrificed depth of vision, and the loss is more keenly felt than the gain. When Howells is at his best, he penetrates superficial actuality to see deeply into the reality of individual human beings, into the amalgamated but ambivalent moral and social condition of man (*A Modern Instance*, in spite of its flaws, may still be his best). But when social considerations upstage character, when characters are denied their particularized reality and become actors designed to play preconceived sociological roles, when Howells moves away from the direction established by his first two novels and begins telling how it is—and how it should be—rather than *seeing*, his fiction loses some of its honesty and some of its early charm.

Washington Irving: Nonsense, the Fat of the Land and the Dream of Indolence

WILLIAM L. HEDGES

Any serious consideration of Washington Irving (b. 1783) must begin with his humor. That's a kind of joke, daughter. Or to say it's a joke's a joke—to get you into the right mood for the nonsense to come. After all, as Psalmanazar the imposter says on the title-page of *Salmagundi; or, the Whim-whams and Opinions of Launcelot Langstaff, Esq., and Others*, "In hoc est hoax." Psalma is close to being Salma. And Langstaff and others are Washington Irving, his brother William and James Kirke Paulding.

Now hear one of the most beautiful paragraphs in American literature, from *Salmagundi*, No. 1, January 24, 1807.

As everybody knows, or ought to know, what a SALMA-GUNDI is, we shall spare ourselves the trouble of an explanation—besides, we despise trouble as we do everything that is low and mean; and hold the man who would incur it unnecessarily, as an object worthy our highest pity and contempt. Neither will we puzzle our heads to give an account of ourselves, for two reasons; first, because it is nobody's business; secondly, because if it were, we do not hold ourselves bound to attend to anybody's business but our own; and even *that* we take the liberty of neglecting when it suits our inclination. To these we might add a third, that very few men *can* give a tolerable account of themselves, let them try ever so hard; but this reason, we candidly avow, would not hold good with ourselves.[1]

I am perfectly serious in my admiration for the precariously controlled flippancy of this paragraph, the mad consistency and symmetry of its illogic, the sudden illumination of "very few men *can* give a tolerable account of themselves."

Between 1800 and 1810, or even 1820, American intellectual life, caught in the conservative reaction to revolution and terror in France and general war in Europe, stultified considerably. The widespread fear of anarchy and atheism that swept the country at the turn of the century brought in its wake suspicion of new ideas generally. The early work of the English romantics, as we know, was very coolly received for the better part of a generation. Official culture tended to retreat into ponderous justifications of well-established attitudes and "truths." This was particularly the case in Federalist New England. In New York, however, a booming city with a heterogeneous population, it was not so easy to maintain an official culture. There upstarts like the Irvings could get a hearing. *Salmagundi and Diedrich Knickerbocker's History of New York* (1809) both preserve certain amenities. They hold on to the fiction of affiliation with a tradition of gentility, to which Irving was powerfully attracted. But it is a feeble fiction, borne on the stooped shoulders of a few old bachelors and constantly threatened by the leveling energy of bourgeois republicanism, from which Irving could not divorce himself, try as he might.

That energy affronts readers in the first number of *Salmagundi* with the ambiguous threat of shock and confusion: "we *care* not what the public think of us; and we suspect, before we reach the tenth number, they will not *know* what to think of us." And it burlesques the form of the periodical essay almost into extinction: "Our intention is simply to instruct the young, reform the old, correct the town, and castigate the age; this is an arduous task, and therefore we undertake it with confidence." The antididacticism of the first number is jubilant and defiant: "In two words—we write for no earthly purpose but to please ourselves."

As a matter of fact, in its distaste for bourgeois vulgarity and the petty corruption and demagoguery associated with republican politics *Salmagundi* occasionally succumbs to a didactic urge, shows more interest in getting a message across than in mocking the medium. But even when most bent on correcting the town and castigating the age, the voices that speak through the masks of Launcelot Langstaff, Anthony Evergreen, and Will Wizard, the old-bachelor "editors," or Mustapha Rub-a-Dub Keli Khan, *Salmagundi*'s "citizen of the world," are never for long gentlemanly, urbane, self-assured. The voices are too young, at times too shrill and raucously vituperative. Unconsciously the Irvings and Paulding violate the identities of their personae even when they are not trying deliberately to do so.

Playing with the worn-out periodical-essay apparatus they begin to develop the nonsense comedy which *Knickerbocker* brings to fulfillment. It is a comedy of distraction and disorientation in which the pretense of composure and authority maintained on the surface is systematically undermined and the reader is subjected to what at times becomes a deluge of non sequiturs and digressions, reversals and contradictions, abrupt shifts of style and tone, and jumblings of fact and fiction. Characters in this comedy tend, as we now so appropriately say, to self-destruct before the reader's eyes—which is what happens most dramatically with that supposedly knowing or knowledgeable persona, Diedrich Knickerbocker, his ineptitude occasionally reducing him to a kind of blathering idiocy. At its best —which is generally *Knickerbocker*—this comedy offers burlesque going berserk, satire and social comment dissolving into mystification, the impulse to mock and criticize being overtaken by a delight in fantasizing.

In an article in the sixth number of *Salmagundi*, for instance, which starts as parody of inept drama criticism, Will Wizard describes going to a performance of *Othello* and getting into a three-cornered argument on several trivial issues. Though his own critical credentials have been mocked in an earlier number, he begins this evening as the voice of sanity, while his two friends strain at the text to discover "new Readings" of particular lines in the play. When Wizard offers an outlandish interpretation of his own, the reader initially takes it as an ironic rebuke of the two pedants. But then Wizard embarks on a baffling hyperbolic spiel which weaves in and out of seriousness and lasts until the end of the article—whereupon he announces in a P.S. that he's just been informed that *Othello* hasn't been produced in New York for years.

Salmagundi is a sequence of fun-house mirrors which distort reality into scarcely recognizable shapes. It wastes hard-hitting satire on embodiments of folly and vice broadly caricatured into pure fictions. Except for a few actual people like Cooper the actor and two dress-designers, Mrs. Toole and Mrs. Bouchard, New York in *Salmagundi* is a city inhabited by a diminutive breed afflicted with names like Dimple, Sparkle, Dashaway, and Ding-Dong, Shivers and 'Sbidlikensflash, Pindar Cockloft and Ichabod Fungus—and Langstaff et al. This is a society of pompous nonentities strutting and fretting to become "little great" men and women. The trick is to look, act, and sound important. Everything is show, gaudy style, and empty rhetoric. The magazine carries a fairly standard satirical awareness to an extreme by turning democracy into "logocracy," a government of words. Partisan newspaper editors become "slang-whangers." And the chief logocrat, President Jefferson, a "man of superlative ventosity," who, in the face of the British and French threat to American commerce, "talks of vanquishing all opposition by the force of reason and philosophy," becomes "a huge bladder of wind." [2]

But *Salmagundi* is implicated in the linguistic overkill which it satirizes. Its appetite for words is insatiable. It laps them up wherever it finds them, mixes them together (into a salmagundi) and regurgitates them with joyful abandon —old words and new, proverbs and Latin phrases, scraps of verse from Shakespeare or anywhere, and, as part of its pseudo erudition, an endless string of names, especially of books, authors, and characters. Burlesque and travesty serve *Salmagundi* in part as an excuse for verbal incontinence. Irving had written slang-whang himself a few years earlier for his brother Peter's newspaper *The Corrector* in support of Aaron Burr. And *Salmagundi*'s attacks on logocracy and little great men in politics descend at times almost to that level, though, for the most part the abuse is not personal. Reducing words to nonsense, the magazine at once suggests the vanity of most verbalizing and testifies to the determination of a provincial society to make itself heard whatever proprieties it violated.

Knickerbocker is Irving's masterpiece, his best book—which is not to deny the superiority of a few individual stories and sketches in later works. Begun with his brother Peter as a burlesque of a guidebook to New York City, it turned into a sustained mock-history, structurally unified around its subject and held together in spite of Knickerbocker's eccentricity by Irving's ability (Peter dropped out before the project advanced very far) to modulate effectively through perpetual shifts of style and tone. Deflating the myth of the greatness of the American past, *Knickerbocker* reduces the New Netherlands to insignificance by establishing its golden age as the reign of indolence under Governor Van Twiller, when fat Dutchmen lolled in the lap of an abundant land, smoked their pipes, kept their mouths shut and were not unduly bothered by the outside world. Troubles began under Governor Kieft (William the Testy), who lost his Dutch cool as political factions arose (the beginnings of logocracy) and tensions with New England developed. Like Jefferson, Kieft tried to govern and defend the land by speeches and proclamations—to no avail. In the end came valiant Peter Stuyvesant, peg-legged and doomed to defeat, a strong executive who rose above faction, fortified the city, fought a furious and insignificant war with New Sweden (described in low-burlesque mock-epic style), prepared to make a heroic stand against the British—and was forced into an ignominious capitulation.

Knickerbocker exposes, as no American book had dared to before and not many others did for a long time afterward, the gross, overdeveloped appetites—for land, wealth, food, drink, sex, pleasure generally—the "frank evaluation of progress in terms of exploitation," as Parrington called it,[3] which has shaped America as much as have its humane aspirations. Though the focus is on New York, the satire manages to take in every section of the country, especially New England. Some of it is sharp, biting sarcasm—against puritan bigotry, for instance, or European exploitation of the Indians—but, over all, the humor is tolerant. The nonsense will not allow characters to be taken very seriously, but from time to time the reader's natural longing for someone or something to identify with converts hints of pathos or quaint dignity in a ludicrous posture into authentic sentiment—which of course never sustains itself for long.

In a larger sense the action of the *History* is Knickerbocker's distracted effort to salvage something from the past—to create a past out of nothing, if he has to—and glorify the accomplishments of his ancestors. He comments garrulously as he goes along on the perils of being a historian—and on anything else that occurs to him. The reader follows the combined narrative and commentary almost as distracted as the historian, seldom sure whether what is being said represents total misunderstanding or ingenious insight, whether Knickerbocker is being serious or ironic, or simply can't make up his mind. At times, however, he comes into odd focus as the image of all of us—humanity—pathetic, broken-backed, nearsighted and yet, absurdly, still cheerful, groping through the rubbish of the past (that is, all previous human experience) for clues to an understanding of the present. When he comes to his senses, or almost does, it seems like an heroic achievement, and the commonplace observations he makes—on fame, pride, tranquility, natural beauty, death—take on a strange profundity. Conventional wisdom is revitalized in our odd reenactment with Knickerbocker of humanity's struggle to acquire it.

At the same time, however, one must recognize the nonsense of Knickerbocker humor as psychologically regressive, part of an escape from responsibility and conflict which is characteristic of Irving generally and which is at once the great strength and weakness of his work. Writing for *Salmagundi* was at least temporarily a release from the tedium and learned logic (or was it rationalization?) of the law (he had just passed his bar examination) and the urgings of his family—his father, the rather rigid Presbyterian deacon, and his business-minded brothers—that he apply himself seriously to something. And behind *Knickerbocker* lies perhaps both his grief at the recent death of his fiancée Matilda Hoffman, and a not consciously admitted relief at not having to settle down to business and make himself a good provider. More important, though, the nonsense of the early Irving is a way of registering the confusions of the period without having to take a definite stand on a controversial issue when he doesn't want to. It was a period in which, with the United States still testing new political institutions and Europe still torn by revolutionary upheaval, western intellectual life, having lost its eighteenth-century assurances, had not yet attained those that were to see it through the nineteenth.

To what extent, one wonders, has humor in the United States, the humor of a young culture unsure of itself, been a mechanism of evasion? Discussion of American humor customarily gives Irving short shrift. His comedy is not supposed to be indigenous enough, the language not sufficiently vernacular and the characters by and large not sufficiently distinguished from English comic stereotypes. But the theory which ties "native" American humor so closely to folk experience and the oral narrative tradition seems unnecessarily restrictive. American culture has been urban as well as rural, eastern as well as western, and for many it has been a mixture of influences from several discordant sources against a background of acute awareness of the European past. Even at the pole where American humor seems most to belong to the backwoods it has had one eye cocked uneasily to the East, the intrusion of the dude being apparently one of the major factors which provokes it.

Daniel Hoffman sees in "The Legend of Sleepy Hollow" the "native" pattern of the squatter frightening the dandy reenacted by Brom Bones and Ichabod Crane.[4] But there is an analogous assault on pretensions to cultural authority in *Salmagundi* when the young voices take over the old-bachelor personae—notwithstanding Irving's characteristic ambivalence in the face of the conflict between bumptious vulgarity and overblown gentility. However much subtlety the deadpan innocence of the storyteller in the oral tradition may give it, American humor is nonetheless often hard to distinguish from boorish anti-intellectualism. Its irrepressible low-burlesque energy keeps driving it toward nonsense.

But if the basic motive is hostility to highbrow cultural encroachment, that energy often becomes a relatively detached comic exuberance, a delight almost for its own sake in hyperbolic improvisation or in what Mark Twain in "How to Tell a Story" called the "innocently unaware" stringing together of "incongruities and absurdities." *Salmagundi* and *Duck Soup* are apt titles for the roaring mishmash of verbal styles, screwball characters, and slapstick that American comedy is apt to become—not only in print but in vaudeville, the movies, radio and television as well. The basic and continuing relevance of Irving's humor is clearly evident in the striking similarity between the nonsense of the *Knickerbocker History* and that of *Catch-22*, a resemblance which Joseph Heller seems at least unconsciously to acknowledge when he has Major Major Major, a bored, inept, and insecure squadron commander, in "an act of impulsive frivolity and rebellion" begin signing Washington Irving's name to official documents.[5]

The Irving who wrote *The Sketch Book* (1819–20) and emerged almost overnight as an international success had lived the ten years since *Knickerbocker* torn between the desire to make literature a full-time commitment and the fear of abandoning a career in law and business. Living in England now (he had been working in the Liverpool branch of the family importing firm), he was cut off from the only society which he knew intimately. And financially, since he was now to write for profit, he was in no position to antagonize an audience (as *Knickerbocker* had some of the old Dutch families in New York) by taking a tone of easy familiarity with it—particularly with the English at a time when English criticism was generally scornful of American literary efforts.

But Irving was able to adapt to the exigencies of the situation. He developed a more graceful prose style, spry, rhythmic, concrete, laced with subdued humor and purged of obvious crudities and provincialisms, a style the English especially were comfortable with. And he created the persona of Geoffrey Crayon, Gent., an American traveler and "humble" lover of "the picturesque," who, like an artist following the "bent of his vagrant imagination," has sketched in "nooks, and corners, and by-places" and sadly missed all the obvious important subjects.[6] Crayon is the mildly self-mocking image of Irving himself, now nearly forty years old, unmarried and without a permanent home. Injecting Crayon's personality into his sketches, he both capitalized on and compensated for the superficiality of his genial tourist's view of Europe.

There is something slightly false about Irving's position as a writer from *The Sketch Book* on. He has lost the freedom to speak out bluntly on anything he chooses. Too often now he says things that he thinks readers want him to say. He becomes more of a sentimentalist, for instance, more committed to titillating female readers with stories of broken hearts and lost loves, than he perhaps intended. But much of what he wrote during his long European period (1815–32) is redeemed by his eye for the ludicrous, his affection for mundane reality, and his natural antididacticism.

A low-keyed approach to short fiction was precisely what was needed at a time when, as he well knew, "strange incident and high-seasoned narrative" were all the "rage." [7] Irving was not above trying for gothic or sentimental intensity, but he was much more comfortable in a manner which at least implicitly mocked the sensation-seeking reader. Whole sequences of fiction in *Tales of a Traveller* (1824), for instance, are arranged so that early pieces, much to the annoyance of reviewers at the time, prove to be burlesques of ghost story formulae or of romantic tales of action. They break off abruptly in mystification or risqué humor. Only after trying to jolt readers out of passivity and literal-mindedness and denying them gratuitous horror, is Irving willing to venture on something more serious.

For Crayon to say that Diedrich Knickerbocker wrote "Rip Van Winkle" and swore to the truth of it is to make clear that the story is a fabrication, at bottom a sort of tall tale—"There was this henpecked husband up in the Catskills. His wife pestered him all day long and left him no peace anywhere in the village. So one day he went off into the mountains to do a little light hunting and ran into some little old boys with a keg. They got him drunk and he fell into a nice deep sleep on a beautiful grassy knoll. It was so peaceful, he slept for 20 years. When he woke up and went home, his wife was dead, and he lived happily ever after." Or perhaps the story is something Rip made up to avoid having to tell what really happened during his long absence. The reader's desire for rational explanation is frustrated. But as sheer fantasy, the tale is not so easily laughed off. Lovable and amusing as Rip is, his account of his experience is full of hints of impotence, wasted life, and loss of identity.

Similarly "The Legend of Sleepy Hollow" offers instead of a ghost the very palpable reality of a pumpkin and, presumably, Brom Bones. The man who tells the story to Knickerbocker says he doesn't believe half of it himself and, when asked about its moral, responds with platitudes and nonsense. And yet at its climax Ichabod Crane's terror is something we can identify with and believe in, as we can not in the case of the victim of an overwrought gothic tale. With Irving in *The Sketch Book, Bracebridge Hall* (1822), *Tales of a Traveller,* and *The Alhambra* (1832) we are in at the birth of the short story as a literary form, although he was not himself fully aware of what was happening and was never quite able to duplicate the startling and somewhat fortuitous achievement of "Rip Van Winkle" and "The Legend of Sleepy Hollow." His seriocomic manner slows down action, gives character, though viewed ironically, a chance to manifest itself, and makes setting a vital part of the characters' lives. His best stories (chiefly those with American settings) seem to be conceived as extensions of his sense of locale, of the characteristic atmosphere of a region; and his sketches—of Westminster Abbey or the reading room of the British Museum or a ride in an English stagecoach—presented not as inert description but as Crayon's response to immediate experience, have a way of turning into slight fictions about an entranced but somewhat unsettled traveler. And time is as important as place in his better fiction. With the action slowed down, the illusion of time passing at a natural rate becomes stronger ("The Legend of Sleepy Hollow" is a small triumph in this regard). Stories begin to be structured to a greater extent around single climactic episodes or a few key moments. The sketches are often actually little one-scene narratives.

But Irving did not have a particularly inventive imagination. He relied heavily on stereotyped characters and plots culled from old stories, plays, legends, and folk tales. In "Rip Van Winkle" and "Sleepy Hollow" he successfully adopted German legends to the landscape of the Hudson valley. But he was not always able to revitalize his borrowings. Some of his stories are thin, insufficiently fleshed out, nothing but old stories. The range of experience, activity and feeling he is capable of exploring in fiction is limited.

He has a few simple things to say about desire, fulfillment, and frustration. On occasion he says them compellingly but not enough so to bear constant repetition.

As he grew older he found it easier to write history and biography than fiction—one wishes that he had returned in earnest to satire, burlesque, and nonsense. The historical writing is uneven. Some of it was done in haste and is backed by a minimum of original research. He had trouble deciding whether he was writing primarily for a scholarly or a popular audience. And half-consciously he tended to turn history into fiction, not in the crude sense of fabricating events for which he had no documentary evidence, but by largely neglecting or minimizing the importance of social, political, economic, and psychological factors, the particulars of an age or a time, and reducing the record of the past to the perpetual reenactment, by individuals curiously almost suspended above time, of the drama of human destiny. Thus as Stanley Williams said, *Life and Voyages of Christopher Columbus* (1828), the first and best of Irving's historical works, is really a romance.[8] It transforms its hero into an archetypal pilgrim and martyr—or rather it resurrects those images from some of the early accounts of Columbus. His lot is to suffer almost constant travail on what is more a sustained allegorical journey, a religious quest, than a series of voyages of discovery. Biblical overtones in rhythm and phrasing and an abundance of Christian imagery create the feeling at times of a gospel story. The biography has considerable poetic power.

But Irving lacked the depth of moral insight demanded by a work of such pretensions. His view of the world was always pathetic, the view of Geoffrey Crayon: things don't last. Mutability is the major theme. He never hints at outrage or rebellion as a conceivable response to the absurdity and indignity of man's fate. Neither does he envision active acceptance of that fate as a means of transcending it. Laughing "right merrily at the farce of life" is still Irving's "wisdom," [9] reducing the world to nonsense his instinctive way of coping with the reality of experience. But writing what he alleged to be history did not offer many opportunities for humor.

Irving lived until 1859, becoming increasingly identified with what Santayana was eventually to call the genteel tradition. Travel and voracious reading had made him a learned man. He was a celebrity used to associating with people of distinction and status. Walter Scott had received him at Abbotsford even before *The Sketch Book*. Back home John Jacob Astor was his friend. He had fraternized with royalty in Dresden in 1822–23. A Russian prince had been his traveling companion in Spain, and he had toured the western American prairies with a Swiss count. The external trappings of the latter part of his life comport with the diplomatic dignity and cordiality implied in his being appointed American minister to Madrid, a post he held from 1842 to 1845. Though he did not live ostentatiously, he remodeled an old farmhouse into the modest but stylish mansion, Sunnyside, overlooking the Hudson at Tarrytown. He spent several years after his return from Madrid in bringing out a revised edition of his works touched up to conform to Victorian notions of elegance and propriety. And he labored his last several years putting together the five-volume biography of his namesake, the American patriarch, George Washington (1855–59).

But Irving did not succumb to gentility without putting up resistance. One should not forget that Squire Bracebridge, his idealized English country gentleman, is gently spoofed in *The Sketch Book* and *Bracebridge Hall* as a hobbyhorse-riding anachronism in a way that to a degree recalls the mocking of the old bachelors of *Salmagundi* with their whim-whams and whalebone habits. The follies of the gentry remained for Irving part of the farce of life. He was not by temperament or doctrine an aristocrat. He enjoyed the comforts his success allowed. By and large he simply adopted the conservative political and social attitudes of the wealthy and influential people with whom he associated. In the late thirties, the forties, and the fifties his position was basically Whiggish but not so much so as to preclude his being wooed politically by Martin Van Buren as well as by Daniel Webster—though one may wonder how much less responsive in this expansionist period Democrats were than Whigs to the idea that what's good for business is good for the country.

All his life Irving affected a patrician disdain for the "cares and sordid concerns of traffic," [10] but he objected more to the cares than to the traffic. His commercial success, which has always from the point of view of literary history been taken as his chief significance, is symbolic of a central impulse in his work, the source, I think, together with his humor, of his limited but enduring appeal. By becoming a writer he to a large extent escaped the necessity for "any periodically recurring task, or any stipulated labor of body or mind," for which, he told Walter Scott, he was "peculiarly unfitted." [11] And yet he managed to make a comfortable living for himself. There is a strong element of frank hedonism in his work. He was certainly interested in making money, went to elaborate efforts, in fact, to prevent piracy of his works and make sure that he got royalties from them on both sides of the Atlantic. Nor was he above taking flyers on investments—in a steamboat company, for instance, or a South American copper mine. [12] It was the drudgery of business that was apt to make it a "sordid, dusty, soul killing way of life." [13]

He might be appalled by America's pursuit of the "almighty dollar," a term he coined in describing young western communities gripped by speculative fever. [14] But he was intrigued as well. Something in him responded to the excitement of flush times and the general spectacle of American money-making and conspicuous consumption. In his earliest journal (1803) he recorded his "amusement" at the "outrageous extravagance" of the manners and clothes of the wife of a nouveau-riche Boston tradesman, a woman he encountered at the Ballston spa near Albany. But he also had a grudging admiration for her: "Amidst all her vanity she shews no foolish pride respecting her origin but takes great pleasure in telling how they first entered boston in Pedlars trim." [15] He was on a trip with his boss, Judge Josiah Ogden Hoffman, to inspect a large speculation in land in upstate New York in which the latter was involved. This was the life Irving matured in, a life centered on commerce, finance, and their relation to politics. Electing candidates favorable to business interests was important. Thus the slang-whangers, thus the need to attack Jefferson, whose neutralist policies were depressing New York business. At this period in his career Irving was not too choosy about how he sought to get ahead. He was willing, for instance, to take a political appointment, if he could get it, from a governor whose candidacy he had furiously attacked in *The Corrector*.[16] He might shy away from business and politics, but he never really turned his back on them. He was too close to the gross appetites he satirized. Progress even for him was to some extent exploitation.

In his 1803 journal he also describes, with absolutely no sympathy for the victim (or victims) but considerable enthusiasm for the sport, the three or four-way competition in which he participated to capture and kill a doe trapped in a river in the backwoods. All dignity was abandoned, as several people (including Hoffman and himself) fell or deliberately plunged into the water "to *get in at the death*." A woman came close to drowning, and the doe was divided between two of the parties (Irving's included), the other hunters getting nothing for their trouble.[17] Thirty years later in what eventually became Oklahoma he engaged in a buffalo hunt with the same avidity and, though after making his kill he had a moment of remorse, he took away the buffalo tongue as a trophy and left the carcass behind on the prairie.[18]

For Irving, the American continent was both beautiful and exploitable—at least up to a certain point. As works like "A Tour on the Prairies," *Astoria* (done with Astor's cooperation, 1836), and *Adventures of Captain Bonneville, U. S. A.* (1837) show, he admired the hunters, the explorers, the trappers, the adventurers—the man who made a fortune in the fur trade. All things in moderation, of course. He knew that money corrupts. He knew the voraciousness of both nature and man. His work is full of homilies on how paradises are perverted by greed. But it was not always easy to distinguish between greed and a healthy appetite for affluence. There was a fundamental moral problem here, which Irving never faced—most Americans were not forced to face it until the frontier closed.

In the meantime he wrote repeatedly about dreams of gold, easy money, buried treasure—or better still the escape to the drowsy indolence of rural comfort and abundance, to Communipaw, the village in *Knickerbocker* lost in the American landscape, left behind by history, enviably ignorant "of all the troubles, anxieties, and revolutions of this distracted planet." [19] Irving gives us fantasies of flagrant wish-fulfillment, direct appeals to the regressive instinct— the American dream as a return to the womb, the desire to escape the grind of daily work and the Protestant ethic of frugality and the postponement of gratification, the desire to evade responsibility and remain disengaged, to steer clear of controversy.

This is Rip Van Winkle's escape from his wife. It is the dream lean Ichabod Crane dreams—to marry plump Katrina Van Tassel, gorge himself on her pastries, and gain possession of a rich farmland, all in exchange for singing a few psalms, telling a few ghost stories, and being generally charming. The reader sympathizes with the dream and has the consolation of knowing that, if Ichabod doesn't deserve Katrina, Brom Bones does. The easygoing youth ("Dolph Heyliger," "Buckthorne," Dirk Waldron in "Wolfert Webber") gets the girl—and often the gold or its equivalent—in Irving's mythology, which as his perennial habit of collecting and adapting legends shows, is, in some important respects, a duplication of aspects of folk mythology. The water carrier outwits the avaricious alcalde in a typical story of hidden treasure in *The Alhambra* ("Legend of the Mor's Legacy").

Always in the background, of course, lurks the awareness that contentment and gratification are usually fleeting or illusory. The devil comes on his white horse for Tom Walker in the counting house just as he is foreclosing on a mortgage. The reality of "the dusty world" of "bustle and business" awaits Irving after the "repose and reverie" of his sojourn in the "oriental luxury" of the Alhambra.[20] The tranquility of New Amsterdam under Van Twiller cannot last. Beyond the infantile illusion of peace, harmony, good fellowship, and repose is, obviously, the reality of competition and conflict, where one risks failure—the American nightmare, the haunting fear of loneliness, uselessness, impotence, particularly in Irving's old bachelors—even if beyond failure there is the vision which his sentimentality projects, above all in *The Sketch Book*, of death as a coming home to mother, a delicious surrender to the binder-up of wounds, to comforting arms and consoling words, death as a recovery of the womb.

But the basic dream persists in Irving, the dream of repose on what Fitzgerald called at the end of *The Great Gatsby* the "fresh, green breast of the new world." Irving knows something about ruthless exploitation, about the sorrow of Columbus and its relation to the cunning of men like Tom Walker. But he does not turn John Jacob Astor into a Gatsby or a Sutpen or an Ahab. What he sees and feels most is that gross hedonism which Faulkner was finally to depict definitively in *The Hamlet*, paying as he did so conscious and perhaps also unconscious tribute to Irving. From Katrina Van Tassel to Eula Varner in the bottomland of Mississippi the myth of American fertility runs its course, Ichabod's and Brom's lust for the farmer's daughter, the eatables and the farm hilariously metamorphosed into Frenchman's Bend's dumb wonder at Eula's indolent mammalian splendor and Ike Snopes's love affair with the cow. Faulkner's schoolmaster, the football player from Ole Miss, is Ichabod and Brom combined. Even so, however, he loses Eula. For in Faulkner the dream of abundance in America has given way to the reality of the rape of the landscape. Flem Snopes cannot be laughed off like Tom Walker. And the hope of buried treasure at the Old Frenchman place is nothing but another of Flem's schemes for disposing of worthless property.

8.

Herman Melville
1972

JAY LEYDA

The excitement, if not exhausted, sounds low, lower than at any time since the Weaver and Mumford biographies of Melville introduced to us an unknown writer—after his hundredth birthday. At least on United States and Canadian campuses (where I have sampled with minimum science) the art of Herman Melville has been reduced from discovery to a reading assignment. You can find this change of attitude not only among students, but among most of the instructors who, consciously or unconsciously, determine student receptivity. There's no surprise or shame in this: they are the first and second generations of postwar ex-students who passively watched the reputation of Melville dry up ready to blow away into the same academic desert where too many American artists—Hawthorne and Winslow Homer come to mind—have been discarded. Older teachers sound somewhat embarrassed by memories of their enthusiasm in the thirties and forties for the rediscovered novels, unknown and untouched by the academic world only a little more than half a century ago.

Has the work of Melville changed since he wrote it? Did it need the drama of its late discovery to keep us pleased and stimulated? I suspect that this is not a problem of changing reading tastes. What we once read for joy has been transformed into a "subject," or rather, an object for criticism and interpretation. The man who wrote these works has been pushed aside (again!) by well-meaning persons who tell us what the words really mean—so that there's not much room any more for either man or works. Critical microscopes are brought into play, but I'm no longer sure for what purpose. What is to be gained from a close, a very close hunt for the sexual puns in *Israel Potter*? Is it to learn more about its author than we knew before?

or to draw attention to the ingenuity of the interpreter? I can't believe that either Herman or Israel was uppermost in the mind of the hunting inspector.

There are brilliant analysts who have won the right to interpretation, but their imitators are too often motivated by their schools' and their ambitions' demand to show "more in print"—and if this can be done without leaving your study, all the better. Another academic merit that has done harm to Melville studies: the importance of being the *first* to reveal a find, and to keep it locked up as the finder's property. The quantity of publications produced by the Melville industry (at one time second only to the Shakespeare industry in the United States) is not a measure of its usefulness—or use. We cannot expect second-rate scholars to acknowledge or consider the harm they are doing, to writer and reader, both.

I wish we could hunt the man-artist more seriously. Through his work, of course, the only possible first step. In the labor spent on the definitive editions that this book is celebrating there is a choice offered to the scholars who have assumed this large responsibility: texts can be determined mechanically (to be sure these are the words we were intended to read is no mean contribution); or this work can be undertaken as an opportunity to learn more exactly about the spirit and the flesh that produced these often mysterious and "unfathomable" arrangements of words.

This could be a new biographical key, just at a time when Melville's biography needs harder work. With so much left to be known, how can we allow the present state of our knowledge to freeze and become permanently acceptable? Perhaps we have become too content with the biographical materials already at our disposal. And this contentment leads away from simple logic and towards such habitual self-deceit! It's so easy to leap to the conclusion that there can be nothing more. For example, before describing Philarète Chasles as the author of "the unique review of *Mardi* in continental Europe," the biographer would have to demonstrate that some extraordinary combing of nineteenth-century European periodicals had been conducted, and so long as I am not aware that any such search had been conducted by anyone, I fear that I would demand that the biographer dilute his statement to: "the only review, etc., known to me." In general, the words "first," "last," "only," "never," have to be used with greater caution. With most of Melville's letters lost or waiting to be found it is misleading to say, "No letter of his ever mentioned such a desire." I suppose it seems such a miracle that so much survives of a man so uninterested in his own archive that it seems useless to look for more, but the biographical and historical hunt must keep pace with the interpreters' hunt. The reality of the elusive artist can be a never attained goal, but it is a reality all the more worth aiming at.

In search of the artist we might find ways to rescue him from the exclusive property claims of our English departments. Here is at least one of their properties that could be brought back to life in Comparative Literature departments or, for even more sport, let the "interdisciplinary" studies work on him. History, business, habits, philosophy —they all, and much more, belong in the portrait of Melville.

When *The Melville Log* first came out in 1951, it concluded with a sort of masochistic confessional-reprimand-hope called "The Endless Study," actually a pointing to all the paths I was conscious that I hadn't followed. These were still on my conscience when, for a reprint of the *Log* proposed in 1969, I prepared (in Berlin!) a Supplement of documents related to Melville turned up since 1951 by the scholars I knew. I looked again at the things left undone in 1951. Sad to say, almost all of them were still undone— so far as I could learn. No matter what my excuses, I had done ridiculously little in eighteen years to advance "the endless study": I had a chance glimpse of the family house at Gansevoort (now a Masonic Hall) and I had—more deliberately—soothed my conscience at the Franklin D. Roosevelt Library where rumor had made his whaling logs more numerous than they are. There were, as always, the serendipical finds, accidentally revealed in searching for something quite different. Others had done more to reduce my sins of omission: the Morgan Library had acquired the Harper correspondence that I was sure must still exist, and persistent people had made a dent in the armored Special Collections at Columbia University. Completely unforeseen things turned up: it was Hershel Parker who saw the 1860/1867 whale's tooth on the shelves of the New York Historical Society—and now we should be looking for Captain Worth and E. S. Doolittle. And how much more must be waiting to be read and used! In that meanwhile of nearly twenty years you could be sure that destruction had moved faster than discovery. How many family papers and attic archives must have vanished while the people equipped for biographical research played, instead, the game of interpretation.

Some errands not yet run would have to be run beyond the English departments. For example, "The Endless Study" hints that South American ports may be worth investigation. Melville's work, especially *Moby-Dick*, so abounds in references to Latin America that something there must be waiting to be found. We could start with those ports where Melville's whalers stopped for water and supplies. His first whaler spent only two days at Rio de Janeiro, but the West coast of South America was more often visited by the *Acushnet*. (It is unlikely that the *Charles & Henry*, about which we know so little while Melville was on board, could have reached the American coast in those months, but consider Pacific gossip; I've learned how useful the indirect or secondhand sea story can be.) A scholar who reads Spanish should be persuaded to read South American newspapers of the early 1840s. If Santa Marta and Tumbes were not big enough to have their own weeklies, how about looking through the commercial and local columns of the bigger coastal cities' papers—Callao? Valparaiso? Guayaquil? There are such newspaper files in North American libraries. If our explorer finds nothing about the *Acushnet* or the *Charles & Henry*, or how their crews behaved in port, he might find something of equal value: a new source of information on the American whaling fleet, and a new color of romance for the era. He will not come away empty-handed from such untried research. And to add to knowledge, with or without shedding light on Melville's life, brings no shame.

Incidentally, there is a certain virtue in not separating milieu from hero, especially in the drama of Melville's life. He drew so directly from experience, and his concealing veils of art are so much more transparent than those that Hawthorne or Dostoyevsky or Rimbaud drew before us, that to know the crowds and streets and waters that Melville passed through brings us halfway to knowing him and his art. All we can trace of his world pays, biographically.

How little we know about Melville's audience abroad was revealed to me while I was doing a quite different sort of job in the Netherlands. I had to drive daily through Haarlem, and eventually I recalled that a Haarlem edition of *Omoo* had been in someone's bibliography; as it was dated 1847 I had taken the chance in the *Log* of correcting it to be a translation of *Typee*. Here I was—why not drop in at Haarlem's library and any publishers that survived, and know for sure? Before the afternoon ended I was in the dignified old offices of Erven F. Bohn—just as evocative of the past (but with less luxury) as the offices of John Murray—with their translation of (yes!) *Typee* in my hands. There was a charming Dutch frontispiece, that so far as I know was the sole illustration to a work by Melville published during his lifetime, and this duly found its place in the 1969 Supplement. Again "The Endless Study" shook its complaints at me:

It is merely another symptom of incompleteness that the only [pardon!] foreign language comments on M should be from

France, a country that did not (as far as is known) publish his works during the author's lifetime, while the reviews in those countries that did publish translations have not been located—though they certainly exist. Many contemporary translations [including serializations] may [? indubitably!] remain to be discovered.

The use of these waiting materials would go beyond the mere fact of their existence, and in more than one direction. We should learn more about Melville's foreign audience, and begin to learn something about his influence abroad—on Hudson? on Loti? on Gauguin? on Conrad? Work has been done on the influence of European literature on Melville; perhaps it worked in the other direction as well.

And, nearer home: I am always surprised that scholars in promising neighborhoods remain so uncurious about hopeful sources a short drive away:

Has anyone at the University of Wisconsin traced the Cramer family in Milwaukee, or found and examined the files of William Cramer's newspaper, *The Daily* (& *Weekly*) *Wisconsin?* The Cramers' friendship with the Melvilles began in Waterford, New York, before they moved, in 1840, to Milwaukee, where their unlocated correspondence continued.

Won't the University of California at Berkeley please send a search party to the San Francisco hospital—whether or not it still stands—where Stanwix Melville died in 1886?

The Pittsfield newspaper files are so near the Williams campus that my expectation stays alive (in spite of the counter current) that we shall hear news from there of more Melville pages turning up in those newspaper columns. Think of all the anonymous poetry waiting to be read! Did the archive of Joseph Edward Adams Smith (died 1896), Melville's link to the *Berkshire Eagle*, disappear totally?

Has anyone on the energetic campus of Chicago or Northwestern traced the family of Herman Melville Greene (son of "Toby") from his last known address (1894), 111 Warren Avenue?

Have people at Wayne looked in the business papers of the *Detroit Free Press* to trace the copyrighting author of the possibly unique and true history of Mocha Dick—published there on 3 April 1892?

Will the many Galena descendants of Thomas Melville (1776–1845) wait much longer for Illinois scholars before cleaning out their attics?

Is there not an Edinburgh admirer of Melville who will spend a week looking for the descendants of the Revd Robert Swan?

The poor bachelor scrivener, E. J. M. Fly, might be the hardest to follow, from his last Vermont addresses of 1852, but the heated revival of interest in "Bartleby" should make it worth the while of some inquisitive scholar—at Dartmouth?

And so on and on. Should we hope that students and scholars can still be excited by Melville and his work? Perhaps we'll have to look outside the classroom for Melville's next rescuers. They may receive their first lightning bolt in a paperback novel bought from an airport bookrack. (Dr. Henry Murray received his lightning in a book found on a transatlantic steamer—I received mine in the library of an army hospital.) Maybe a poor film or a good opera based on a work by Melville will set off the search.

Films have been known to work on the mind underneath

their rarely satisfactory surfaces, and though Melville may have had little luck in his film "adaptations," there is some evidence that the traces of Melville in them have often left lasting impressions. What films have done with *Typee* (thrice!) can be easily imagined, but how would you have pictured his adventures in that successful first novel? "Bartleby" and "The Encantadas" have reached the screen (the latter a French production) in unsurprising ways. The authors of Welles's *The Stranger* could not resist the temptation to borrow the climax of "The Bell Tower." Scenarios of *The Confidence-Man* and "Benito Cereno" remain in circulation—both ideal for brave film-makers, one would think. But once we thought the same of *Moby-Dick* and *Billy Budd*, and look what we got—not much beyond John Barrymore's striking Ahab and the good intentions of *Billy Budd*'s producers.

The hardest disappointment, of course, was in the latest *Moby-Dick*, directed by John Huston. When begun, his project sounded like a dream: Ahab was to be played by Huston's great father, Walter Huston (do you remember his portrait of the Devil in Benét's *All That Money Can Buy?*), and the scenario was to be by James Agee. The deaths of both these key figures in the project changed the film's nature damagingly. Ray Bradbury became the adaptor (with Huston) and Gregory Peck sloughed off the dark side of Ahab, with results as pale as his painted white rubber antagonist. What astonished me particularly was that, as much as any other nineteenth-century writing, *Moby-Dick* is crammed with film suggestiveness that, if listened to, would make any *Moby-Dick* film original on every level. The balance of imagination with a passionate observation of reality is a beautiful base for film making, and I had thought that Huston would be sensitive to this gift. Agee was aware of the rich mine, but somehow Huston and Bradbury successfully ignored it at every inviting point, and gave us instead a normal condensation of the "story," a process that any long novel must involuntarily endure and be squeezed through on its way to the screen. Melville as an inspiration for film making has to wait longer for his chance, but who knows how many film-goers became his readers, out of curiosity? It would not be strange that through the boldness of his imagery, the meaning and power of his words and his action, that Melville might be kept alive in equally bold films of the future, in theaters or on television screens, quite independent of the enclosed academic world.

Nor need we limit his potentialities to the familiar media. My friend, visiting Prague, saw the repertory of the Laterna Magica there and got "excited when I think what could be done in terms of action and confrontation with three screens and a live Ishmael walking in and out of them as he joins the action or steps aside to comment. I can't help thinking that the Czechs have developed something that will do things for books like *Moby-Dick* and *Crime and Punishment* that no critic could ever do." Another friend, a painter, has conceived, though not realized, a great light and color show to convey the prophecies and philosophy of Melville's *Moby-Dick*.

It is good to see in one of the most recent works of and about Melville, the poems selected by Robert Penn Warren, the personal pleasure of one poet in reading the poems of another. There is a refreshing directness in his comments and a sensibility in his selection that calls to other readers to join him in his discovery. If we're lucky the works of Melville, through these definitive texts, will reach the eyes of other discoverers. The joy of reading his writing, even the least of it, is a treasure to be guarded, not discarded as some minor element in the history of literature. Is is too much to hope that Herman Melville can enter a new stage in our lives?

William Gilmore Simms

THOMAS L. MCHANEY

$\mathcal{S}$ince the publication in 1892 of William P. Trent's American Men of Letters biography of William Gilmore Simms, hardly a decade has passed in the writing of American literary history without some attempt to evaluate the prodigious Simms *oeuvre* and put a label on its author. The more than eighty volumes of fiction, drama, poetry, and occasional prose, plus the editorial work and, since the completion of its publication in 1956, the five volumes of correspondence have, however, defied simple evaluation with as much success as they have avoided easy dismissal. Simms himself has likewise remained a kind of mountainous terra incognita to be speculated upon and squabbled over without being fully explored. The problem remains one of seeing Simms whole, something which can be done only in a full-scale modern critical biography, still the prime desideratum a hundred years after the author's death. This essay does not aim at completeness, but through it I would like to suggest some modifications regarding Simms which seem to evolve naturally out of his most interesting work and previous approaches to it.

The main lines into Simms's life and art are sufficiently well known to require little repetition here. Trent believed him to be a victim of his loyalties to slavery and a repressive slave society which curbed his creative imagination, restricted his thought, and perhaps discouraged even formal experiment. Vernon Parrington, in the second volume of *Main Currents in American Thought* (1927), delivered a paean to what Simms might have been and a broadside at Charleston society for its shabby treatment of its most virile native son; Charleston snobbery and the excessive romanticism of the South, according to Parrington, turned Simms away from his predilection for realism and made him a mediocre writer. The harmful effect of the romantic tradition was also cited by Carl Van Doren in his *Dictionary of American Biography* sketch of Simms (vol. 17, 1933) and in *The American Novel, 1789–1939* (rev. ed., 1940).

Parrington and Van Doren both praised Simms's realism, but, for all the praise, they had curiously limited notions about it. Like most critics after them, they preferred Simms's revolutionary romances to his border novels; they did not much like what Simms was able to extract from the raw frontier. Parrington wrote:

> Contemporary romanticism engrafted on a nature fundamentally realistic developed a pronounced strain in his work which, for lack of an exacter word, we may call picaresque. This comes out at its worst in the crude border tales of *Richard Hurdis* and *Border Beagles*, stories marked by the coarseness of the eighteenth century, backwoods versions of *Jonathan Wild*.[1]

At its best, he felt, this strain in Simms produced a handful of flesh and blood rogues in the revolutionary novels. Similarly, Van Doren wrote of the "rich picaresque energy" of Simms's rogues,[2] likewise favoring the revolutionary material. "Simms was at his best in dealing with the matter of the Revolution; he was less happy with the Frontier. Perhaps the earlier frontier [i.e., Cooper's] had been intrinsically more dignified than the one which Simms had observed along the Mississippi and which had a contemporary comic hero in the very real David Crockett. Certainly Cooper's frontier, lying deeper under the shadow of the past, had been romanticized more than Simms's."[3]

Parrington and Van Doren express a viewpoint that has held up the proper evaluation of Simms's best work. They seem to have encountered something which they cannot, or will not, accept or understand. Cooper can have his romantic and decorous—and largely imaginary—frontier, but Simms is to be denied the real thing as he found it during youthful adventures into the developing areas of the old Southwest and in the course of many trips into the Carolina and Georgia backwoods after he was a mature writer. What Parrington and Van Doren would seem to prefer is a reality of their own choosing and a literary realism like Howells's—decorous and genteel. Unfortunately this view has remained in the minds of many of Simms's commentators. It has caused them to shy away from appreciating his connection with the old southwestern frontier territory and the important and vigorous literature which it produced, a literature that was often violent and macabre, frequently but not exclusively humorous and picaresque, peculiarly realistic, and readily available to Simms not only through his experiences and his inclinations, but also through a tradition that was developing in newspapers and magazines at the very time he was beginning to acquire his skills and habits as a writer of fiction.

Recent criticism has continued to prefer the revolutionary novels to the border romances and to dismiss Simms's ties to frontier realism and humor. In *The South in American Literature* (1954), for instance, Jay B. Hubbell calls the seven novels of the Revolution "Simms's best work" and declares that "we should like Simms better if he had continued to explore the vein he opened in *The Golden Christmas*," [4] that is, a kind of local-color realism about plantation life. Hubbell has little to say about the southwestern realists, allotting all of them only twenty-one pages in his nine-hundred-page study; that fact alone may explain why he does not attempt to connect Simms's work with theirs. Hugh Holman, who has written much on Simms, also seems to be negatively disposed to the Southwest tradition, writing in "William Gilmore Simms and the 'American Renaissance'" that he shares "Edmund Wilson's misgivings" about the "ungrammatical sadism" of George Washington Harris's Sut Lovingood yarns, masterpieces of the vernacular.[5] J. V. Ridgely in his 1962 Twayne series book on Simms develops the notion that all of Simms's novels are essentially "border tales" and that Simms's "real subject" in his "best work is the interaction between civilization and frontier,"[6] but he, too, slights the border romances and claims that Simms was not influenced by such southwestern authors as A. B. Longstreet, William Tappan Thompson, Johnson Jones Hooper, or Joseph Glover Baldwin. Ridgely mistakenly suggests that all the southwestern writing was "comic." The tales, he adds, "were ephemeral; they appeared chiefly in newspapers . . . and, with the exception of a few like those just cited [i.e., works by the men listed above], they were not often collected in book form. Moreover, to Simms, they were subliterary in content and style, and they did little to contribute to that elevation of Southern manners and morals for which he strove."[7]

Ridgely errs and also overstates his case. He leaves out of account the widely read Library of Humorous American Works, the Carey & Hart venture that published almost all the landmark volumes of southwestern humorous, realistic, and sporting writing. Under a succession of publishers, the Library expanded from eighteen to nearly forty volumes and lasted from 1846 to beyond 1869; it included Simms's *As Good as a Comedy; Or, the Tennessean's Story*, published as by "an Editor" in 1852. In the second place, one cannot dismiss the periodical appearances, beginning in the late 1820s, of this writing. Simms, a journalist and editor, may have known much of it in this form. That he found no time to contribute at this ephemeral level does not argue against his interest, since he, as a professional writer, had to make money on what he wrote and there was no money in the freely circulating tales which rival editors clipped from one another's papers. He knew both the amateurs and the few professionals who worked the field. His neighbor from Beaufort, S. C., William Elliott, contributed sporting sketches to the *American Turf Register* as early as 1829 and collected the sketches of two decades into one of the little known but excellent volumes of sporting literature, *Carolina Sports by Land and Water* (Charleston: Burges & James, 1846). Simms tried to persuade Elliott to contribute to his *Southern Quarterly Review* in letters mentioning the work of another friend, Henry William Herbert, author of *Frank Forrester's Field Sports of the United States, and British Provinces, of North America* (1849) and other books in the field.[8] Simms knew the achievement of Johnson Jones Hooper, creator of Simon Suggs, and Joseph Glover Baldwin, author of *Flush Times of Alabama and Mississippi*, well enough to write Evert Duyckinck his regrets that they had not been included in his *Cyclopedia of American Literature*.[9] He probably knew William Tappan Thompson, author of *Major Jones's Courtship* [10] and other volumes, when Thompson edited the weekly magazine, *Western Continent*, in 1846, and was announcing forthcoming contributions by Simms.[11] Simms probably also knew W. T. Porter's *Spirit of the Times*, the chief popularizer of southwestern writing, even though it is not mentioned in his letters. As Perry Miller points out in *The Raven and the Whale*, the "myth persists that Porter's sporting journal was disdained by genteel Americans, that his pioneering ventures into native American humor went unappreciated by all but gentry of the track," but the Knickerbocker editors and writers knew it and so, undoubtedly, did the Young Americans, with whom Simms—along with Melville—was associated.[12] Finally, even if Simms had been disdainful of this writing or if he was not "influenced" by it, he still would have been capable of adapting its subjects, styles, characters, and points of view into his own more ambitious fiction. If he had never known any of the writers or their work, even, he was, like those authors, on the scene. He knew the backwoods. He had witnessed the flush times. He was searching his region for literary materials. Without an example to follow he would have turned in a similar performance.

Simms possessed the raw material that the life of the

frontier provided. The spirit with which he approached it literarily is suggested in a letter he wrote to Phillip C. Pendleton in 1841 defending the language and subject of a racy tale, "Loves of a Driver": "To be truthful, a true writer—an earnest man, full of his subject and having no sinister, and only the direct object, must lay it as bare as possible. He must roll up his sleeves to it, and not heed the blushes of the sophisticated damsel, who is shocked at the bare, brawny arms. Convention is always the foe to truth; and the literature of a country, and the literary men thereof . . . must stick to nature and scorn the small requisitions of little cliques and classes." [13] Among the writers who will "do justice to us," he writes (before the tradition had brought forth Thompson, Harris, and others) are Elliott and Longstreet.[14] The writer of such sentences, Arlin Turner observed when reviewing Simms's letters, "was surely a realist by both temperament and conviction." [15]

Simms wrote too hastily, as he himself repeatedly recognized. The literary fashions of the day were against his natural bent. He rarely transcended the conventions of form and style which he had inherited from Cooper, Scott, and others. Invariably, he hobbled his romances with the obligatory love interest, stilted dialogue and all. But he wrote with intense and determined honesty within the boundaries he accepted and he found ways to include into his romantic novels good solid chunks of the raw humor, the violence, and the realism of the frontier. Carl Van Doren found him "a more veracious novelist than Cooper." [16] Hubbell remarks that, "As the Border Romances show, Simms saw as clearly as William Faulkner or Robert Penn Warren the strain of violence in Southern life—in life in all lands, for that matter—the strain of violence and disorder which sentimental readers and writers have always been disposed to ignore." [17] Donald Davidson suggests that the "best fiction of Simms is not a long step away from saga and folk tale" and that " 'folkishness' is an all-pervasive quality" in his best writing. "It is an organic quality, not something added for picturesqueness. It belongs to the grand and moving comedy of the frontier as Simms conceived the image of the frontier. No other writer of Simms's generation explored its richness as fully as he did. It was left to Samuel Clemens, long afterwards, to rediscover in *Huckleberry Finn*, something of its efficacy and meaning." [18]

With the exception of Davidson, such favorable comments about Simms's realism have come from critics who, as we have seen, still low-rated the border tales and who, generally speaking, failed to discuss his short fiction, especially the stories which directly reflect the realism of southwestern writing (some of them, admittedly, unavailable heretofore).[19] A proper view of Simms, however, will have to take the border romances and the short stories into closer account. Here is the Simms with the rolled-up sleeves whom we need to recover.

Simms's first novel, *Guy Rivers* (1834),[20] is a border romance set on the Georgia-Tennessee line in the gold-mining district that prospered in the 1820s. The plotting is poor. The love interest will not do at all. But Simms had ambitions for his novel. The villain, however poorly realized, is a Byronic figure; he has his mark of Cain, his mysterious past, and a final fall from all possibility of salvation. The frontier, however, is what has made him this way. Life on the border leaves him, in the end, an embittered man who curses God, saying "I have gained nothing by [Christ's] death. Men are as bad as ever, and wrong . . . has been as active . . . a principle of human action as before he [sic] died. It is in his [sic] name now that they do the wrong." [21] Despite many general faults, Simms's best work in the novel is that which reflects the southwestern literature that was just appearing in newspapers and magazines. The Yankee pedlar, Jared Bunce, defends himself against charges of selling defective clocks and tinware in the neighborhood:

A clock is quite a delicate and ticklish article of manufacture, you see, and it ain't everybody that can make a clock, or can make it go when it don't want to; and if a man takes a hammer or a horsewhip, or any other unnatural weapon to it, as if it was a house or a horse, why, I guess, it's not reasonable to expect it to keep in order, and it's no use in having a clock no how, if you don't treat it well.[22]

. . . .

The tin wares I sell stand well enough in a northern climate: there may be some difference in yours that I can't account for; and I guess, pretty much, there is. Now, your people are a mighty hot-tempered people, and take a fight for breakfast, and make three meals a day out of it . . . so here, now, as far as I can see, your climate takes pretty much after the people, and if so, it's no wonder that solder can't stand it. Who knows, again, but you boil your water quite too hot? [23]

When his calico prints depicting natural scenes prove to be miscolored, the prosecutor warns him, "I'll tell you what, Master Bunce, it won't do to take natur in vain. If you can show me a better painter than natur, from your pairts, I give up; but until that time, I say that any man who thinks to give the woods a different sort of face from what God give 'em, ought to be licked for his impudence if nothing else." [24]

Simms's comedy is good, but it is more than comedy. It is accurate, like the legal complications that invariably snare the innocent heroes of the border novels and reflect, as Arthur Hobson Quinn has noted, the realities of the frontier.[25] Yankee pedlars as stock figures of American humor aside, Simms uses Bunce to dramatize something real about the temper and provinciality of the backwoods. The scenes are as effective as Faulkner's horse deals in illuminating by art a small corner of southern, American, and, ultimately, generally human life.

Mark Forrester, the frontiersman of *Guy Rivers*, plays a small role, but he is well drawn, as are the band of renegades and squatters who try to hold the gold fields against the regulators who come to drive them out. Accurate, too, is the explanation of Ralph Colleton's presence at the affray: "Here was incident, excitement—and with all the enthusiasm of the southern temper, and with that uncalculating warmth which so much distinguishes it, he determined, without much regard to the merits of the question, to go along with the party." [26]

Martin Faber, (1833) the confession tale, and *Guy Rivers,* the border novel, were both well received, but for his second novel Simms turned into another field. *The Yemassee* (1835) is the first of his colonial romances. It is also the novel which most of his modern critics prefer. Simms parallels and improves upon Cooper in *The Yemassee,* perhaps one reason the novel has received so much attention. His Indians are well-imagined (he admitted inventing their mythology),[27] though a little precipitous, and the portraits of Sanutee and Matiwan are justly admired. Also worthy of admiration, however, are fine examples of a kind of unflinching realism that doesn't appear in American writing until much, much later. The death of Macnamara is one example: "At that moment a tall chief of the Seratees, with a huge club, dashed the now visible skull down upon the trunk. The blow was fatal—the victim uttered not even a groan, and the spattering brains were driven wide, and into the upturned face of Harrison." [28] Simms also had his sleeves rolled up when he detailed the struggle between Grayson's wife and an Indian who tries to enter the blockhouse window:

Excited and nerved, she drew the extended arm of the Indian, in spite of all his struggles, directly over the sill, so as to turn the elbow completely down upon it. With her whole weight . . . she pressed the arm across the window until her ears heard the distinct, clear crack of the bone. . . . He fainted in his pain, and as the weight increased upon the arm of the woman, the nature of her sex began to resume its sway . . . a strange sickness came over her; and she was just conscious of a crashing fall of the heavy body among the branches of the tree at the foot of the window.[29]

The Yemassee was also a success, but Simms again refused to capitalize upon his previous formulas. In the same year he published the first revolutionary romance, *The Partisan* (1835). This exploration of subject and theme and, to some degree, of form, is itself a measure of Simms's integrity as an artist, but all these early novels are apprentice fiction. Simms was to do better work, and, I submit, much of it is found in the two subsequent border novels, *Richard Hurdis* (1838) and *Border Beagles* (1840), and in *The Cassique of Kiawah* (1859), like *The Yemassee* a romance of the colonial period and Simms's last novel to reach book form.

The Cassique of Kiawah — to jump ahead in time and consider it with its companion novel — has been neglected at the expense of *The Yemassee*. Yet it is a far more even book and the story more compellingly told. In it, Simms works the backwoods and the frontier vernacular at great length. He displays a rich imagination in the creation of character and event; he skillfully works abrupt shifts in time and scene; and he resists the convention — which Hawthorne could not escape — of making the dark, romantic heroine lose her love and life in a conflict with the saintly blonde, no small triumph in American fiction of the period. Zulieme Calvert is a sprightly figure out of romantic literature and, due to her innocence, she is often shallow, but she is also a complex woman often capable of speaking with a voice of her own, as when she tells how she came to marry her moody privateer, Harry Calvert:

"He was a great doll for me, and it was in playing together that we made love and carried on our courtship. It was very funny. . . . I taught him how to dance our Spanish dances . . . and I chased him through the orange-groves, and found him out where he used to hide himself; for he loved too much to hide himself among the thick groves; and he looked so sad when I found him; but I cheered him up, and he would smile, and sing and dance with me, all so good; till, one day, he started up in a sort of passion, and looked very grand, and said I should be his little wife; and I said, 'Yes, why not? It will be so funny to become a wife.' And so the priest married us. But he's changed since then—he is not funny now. He's so serious, and so cross!—all you English are so cross and quarrelsome." [30]

Privateering, mutiny, intrigue, Indian warfare, backwoods life and character—all this is laid against some fine portraits of early Charleston. Ben Backstay, the old backwoodsman, in chapter 9, and Sam Fowler, the renegade sailor who stirs some of Calvert's crew to mutiny and a swearing over the Jolly Roger, in chapter 30, are both nicely done. The satire of society pretensions in general, through Mrs. Masterson, and Charleston society particularly, through Mrs. Perkins Anderson, though it all applies to the seventeenth century, may lend some support to Trent and Parrington's speculations about Simms's relations with his native town. Ligon, the grim frontiersman, is a well-drawn Indian-hater. The ironic contrast between the two brothers—each of whom has a blind spot regarding things closest to him—works; in the end, their lives do not come out well, though not tragically, either. That, as the saying goes, is life.

Cassique is, as Carl Van Doren has written, a "stirring and varied romance of seventeenth-century Carolina," [31] and it is hard to understand why it has lagged so far behind *The Yemassee* in popularity, except that it has not been readily available, in the twentieth century, while *The Yemassee* has been reprinted often. It is true that *Cassique*, like Simms's tales of South Carolina in the Revolution, superficially seemed to merit the charge of too narrow a provincialism in its own day, but the detail which possibly put off readers in the nineteenth century should not matter now any more than it does in *Moby-Dick*. Hopefully, the republication of *Cassique* in the Simms edition from the University of South Carolina Press will bring it a new group of readers and help to adjust its current standing.

Following *The Yemassee* and *The Partisan* in 1835,

Simms wrote *Mellichampe* (1836), another novel of the Revolution, and then returned to the border series for two novels, *Richard Hurdis* (1838) and *Border Beagles* (1840). *Richard Hurdis* represents another experiment by Simms. Like *Martin Faber*, it is a first-person narrative, but in a different form and tone from the confessional tale. The device, in this case, does not always work, especially whenever Richard must reveal events (as in chaps. 10 and 11) beyond his experience, but Simms deserves credit for the attempt; Melville and Hawthorne, in *Moby-Dick* and *Blithedale Romance*, were not able to solve the problem any better technically, though their failures were not quite so obvious as Simms's. Anomalies aside, the device does allow Simms, through Hurdis, to reflect upon the "besavaging" effect of the frontier: "a rude indifference to the claims of one's fellow, must follow every breaking up of the old and stationary abodes. The wandering habits of our people are the great obstacles to their perfect civilization. These habits are encouraged by the cheapness of our public lands, and their constant exposure for sale. The morals not less than the manners of our people are diseased by the license of the wilderness." [32] As Ridgely states in his book on Simms, such observations form a portion of Simms's attitude toward the frontier and its effects, conflicts which he dramatized in much of his fiction, especially in the border tales. Characters like Guy Rivers and Foster; John Hurdis; Gorham and Voltmeier; and Lt. Molyneaux of *Cassique* all give evidence of divided consciousnesses which have been heightened by contact with the savage and lawless.

Richard Hurdis is filled with well-rendered material done after the fashion of the realistic writers of the Southwest. Chapter 43 is as good a diddling scene as was ever invented by Hooper or George Washington Harris. Chapter 36, in which John Hurdis tries to gun down the emissary of the outlaws, is a true, if simple, study of human cowardice. Emmeline Walker's death in chapter 40 is startling. In effect, she dies of a broken heart, suffering shock, madness, and death over the murder of her betrothed, like so many daughters of sentimental fiction, but there is little sentimentality in the way Simms handles it. As she resists medication, Hurdis forces a wineglass upon her: "In our efforts we were at length forced to pry her teeth apart with our fingers, and to force the glass between them. It was an error to have used the wineglass in such a situation . . . for no sooner had we put the edge of the glass between her divided teeth, than they closed upon it, crunching it into the minutest fragments. . . . I dropped the fragment of the glass which remained in my hands, and grasped her instantly by the throat. I grasped her almost as tightly as I should have done a mortal foe. It was a desperate resort for a desperate situation. I nearly strangled her, but it was the only thing that could have saved her from swallowing the broken particles. With my fingers, while the jaws were stretched apart, I drew out the bits of glass, which were numerous, though not without cutting her mouth and gums in a shocking manner. The blood ran from her mouth, and over the side of her pallid face, staining its purity; and her tongue, bleeding also the while, hung over the lips." [33]

One cannot imagine that Simms invented such passages to please the "ladies of United Columbia" to whom most of the sentimental and romantic fiction since William Hill Brown's *Power of Sympathy* had been "dedicated." Simms was exploring new ground, and however badly he was often doing it, he still opened up material and methods for writers to come and helped to prepare an audience for them, if only by confronting his readers with scenes like the one above in what they supposed were romantic novels in the old style.

Border Beagles, which continued to concentrate upon outlawry, contains a greater variety of humor and realism. Tom Horsey, the would-be frontier thespian, is an extravagant and funny characterization whose constant dra-

matic quotations and descriptions of frontier theatrics reflect Simms's own strong interest in Elizabethan and
contemporary drama.[34] The theatrical material also antici-
pates another part of southwestern writing, as found, for
example, in Sol Smith's account of acting and theatrical
management along the rivers and in the towns of the
Southwest.[35] In *Border Beagles* Simms is also good on
"gouging," a recondite backwoods skill (see Tom Horsey's satirical remarks about young Mabry in chap. 10,
entitled "Closing Up Peepers According to 'The Science'"); good in the "stick, fist or hug?" challenge between Denis O'Dougherty and Dick Jamison (chap. 21);
and good with the dwarf, Dick Stillyards (esp. chap. 26),
who is an improvement upon, as his role is an amplifica-
tion of, the half-wit Chub Williams in *Guy Rivers*. There
is satire worthy of Twain in the bandit's admonition to
Tom Horsey that only complicated schemes can catch
the support of the Americans: "Tell them of small
schemes which are possible and practicable, and which
might yield them moderate profits and be of some service,
and they will turn up their noses in disgust. They despise
little projects. But get up a grand Religious Steam Association; or a company for connecting Pensacola with San
Jacinto by means of a chain of floating bridges . . . propose some such modest matters to them as these, and
they'll take stock directly." [36] *Border Beagles* is currently
far from being admired, though Donald Davidson was
willing, as I am, to put it with Simms's best.[37] An age that
has discovered the delights of Melville's *The Confidence
Man* may find the novel more to its liking.

Voltmeier was Simms's last novel, serialized shortly before his death (1869) and not published in hard covers
until 1971, when it appeared as volume 1 of the South
Carolina Simms edition. It is another faulty book, but the
fine things, the vital characters, the ambitious view, the
same honesty that marks his better writing are in it. *Voltmeier* fuses the gothic with the backwoods; it was a good
idea, one that ought to work today for one of our writers

of black humor. As before, Simms failed with his villainous main character; he has not been able to create an Ahab, and he is not able to explain Voltmeier's peculiar occupation or his destiny. Toward the end of the book, everything begins to fall apart. But it was poor Simms in this novel, and not the image the author worked with, who was in his last flurry as *Voltmeier* was being composed. Despite Simms's illness and fatigue, Swipes, Brown Peters, and especially Mother Moggs are well done, as is Brownlow the lawyer; the scenes with these characters pulse with life and racy dialogue. There is one of those startling and detailed episodes of violence when Voltmeier, symbolically struggling to master his darker self, breaks a wild stallion by forcing it, finally, to leap to its own destruction against a mountain wall. Simms handles the love interest with greater skill than he had been able to before, submerging it, in effect, and speeding it along out of sight as an undercurrent. Otherwise, the novel reflects but dimly his earlier work, and, in fact, the germ of *Voltmeier* may be in one of the pieces from *The Wigwam and the Cabin* (1845–46), a fast-paced little folktale called "The Last Wager." From that volume of stories, "The Armchair of Tustenuggee" and "The Snake of the Cabin" also are particularly deserving of attention. "Grayling," the ghost story which Poe liked, seems pale and contrived beside Poe's own work, but much of the collection admirably fits Donald Davidson's contention about the folk quality of Simms's writing.

Most of the handy phrases by which Simms has been described are obviously incomplete. He was a bigger and tougher writer than he has been given credit for being. The wonder is, when the evidence of his voluminous correspondence is ranged alongside his editorial work, that he had time for belles lettres at all. Yet write he did. Unfortunately, he came of age professionally on the eve of the Panic of 1837, and William Charvat has shown the effects of the ensuing depression on the business of literature.[38] He faced the competition not only of the scribbling women and the pirated Victorians, but also of his American peers from New England and New York, who had slightly better entrée than he did into the important centers of publication. He did not live up to his promise, and it has been necessary for almost everyone who has written about him to try to say just why. Trent and Parrington, it is now agreed, were wrong. Hugh Holman and Donald Davidson have pointed out some of the hardships he endured, which certainly must have taken their toll in spirit and energy. Simms had more experience of the rawness, unpredictability, violence, and varied tragedy of human existence than any major American writer until we get to Twain and Crane. He lost parents, wives, children, home, library, estate, "country," fortune and fame, but something in him never gave in to these circumstances, and perhaps what would not give in to them, would not—somewhat like Hawthorne's backing away from the deep-diving mind of Melville—or could not use them fully for artistic purposes either. He seems, artistically, never to have driven life into a corner. He never fully expressed its tragedies or its joys or created a character with the fullness of strength and spirit which he himself must have understood and possessed.

Simms, as Hugh Holman has noted, chose to be a "man of letters." That is not a very happy occupation in America, looked at over the long view, for all that many still covet the title. What it has meant, unless some accident of wealth freed the man from the marketplace, is hustling for the literary buck: following "trends," breaking concentration, diluting talent in a hundred varied enterprises. In the midst of doing just this, however, as A. S. Salley has said, Simms kept his eye on the goal of making a true contribution to American literature, resting his case, at the last, with posterity and Providence.[39] Simms's case is still out, but I think that if we can persuade the jury to consider all the evidence, a favorable verdict is assured.

Henry Thoreau
and the Reverend
Poluphloisboios Thalassa

JOEL PORTE

En ce qui touche ma rêverie, ce n'est pas
l'infini que je trouve dans les eaux, c'est la
profondeur.

Gaston Bachelard, *L'Eau et les Rêves*

. . . we looked off, and saw the water
growing darker and darker and deeper and
deeper the farther we looked, till it was awful
to consider . . .

Henry Thoreau, *Cape Cod*

H

His riddles were worth the reading," [1] Emerson notes, after quoting Thoreau's familiar parable of the hound, the bay horse, and the turtledove, whereby Emerson seems to grant his friend precisely that "pardon" for his "obscurities" which Thoreau had requested while introducing his mysterious little fable in *Walden.* "There are more secrets in my trade than in most men's," Thoreau apologized, "and yet not voluntarily kept, but inseparable from its very nature." [2] Although it might be said with justice that this particular riddle is scarcely worth all the ink that has been shed over it, both Thoreau's plea and Emerson's concession seem much to the point. There *is* an enigma at the heart of Thoreau's quest, but we are emphatically cautioned not to attempt any solution of Thoreauvian mysteries that overlooks his "trade"—which is, of course, literature ("my work is writing"),[3] or, better, poetry. We are advised, that is, to seek to fathom Thoreau's secrets in a spirit of imaginative extravagance that corresponds to his own. "Nothing remarkable was ever accomplished in a prosaic mood," he insists in *Cape Cod,* for we must put ourselves "in a frame of mind fitted to behold the truth." [4] There is "a mystery in all things," Thoreau noted in 1841, in the course of a long explication of Emerson's "The Sphinx"—"in infancy, the moon, fire, flowers, sea, mountain"; but "poetry is the only solution time can offer." [5]

What Thoreau meant, or achieved, by an extravagantly imaginative—an inherently poetic—approach to his world, is the heart of the matter, as I see it, and thus constitutes my fundamental concern. But since I shall root my discussion in Thoreau's *elementary* interest in and attraction to water, I must ask the reader to anticipate this subject (and particularly to focus both eye and ear on *Cape Cod* in the near distance). The concept, and critical practice, of associating the material fantasies of a given creative artist with a marked tendency toward one of the four elements—fire, water, air, or earth—is borrowed from the great phenomenological philosopher-critic, Gaston Bachelard (a devoted reader, be it noted, of Henry Thoreau), whose general theory of the creative imagination also has remarkable pertinence here. Like Thoreau, Bachelard makes a crucial distinction between nighttime dreams and daytime reveries. The first, as Thoreau says in *A Week*, "are the touchstones of our characters"; [6] they belong to the realm of psychological analysis. But there is a mystery *in* things, or in our relation *to* things, which can best be explored through daydreams. "The dream worlds of wide-awake, diurnal reveries," Bachelard writes, "are dependent upon truly fundamental phenomenology." When these reveries become authentically poetic, they constitute "hypothetical lives which enlarge our lives by letting us in on the secrets of the universe. A world takes form in our reverie, and this world is ours. This dreamed world teaches us the possibilities for expanding our being within our universe." [7] Thoreau's own formulation in *A Week* is more succinct: "Our truest life is when we are in dreams awake." [8]

As we know, Thoreau's reveries persistently concern that pastoral universe of things and nonhuman creatures in which he wished to immerse himself—that "woodland vision" of Walden Pond which, he says, "for a long time made the drapery of my dreams." [9] But his most impressive, most extravagantly poetic, indeed most puzzling imaginings have to do with what he called the "Wild"— nature as sheerly alien matter, awesomely personified in "Walking" as a "vast, savage, howling" beast. [10] This essay, in fact, is a kind of touchstone of Thoreau's imaginative life, a fascinating and particularly revealing compendium of unbounded Thoreauvian fantasy. And the ever-present danger of approaching Thoreau's writing in the wrong frame of mind—in the spirit of ratiocination rather than of reverie—is especially sharp here. What are we to make, for example, of this remark about "Walking" offered by Leo Marx in 1962:

Now he speaks as an extreme primitivist-anarchist. . . . It is one thing to repudiate the workaday world, as he had once done, for aesthetic purposes: to clear the ground for concentrated perception; but it is quite another to propose this regressive attitude as an overall prescription for living. In the end Thoreau's doctrine of "wildness" becomes indistinguishable from the shadowy bliss of infantile mindlessness.[11]

Perhaps the decade that has passed since that observation was published is a sufficient comment on its impertinence, for Thoreau's self-proclaimed "extreme statement" seems to have inspired a whole generation of budding ecologists (let us recall that the Sierra Club's lovely and influential *"In Wildness is the Preservation of the World"* was also published in 1962). But I cannot refrain from pointing to the curious kind of critical *trahison*, the subtle—though perhaps not entirely intended—disparagement that laces the phrase "for aesthetic purposes." Thoreau's repudiation of State Street was as serious and sustained as his devotion to literature; and his aesthetic purpose was consciously "to make an extreme statement" if so he might "make an emphatic one." [12] He traded not so much in prescriptions for living as in imaginative release and recreation.

There is, however, a totally valid and unanswerable criticism that can be leveled against "Walking": namely, that Thoreau's set of clichéd variations on the theme of "westward the course of empire takes its way" is virtually indistinguishable from the mindless political sloganeering in favor of expansion that Henry Nash Smith has so ably documented in *Virgin Land*.[13] Unquestionably, the true force of "Walking" does not lie in that direction, but rather in its radical revelation of that "syntax of metaphors," those "metaphorical coordinations," which in Bachelard's view are the hallmarks of a consistently poetic mind.[14]

Fundamental to the metaphoric syntax of "Walking" is

a set of religious tropes that are clearly intended to under-line the seriousness of Thoreau's quest. *Sauntering,* of course, Thoreau etymologizes at the outset as walking *à la Sainte Terre*—to the Holy Land. He is a walker in this sense, but his ultimate goal, his *Sainte Terre,* is an awe-some, forbidding, even grim place, for he expects his life as a pilgrim to be "a divine tragedy" and warns whosoever would join him that we must be "prepared to send back our embalmed hearts only as relics to our desolate king-doms." [15] Although Thoreau does not believe in the Fa-ther, Son, and Holy Ghost, as he tells us in *A Week,* because in all his wanderings he "never came across the least vestige of authority for these things," he offers his own Trinity in "Walking": "I believe in the forest, and in the meadow, and in the night in which the corn grows." [16] He is sauntering toward the dark, holy Wild, and though he is presumably "in search of the springs of life" (a phrase that resonates widely in Thoreau's writings), his journey will necessarily carry him toward scenes of ex-plicit "dreariness" and terror. He will look for "an im-permeable and unfathomable bog" or "the darkest wood, the thickest and most interminable, and . . . most dismal swamp." This will be his "sacred place," his "*sanctum sanctorum.*" At the height of his seeming enthusiasm for this divine devastation, Thoreau ventures his most extreme —and perhaps most problematic—exclamation: "Give me the ocean, the desert or the wilderness!" [17]

We shall have occasion to reconsider this heady chal-lenge shortly. Let me only note in passing that, despite his clearly hyperbolic (though distressingly masochistic) tone, Thoreau's extravagantly bleak vision here of the ulti-mate he seeks is entirely consistent with his familiar state-ment in *Walden* that he craves only reality, "be it life or death." [18] But there is another, complementary set of meta-phoric coordinates in "Walking" that invite special atten-tion, whereby Thoreau expresses the more attractive, life-enhancing aspect of his reverie on sublime wildness.

Everywhere in Thoreau's writings the site of his religious experience is given a location in space which he calls, variously, the "frontier," the "border," or the "neutral ground." As Edwin Fussell observes, "Pilgrim and Pathfinder, Thoreau was forever playing with the words frontier and front, trying to detach them from literality." [19] In a very important sense, however, this "place" has physical reality for Thoreau: it is the dream-site where the supernal, or supremely poetic, experience impinges on mundane consciousness. As such, it invites what Bachelard calls a "topoanalysis," or "the systematic psychological study of the sites of our intimate lives." [20] In context, Bachelard is thinking of houses—particularly of Thoreau's hut—but the concept lends itself in a suggestive way to "Walking." The "border" figure appears in what is presumably its purely metaphoric form in this sentence: "I feel that with regard to Nature I live a sort of border life, on the confines of a world into which I make occasional and transional [transient] and transient forays only . . ." [21] The Wild, as an ideal, we surmise, is something Thoreau experiences only sporadically. There is another passage in "Walking," however—one with the deepest reverberations in Thoreau's reveries—where that border experience is made flesh and dwells with the poet.

There are some intervals which border the strain of the woodthrush, to which I would migrate,—wild lands where no settler has squatted; to which, methinks, I am already acclimated. [22]

The site, as it were, of Thoreau's most intimate experience of wildness *borders* where this particular bird sings; it lies *next to* the wood thrush. Any devoted reader of Thoreau's journal will recall that he was virtually obsessed by the wood thrush; its real importance in Thoreau's life can scarcely be overemphasized. In addition, this sentence bears an interesting and revealing relation to a curious passage in the "Spring" chapter of *Walden*. To glance at that first:

I heard a robin in the distance, the first I had heard for many a thousand years, methought, whose note I shall not forget for many a thousand more,—the same sweet and powerful song of yore. O the evening robin, at the end of a New England summer day! If I could ever find the twig he sits upon! I mean *he;* I mean *the twig.* This at least is not the *Turdus migratorius.*[23]

With the obvious substitution of the robin for a nightingale, Thoreau is without question under the influence of Keats's great ode in his consciously poetic first sentence (compare Keats's "the self-same song . . ." etc.).[24] And there is a clear connection for Thoreau between the robin and Walden Pond ("the water laves the shore as it did a thousand years ago")[25]: they are both representations of the correspondence between the timeless profundity of pastoral nature and the depth of the poet's eternal spirit. But the rest of the passage has an odd emphasis: though this robin of robins is a kind of Platonically ideal bird ("not the *Turdus migratorius*"), it is the quiddity of the bird, *this robin,* and *his perch,* which Thoreau longs for: "I mean *he;* I mean *the twig.*" *He* is also "not the *Turdus migratorius*" because he sits patiently and securely, beckoning Thoreau to a particular place—the actual site where the poet's pastoral reverie may be fulfilled. Though briefly, Keats unites in imagination with his nightingale. Thoreau fails only because he insists in some sense on realizing his dream, on having actual contact with the natural-divine "other."

The wood thrush affects Thoreau more profoundly than the robin because it is the voice of that *wild* nature which Thoreau particularly seeks: "This sound most adequately expresses the immortal beauty and wildness of the woods. I go in search of him. He sounds no nearer. . . . though I am scarcely more than a rod off, he seems further off than ever." [26] In other journal entries, this elusive bird of wildness gathers to itself an illuminating set of metaphoric attributes. Thoreau associates it with water: its song is a "stream" that embodies "the liquid coolness of things that are just drawn from the bottom of springs"; it is "a medicative draught" to his soul, "an elixir" to his eyes, and "a fountain of youth" to all his senses. [27] And the waters of the thrush are profound ones ("the bottom of springs"): "he deepens the significance of all things seen in the light of his strain"; for Thoreau, "he touches a depth in me which no other bird's song does." [28] These fathomless waters of song are "divine," the "truest and loftiest preachers" on earth; they are Thoreau's preferred religion, "the gospel according to the wood thrush." [29] Finally, corresponding to the belief expressed everywhere in Thoreau's writings that the poetry of Homer represents literally the voice of the Wild ("it is as if nature spoke"), the wood thrush is proclaimed the Homer of birds: "Men talk of the *rich* song of other birds,—the thrasher, mockingbird, nightingale. But I doubt, I doubt. They know not what they say! There is as great an interval between the thrasher and the wood thrush as between Thomson's 'Seasons' and Homer." [30] That *interval*, the space between ordinary nature and the Wild, is the borderland of Thoreau's ecstatic reverie, where, as he says in *Walden*, "both place and time were changed" and he "dwelt nearer to those parts of the universe and to those eras in history" that most attracted him. [31] Or, to return to the journal:

This minstrel sings in a heroic age. . . . I long for wildness, a nature which I cannot put my foot through, woods where the wood thrush forever sings, where the hours are early morning ones, and there is dew on the grass, and the day is forever unproved, where I might have a fertile unknown for a soil about me. . . . A New Hampshire everlasting and unfallen. [32]

Readers unsympathetic to Thoreau's rhapsodic praise of the Wild might be excused for disparaging him as "an ex-

treme primitivist" mindlessly ranting in his "most unrea-
sonably and unrealistically reckless" fashion,[33] but the
truth remains that we cannot really have Thoreau on any
other terms. "His love of wildness was real. . . . This was
a religion to him; to us, mythical." [34] Though his quest for
the "fertile unknown" might appear to be psychologically
dubious and socially and economically regressive, it represents the central commitment of his life and art: an experiment in imaginative *re-creation* through contact with the
elementary sources of life. Beneath the undeniably miscellaneous character of everything Thoreau wrote palpitates
this theme. *A Week*, for example, has not generally made
its point.[35] It is Thoreau's search back in time, inland spa-
tially, for the origins of all things: of history (particularly
American), of religion, of literature, of nature, of being
itself. When he reaches "Unappropriated Land" and at-
tains the summit of Agiocochook, Thoreau implies that he
has not only discovered the source of the Concord and
Merrimack rivers, but of all seas and mountains, indeed of
primal daylight.[36] It is, as he quotes from George Herbert,
"the bridal of the earth and sky," the marriage of Gaea
and Uranos, at which he is present.[37]

   A Week is very consciously, and even humorously, an
elemental book. "There are earth, air, fire, and water,"
Thoreau asserts with Empedoclean certainty in the "Sunday" section, and the next day he continues: "The greatest
appreciable physical revolutions are the work of the light-
footed air, the stealthy-paced water, and the subterranean
fire." [38] Nor is Thoreau purely objective concerning what
Bachelard calls "the natural dialectic of fire and water." [39]
He makes an impassioned plea for the element that most
attracted him: "Cold and damp,—are they not as rich experience as warmth and dryness?" [40] In the opening pages
of "Wednesday" Thoreau seems to cast his lot for Thales
(though Heraclitus was to get his due in *Walden* when the
Hermit "sacrificed . . . to Vulcan" as he warmed his hut),
for he becomes fascinated by a smaller bittern, "a bird of

the oldest Thalesian school" who "no doubt believes in the priority of water to the other elements." [41] Studying this "relic of a twilight antediluvian age" with its "melancholy and contemplative" air, Thoreau wonders whether it may not have "wrested the whole of her secret from Nature." He thinks that if he could penetrate to the core of the bittern's "dull, yellowish, greenish eye"—descend, that is, into the very heart of water—he might reach the bottom of his own soul.[42]

"In order for a reverie to be pursued with sufficient constancy to produce a written work," theorizes Gaston Bachelard in *L'Eau et les Rêves*, "in order that it not be simply the vacancy of a fugitive hour, it must find its *matter*, it is necessary that a material element nourish it with its own substance, its own pattern, its own specific poetics." Poetic thought, like pre-Socratic philosophy, must be marked by the elemental temperament of the poet, "linked to a primitive material reverie." [43] It would, of course, be absurd to insist narrowly and rigidly on any particular scheme of things in this regard. Bachelard says elsewhere that he is talking about "orientation," that "it is not a question of being rooted in a particular substance, but of tendencies, of poetic exaltation." [44] The true poet must have a concretely material imagination in order to be interested in the world and to interest us in *his* world, and this material imagination will always have a specific tendency.

Can there be any doubt about Thoreau's primary orientation toward water? [45] (In this respect of course he is not singular in his literary generation, for one thinks naturally of Poe, Melville, and Whitman.) We have only to glance at the titles of the two books Thoreau published in his lifetime to confirm this observation, and if we add *Cape Cod* we have a kind of aqueous Trinity: in *A Week*, the book of the River; in *Walden*, the book of the Pond; and in *Cape Cod*, the book of the Sea. For this last, despite its historical and humorous digressions, is thoroughly permeated and controlled by that "unwearied and illimitable ocean," that "grand fact," which Thoreau tells us he specifically went to see—which, indeed, he was "determined" to get "into" himself.[46] In "Walking," as we have noticed, Thoreau begged for "the ocean, the desert or the wilderness." In his professedly unsentimental journey to the Cape, where "everything told of the sea," he found all three impressively combined ("the abyss of the ocean is nearly a desert"; "the ocean is a wilderness reaching round the globe").[47] Searching for the "springs of life," he found at Cape Cod the "spring of springs, the waterfall of waterfalls," a teeming jumble of actual and inchoate life perpetually being created and destroyed.

The Greeks would not have called the ocean ἀτρύγετος, or unfruitful, though it does not produce wheat, if they had viewed it by the light of modern science; for naturalists now assert that "the sea, and not the land, is the principal seat of life." . . . "modern investigations," to quote the words of Desor, "merely go to confirm the great idea which was vaguely anticipated by the ancient poets and philosophers, that the Ocean is the origin of all things." [48]

Here, on the "neutral ground" of the seashore, by the side of this mysterious element—at once "unfruitful" and "the origin of all things"—in which "the animal and vegetable kingdoms meet and are strangely mingled," Thoreau prepared himself for something like "the experience of Noah —to realize the deluge." It was primarily not a scientific but a poetic attitude and religious expectation that Thoreau brought to "the shore of the resounding sea." [49]

This last phrase in fact, drawn from a line in the *Iliad* (1. 34) that especially affected Thoreau, to judge by the frequency with which he returns to it, embodies the quintessence of oceanic poetry and religion. For Greek is Thoreau's *elemental* language, and Homer is its truest practitioner. His song, like that of the wood thrush, is the actual voice of that divine watery Wild which Thoreau sought:

We were wholly absorbed by this spectacle and tumult [of the sea], and like Chryses, though in a different mood from him, we walked silent along the shore of the resounding sea,

Βῆ δ'ἀκέων παρὰ θῖνα πολυφλοίσβοιο θαλάσσης.

I put in a little Greek now and then, partly because it sounds so much like the ocean.[50]

In *Cape Cod*, Thoreau puts in more than a little Greek, for as Sherman Paul notes, "allusions to Homer, especially for the sound and color of the sea," are particularly numerous.[51] Here we have a crucial example of that *"philological side"* to Thoreau's writing which Ellery Channing said deserved thoughtful consideration,[52] though it is not so much a question of etymological interest as of the very sound and texture of words. "At times the sound of a vocable, or the force of a letter, reveals and defines the real thought attached to a word," observes Bachelard in a remarkably Emersonian mood. For someone extremely sensitive to words,

language having achieved complete nobility, phonetic phenomena and the phenomena of the logos harmonize. But we should have to learn how to meditate very slowly, to experience the inner poetry of the word, the inner immensity of a word. All important words, all the words marked for grandeur by a poet, are keys to the universe, to the dual universe of the Cosmos and the depths of the human spirit.[53]

So πολύφλοισβ[οι]ος θάλασσα suggests to Thoreau the possibility of an actual religious revelation being uttered from the depths of wild nature to the receptive soul:

The attention of those who frequent the camp-meetings at Eastham is said to be divided between the preaching of the Methodists and the preaching of the billows on the back-side of the Cape, for they all stream over here in the course of their stay. I trust that in this case the loudest voice carries it.

With what effect may we suppose the ocean to say, "My hearers!" to the multitude on the bank! On that side some John N. Maffit; on this, the Reverend Poluphloisboios Thalassa.[54]

Even the revivalists are compelled by the power of water, for they too "stream over" to view the ocean. But for Thoreau Christianity can scarcely compete with the voice of the Wild. And he puts in a little Greek now and then to render physically present for us the force of what Wallace Stevens calls this "speech belched out of hoary darks," this "one vast, subjugating, final tone."[55]

Like Stevens's Comedian, however, Thoreau faces obvious problems in transcending Kantian prohibitions. "Here was the veritable ding an sich, at last" (indeed Thoreau calls the Cape and its ocean "the thing itself"), and here, as Crispin discovered, "was no help before reality." Both Crispin and Henry David are in danger of being "washed away by magnitude."[56] Emerson noted with justice, in his memorial sketch of Thoreau, that he had "a natural skill for mensuration," but as Emerson moved from the scale of commodity to a more transcendental point of view, he unintentionally contradicted himself in an interesting way: "To him there was no such thing as size. The pond was a small ocean; the Atlantic, a large Walden Pond."[57] Despite Emerson's confidence, not even Thoreau's customary tricks of rhetoric could carry him, a man used to measuring things by eye on a pastoral scale, over the shattering "immensity" of this "illimitable" ocean. As he stood looking on "the roaring sea, θάλασσα ἠχήεσσα," Thoreau became "gradually convinced," with Yankee understatement, "that fishing here and in a pond were not, in all respects, the same."[58] He is roughly in the situation of Stevens's "Doctor of Geneva":

> Lacustrine man had never been assailed
> By such long-rolling opulent cataracts. . . .

> [The sea] found means to set his simmering mind
> Spinning and hissing with oracular
> Notations of the wild, the ruinous waste . . .[59]

Thoreau's ocean reveries darkened under the pressure of a particular perception the significance of which attentive readers of *Walden* will be quick to notice:

As we looked off, and saw the water growing darker and darker and deeper and deeper the farther we looked, till it was awful to consider, and it appeared to have no relation to the friendly land, either as shore or bottom,—of what use is a bottom if it is out of sight, if it is two or three miles from the surface, and you are to be drowned so long before you get to it, though it were made of the same stuff with your native soil?—over that ocean, where, as the Veda says, "there is nothing to give support, nothing to rest upon, nothing to cling to," I felt that I was a land animal.[60]

This quasi-anacoluthic sentence, with its painfully suspended period, perfectly enacts the anxiety it expresses: the ocean appears to have no bottom. Thoreau is faced with a crucial dilemma, for the question of a *bottom* is fundamental to him. We recall his passionate concern in *Walden* to find "a hard bottom and rocks in place, which we can call *reality*, and say, This is, and no mistake," [61] leading of course to his compulsion to measure Walden Pond; for although it is commonly believed to be bottomless, Thoreau is determined to fathom it. In large measure the optimistic assurances of *Walden* are based on Thoreau's belief that bottoms exist *commensurate* with man's ability to discover them. He concludes the book with an unequivocal assertion in this regard—"there is a solid bottom everywhere"—followed, however, by an illustrative anecdote which, in the light of *Cape Cod*, is finally not so funny:

We read that the traveller asked the boy if the swamp before him had a hard bottom. The boy replied that it had. But presently the traveller's horse sank in up to the girths, and he observed to the boy, "I thought you said that this bog had a hard bottom." "So it has," answered the latter, "but you have not got half way to it yet." [62]

Reinforcing the dubiousness of the humor here, that sentence from *Cape Cod* reverberates: "of what use is a bottom if it is out of sight, if it is two or three miles from the surface, and you are to be drowned so long before you get to it?" [63]

Thoreau claimed in *Walden* that he craved only reality, "be it life or death." Now, in the sea, he found a "fertile unknown" which he could not put his foot through because there *was* no bottom, and it made him ponder nervously. "Severance / Was clear," as Stevens writes:

> The last distortion of romance
> Forsook the insatiable egotist. The sea
> Severs not only lands but also selves. [64]

Thoreau found that the self of *Walden*, the "I" which could measure its own depth in the depth of Walden Pond, was now literally and philosophically at sea. [65]

In this connection probably the most fascinating passage in *Cape Cod*, and the one that stands in the most striking contrast to *Walden*, concerns Thoreau's careful investigation of a "Charity-house," or "Humane-house," placed along the shore as refuge for shipwrecked sailors. In Thoreau's hands, this description of the locked and windowless hut, as seen through a knothole, becomes a parodic deflation of the comforts of home and of the assurances held out to us by exhortations to spiritual self-examination and religious faith, vis-à-vis the dark depths of the Wild.

Looking with the eye of faith, knowing that, though to him that knocketh it may not always be opened, yet to him that looketh long enough through a knot-hole the inside shall be visible,—for we had had some practice at looking inward,—by steadily keeping our other ball covered from the light meanwhile, putting the outward world behind us, ocean and land, and the beach,—till the pupil became enlarged and collected the rays of light that were wandering in that dark (for the pupil shall be enlarged by looking; there never was so dark a night but a faithful and patient eye, however small, might at last prevail over it),—after all this, I say, things began to take shape to our vision,—if we may use this expression where there was nothing but emptiness,—and we obtained the long-wished-for insight.[66]

Then, with an ironical flourish borrowed from the opening of book 3 of *Paradise Lost* ("Hail, holy Light!"), this diminished "I" ("eye," "pupil") offers us his desolate "insight":

A little longer, and a chimney rushed red on our sight. In short, when our vision had grown familiar with the darkness, we discovered that there were some stones and some loose wads of wool on the floor, and an empty fireplace at the further end; but it *was not* supplied with matches, or straw, or hay, that we could see, nor "accommodated with a bench" [as advertised in a "Description" of the Cape that Thoreau read]. Indeed, it was the wreck of all cosmical beauty there within.

Turning our backs on the outward world, we thus looked through the knot-hole into the Humane house, into the very bowels of mercy; and for bread we found a stone. It was literally a great cry (of sea-mews outside), and a little wool. However, we were glad to sit outside, under the lee of the Humane house, to escape the piercing wind; and there we thought how cold is charity! how inhumane humanity! This, then, is what charity hides! . . . So we shivered round about, not being able to get into it, ever and anon looking through the knot-hole into that night without a star, until we concluded that it was not a *humane* house at all, but a sea-side box, now shut up, belonging to some of the family of Night or Chaos.[67]

We might well speculate on the possibility of Melville's having read this passage while composing *The Confidence-Man*,[68] but let us not lose sight of Thoreau. He discovers that this uninviting hut by the sea is merely a poor imitation of a *human* house, for instead of light, warmth, and nourishment it contains only a cold chimney and a bit of disorder. In fact, through a kind of terrible attraction, it has been appropriated by the sea and has ceased to be a human habitation at all. Its secrets are not human ones, but rather the elemental

> secrets of the hoary deep, a dark
> Illimitable Ocean without bound,
> Without dimension, where length, breadth, and highth,
> And time and place are lost; where eldest Night
> And *Chaos,* Ancestors of Nature, hold
> Eternal *Anarchy.*[69]

From a structural point of view, the situation presented in this section of *Cape Cod*—the situation, that is, of a hut next to a body of water—corresponds to the central motif in *Walden;* but the differences in meaning are crucial and worth close examination. In his "topoanalysis" of "inhabited space . . . the non-I that protects the I," Gaston Bachelard—thinking especially of Thoreau—describes the hut as a "centralized solitude" that "gives us access to absolute refuge." [70] I believe we can and should extend the notion to Walden Pond itself. The pond, like the hut, is "inhabited" by Thoreau. It is "like a hermit in the woods," [71] and Thoreau identifies with it thoroughly. Both hut and pond are scaled to human size and can be comprehended and measured by Thoreau. Though the hut is associated with fire and the pond with water, both express and enclose Thoreau's vital self: fire is the self that rises; water the self that descends.[72] One might say finally that the hut and the pond represent two forms of intimacy.

In the hut by the sea, on the other hand, the chimney is bare and there is no fire: the self is annihilated. Insofar as this hut represents Christianity, it is an *inhuman* "Humane-house," an uninhabited ark of divinity, express-

ing the emptiness and despair Thoreau finds in the "profundity" of religious promises. But to the extent that this
cheerless habitation has simply been assimilated by the
sea, it stands for the awesome *bottomlessness* of the Wild.
Thus this hut and the body of water it lies beside may be
seen as two forms of immensity, or boundless depth,
inspiring in man a sense of alienation, terror, and helplessness. The only possible reactions, as in *Moby-Dick*,
are defiance (Ahab), reverence (Starbuck), or a species
of cosmic humor (Ishmael). Thoreau's response contains
none of the first, some of the second, and a good deal of
the third. Perhaps it is this last that accounts for the
frequent descriptions of *Cape Cod* as Thoreau's "sunniest,
happiest book," [73] despite the undeniable seriousness of its
oceanic reveries.

What lesson, then, did Thoreau learn from the sea, what
was the doctrine preached by the Reverend Poluphloisboios Thalassa? Mainly this, it seems: that a man who has
gotten the Wild into his soul may stand anywhere and put,
not only all America, but every place and thing behind
him. Some lines from Santayana's "The Genteel Tradition
in American Philosophy" may be useful here. We recall
that Santayana delivered this talk in 1911 during his first
visit to California. In his summation he, too, appealed to
the lesson of the Wild, to the voice of the forests and
sierras of the great West:

In their non-human beauty and peace they stir the sub-human
depths and superhuman possibilities of your own spirit. It is
no transcendental logic that they teach; and they give no sign
of any deliberate morality seated in the world. It is rather the
vanity and superficiality of all logic, the needlessness of argument, the relativity of morals, the strength of time, the fertility of matter, the variety, the unspeakable variety, of possible
life. . . . Everywhere is beauty and nowhere permanence,
everywhere an incipient harmony, nowhere an intention, nor
a responsibility, nor a plan. . . . They allow you, in one

happy moment, at once to play and to worship, to take your-
selves simply, humbly, for what you are, and to salute the
wild, indifferent, non-censorious infinity of nature. . . .
through wonder and pleasure, you are taught speculation. You
learn what you are really fitted to do, and where lie your
natural dignity and joy, namely in representing many things,
without being them, and in letting your imagination, through
sympathy, celebrate and echo their life. Because the peculiar-
ity of man is that his machinery for reaction on external
things has involved an imaginative transcript of these things,
which is preserved and suspended in his fancy; and the interest
and beauty of this inward landscape, rather than any fortunes
that may await his body in the outer world, constitute his
proper happiness.[74]

The sea, with its annihilating force, teaches us that our
world can be possessed only in imagination—that it is the
imaginative spirit alone, as Emerson once said, which
builds itself a permanent house, world, and heaven. Thoreau's faith in the constitutive power of poetry was the
same and his conclusion, already quoted, deserves to be
heard again: "Our truest life is when we are in dreams
awake." [75]

Mark Twain
The Triumph of Humor

JAMES M. COX

In 1909, one year before Mark Twain died and seven years before the death of Henry James, W. C. Brownell published *American Prose Masters*, still one of the most remarkable criticisms of American writers ever written. The writers Brownell included were Cooper, Hawthorne, Emerson, Poe, Lowell, and James. He omitted Melville, Thoreau, Whitman, and Mark Twain. Melville was, of course, practically unknown by anyone at the time Brownell wrote. Whitman was primarily a poet. As for Thoreau, Brownell may have considered him too much of an eccentric version of Emerson to be included. Of the writers Brownell chose to select, only Lowell seems out of place, and even here Brownell was not far amiss, for he concluded that Lowell was indeed the weakest member of his group and predicted that his stock would continue to fall.

That leaves us with Mark Twain. Certainly no one today would omit Mark Twain from a list of major American writers—we would never call such a group American prose masters, for we would not feel the need to set our major writers against a prior international critical standard. We are both more confident and more evasive about our literature than Brownell would have ever wished to be. There are good as well as bad reasons for our confidence. We are more powerful, literarily as well as politically, than we were in 1910. The emergence of Frost, Eliot, Hemingway, and Faulkner has made a real difference in how we look at the nineteenth century, for it has shown that the nineteenth century was leading to something which not even someone so perceptive as Brownell could see. At the same time, our complacent assurance about a national literature reveals something of a wish not to compare our literary strength with that of other nations.

Thus we speak of major American writers rather than American major writers.

Brownell had a very different vision. He was genteel—and he represented the genteel tradition at its best, reminding anyone who reads him just how valuable that tradition could be. It was, after all, that tradition which somehow stood behind, if it did not produce, James and Eliot; it was the tradition which gave us our strong international impulse. And in omitting both Mark Twain and Whitman, Brownell was not revealing the narrowness so much as the strength of his identity, just as, in the very title of his book he was asserting his conviction that there were indeed master writers in this country.

For Whitman and Mark Twain are distinctly outside the genteel tradition. The truth is that they are not men of letters. They are instead writers in a primary rather than a literary sense. Incapable of the seclusion of Hawthorne, the determined withdrawal of Melville, the conscious artistry of James, they seem to declare themselves into being directly out of nothing, and they talk till they die. Their deepest instincts seem to be in their voices. But the paradox is that both men are *writers*, not merely speakers. What both were able to do was to relate the idea of the voice to the act of writing, as if the voice had literally embodied the writer.

Thus Whitman, emerging out of journalism before the Civil War, proclaimed himself a poet who would create all his readers in his own image—that of poet. In his radically democratic poetic program, he was determined to make himself equal to the reader at the same time he made the reader equal to himself. That is why there is, in all his poetry, the eternal effort to create a host of readers, both en masse and in intimate singularity, to embody his disembodied words. Yet even in the bardic promise to create his readers as poets, there is a sense of solitude and even wistful isolation. Thus if Whitman is hortatory and homiletic in calling forth his vast audience, he also knows that his audience may never be vast at all. He has remarkable strategies for meeting this issue. The pronoun "you" referring at once to a plural and singular audience, the call of and to death, and the proclaimed and whispered love of his readers are all in their way resourceful masks which do not hide so much as they make possible a fugitive self behind the words which may be sounding in a void. Whitman's very awareness of the potential unreality of his words was no doubt related to his welcome of the Civil War. For the war itself provided an assurance that the masses of idealized heroes he had prophesied from 1855 on had indeed materialized; it proved that Whitman himself had materialized in the role of male nurse to attend, comfort, and write home for them; and it provided Whitman with more dramatic experiences to convert into poetry. Thus, when Lincoln was assassinated at the end of war, Whitman was utterly prepared to memorialize the moment in an elegy. In the person of Lincoln, and in Whitman's poetic identification with that person, Whitman could at once personally and publically represent his nation.

Whatever Mark Twain shares with Whitman, he is vastly different. First of all, whereas Whitman was the veritable incarnation of the Poet of the Union, Mark Twain was a traitor. And when, two weeks after he joined the Confederate army, he "resigned"—as he later referred to his desertion—he was a deserter. He had in the space of a month committed two capital crimes. This criminal aspect of Mark Twain is not to be lightly cast aside as merely a part of the circumstances of birth. For Mark Twain in Virginia City and again in San Francisco showed determined tendencies to break the law as well as to attack directly the guardians of law and order. Surely this outlaw in Mark Twain is deeply a part of his humor, and surely our own experience of almost ten years of increasingly futile war should make us sensitive to that presence.

Then too, there is Mark Twain's popularity. Whereas Whitman sought to reach all people and failed, Mark Twain sought to reach them and succeeded. And he not only sought to reach them; he was determined to please them. It is just this determination to get on in and get along with the dominant society which has brought down on Mark Twain's head the persistent charges that he betrayed his genius. Van Wyck Brooks's *The Ordeal of Mark Twain* is the classic expression of such a charge. Yet it is just this triumphant determination to reach as well as to represent the majority which makes Mark Twain a national writer of the scope and character of Whitman.

And yet Mark Twain's determination to reach his audience is vastly different from Whitman's. If Whitman in visibly yearning to project himself into and upon everyone creates in the process a fugitive almost surreptitious self which secretly waits for the intimate seeker, Mark Twain reaches his audience so simply, easily, and effortlessly that he in turn creates a self which expresses contempt for his communicants. The more Whitman yearns, the more inaccessible he becomes; the more Mark Twain fulminates, the more he is embraced. Thus at the end of his life, when he was able to utter his most comprehensively damning definitions of man, Mark Twain was never more loved and acknowledged as the very epitome of his nation's spirit.

Finally there is the difference in their achievement. Whitman breaks down poetic form, to emerge with "free" verse—a poetry which, by annihilating rhyme and measure, regains connections with much older scriptural line and vision at the same time that it prophesies its own future dominion. Mark Twain, on the other hand, breaks down literary language by writing so directly, so clearly, so transparently that his very style is an overt criticism of all literary language which has preceded him. Indeed, he makes prior writing *seem* literary. Now what gives his transparent style its edge is nothing less than the identity of master humorist which the very name Mark Twain signifies. For if Walt Whitman was the prophet and the poet of Walter Whitman, then Mark Twain is at once the humor and the genius of Samuel Clemens.

And as humorist he releases the criminal, the misanthrope, the social climber, the vulgar businessman, and above all the "low" artist into the dominant society. The very identity of humorist mediates the polarities of that dominant society, uniting the refined and the vulgar, the patrician and plebeian, the theoretic and the practical, the man and the child, the present and the past, the civilized and the savage, the judge and the murderer, the artistic and the commercial, the North and the South, God and the Devil. But merely to say humor mediates these opposites is to imply that it stands neutrally between them (which is no doubt why mediation rather than arbitration has become in these late days, such a popular word in literary criticism as well as in politics). If Mark Twain mediated those opposites, he nonetheless seemed always to emerge from the "lower" realm of each pair. He brought with him the experience, the dialect, and the vulgarity which invaded the parlor. Thus he would always be the boy among adults, the Westerner in the East, and finally the American in Europe. I do not mean at all that he did not placate authority, but he just as clearly always threatened it. If he played the boy among men, it was nonetheless the *bad* boy. And if he always sought to secure the indulgence of the dominant society, he nonetheless invaded that society in his easy way. And though he had to appear disarming, he never really did disarm himself.

To be sure, he wrote weak pieces; but so did Thoreau for all his concision, so did Emerson for all his high purpose, so did Emily Dickinson for all her sensitivity, and so even did Henry James for all his artistry. The difference between Mark Twain's "bad" literary art and theirs is that his seems somehow not out of but *in* character; his failures are thus not seen as accidents or misfortunes but as an essential aspect of his imagination. All of which brings us squarely back to face his identity as humorist.

He himself often lamented the identity. It was after all his burden, just as much as another writer's burden might be tragic vision, painful insight, or wounded memory. But whereas these other burdens can be tricked out as the deep responsibilities of serious writers—the responsibilities which enable the literary critic to wax eloquent about the toils of the imagination—the humorous writer has only his humor, and the only way the critic can get *him* into the fold of literary respectability is to invest the humor with serious-ness and tragedy and prophecy. It is really small wonder that Mark Twain lamented his identity. He could see that his very hold on literary respectability depended on being considered a serious writer behind the humor. And to this day the terms in which he is praised turn on converting the humorous identity into a "serious" force. Who has not read that *Huckleberry Finn* is, behind or above or beyond or beneath its humor, one of the great tragic books of American literature? Or that Mark Twain himself was, at heart, the most somber of men, or the most neurotic, or the most anguished, or the most suicidal? Or that, behind the clown's mask, there is the age-old cry of pain and passion? Or that Mark Twain's humor cannot conceal his outrage at the social wrongs in his own time and in all history?

This is not to say that these statements have no truth in them; it is to disclose them as strategies of dealing with humor. They are modes of making Mark Twain "literary," and everyone of them discloses an implicit acknowledg-ment that humor is, if literature at all, a distinctly lower order of literature unless it can be shown to be essen-tially serious. It was just this strategy which both William Dean Howells and Albert Bigelow Paine used in their determined effort at the time of Mark Twain's death to secure for him a place in high literature.

Conversely, those who wish to criticize Mark Twain rest their deepest claim on the fact that he isn't a serious writer. Certainly this is essentially Van Wyck Brooks's point—all of which did not prevent Brooks from writing one of the finest books ever written about Mark Twain. Even so, there is in Brooks's criticism, and in much of the criticism which has echoed it, the rueful complaint that Mark Twain betrayed the high genius that was in Samuel Clemens. Now that "genius," which Brooks and so many others have adumbrated, is finally the conventional literary genius; and though Brooks was deeply aware of Mark Twain's fresh, powerful style—as who is not—he continually attempted to see it in conventional literary terms. From Brooks and the other critics in his category there comes another series of lamentations. Such critics acknowledge Mark Twain's greatness, but, since there is no clear pattern of conventional literary causation, they tend to see it in terms of luck or accident. Moreover, there is a parallel tendency to gloat over Mark Twain's failures in taste or lack of literary knowledge. For example, the same critic who sees nothing whatsoever amiss in Whitman's relative ignorance of Mark Twain's work, finds Mark Twain's failure to demonstrate profound understanding and appreciation of Whitman a characteristic *limitation* of Mark Twain's mind. And who has not known Jamesians who, at the same time they regret Mark Twain's joke about *The Bostonians*, see nothing amiss in James's relative silence about Mark Twain. Mark Twain scholars know, of course, that Mark Twain had, in his later years acknowledged that Henry James was a great master (though there may have been a deeper joke in that acknowledgment than in the earlier disparagement of *The Bostonians*); but only now has Leon Edel revealed that Henry James admired Mark Twain.

Actually, Mark Twain's announcement to Howells that he would rather be damned to John Bunyan's heaven than read *The Bostonians,* is a much more profound acknowledgment of the presence of Henry James than James was ever able to make about Mark Twain, and we should be grateful that Mark Twain made that joke. His capacity to bring down two writers with one shot is a measure of his compression; the fact that both writers were great is a measure of his nerve and force. We should also be glad that Mark Twain said that the test of a good library should be the absence of novels by Jane Austen. Such remarks are proof of Mark Twain's mettle. They should be as welcome in the literary world as we hope his jokes about ministers and religion are welcome in the clerical world. Surely we hope that the devout persons of this earth will enjoy Mark Twain's observation that, judging by the prices charged the tourist to go sailing on the Sea of Galilee, it is no wonder that Christ walked. And we also hope that the descendents of the Aldrich family will have to laugh about Mark Twain's contention that the only way he could learn to like Mrs. Thomas Bailey Aldrich would be on a raft at sea with no provisions in sight.

Now we know that, among the reverent, Mark Twain's irreverence may be hard to take, just as it might be hard for the great-grandchildren of Thomas Bailey Aldrich to take that joke about their ancestor. The reason we know, or ought to know, is that the jokes about Shakespeare, about Jane Austen, about Walter Scott, and about Henry James have been hard to take in the literary establishment, just as the jokes about Michelangelo and Leonardo do not sit very well with lovers of art. They have been as hard, in general, for us to take as the famed Whittier Birthday speech was hard to take for the genteel literary world. We can take that joke on Whittier, Emerson, Holmes, and Longfellow because first of all, Emerson was senile and apparently was serenely unaware of anything that went on at that occasion, and, second, because Whittier, Holmes, and Longfellow aren't *our* candidates for gentility. Ours would be Melville, Whitman, and Henry James, and sometimes even Mark Twain himself, though he has fairly well succeeded in remaining outside the charmed circle.

The point is that the genteel tradition will never die; its membership merely changes. If it now includes writers different from the Brahmins, that is because it includes us as its audience. So there we are, trying in our way, much as Howells tried in his, to get Mark Twain into the circle, yet still wondering whether he belongs.

Of course we do know what he accomplished, for time has given us a perspective which even a writer so acute as Howells lacked. The essence of that accomplishment was to bring a greater range of art and life under the dominion of humor than anyone would have imagined possible. It is well to remember that the very word *humor* was originally a term in the old physiology denoting the fluids which supposedly governed a person's dominant temperament. The term was gradually detached from its original meaning, and by the beginning of the eighteenth century it had come to refer to a genial temperament. Thus, throughout the eighteenth century until well into the nineteenth, the tradition of the amiable humorist developed. Having a sense of humor—something which would have puzzled Ben Jonson—came to be seen as a valuable trait. It was the saving grace of the bilious satirist, just as it was the leavening principle of consciousness for the austere moralist. With the increased bowdlerization of the Victorian period, the humorist, though he was released much more fully into society, ran every risk of being either patronized or emasculated in the acceptance. The very constriction of the identity was surely part of what drove Dickens to abandon Boz and go on under his own name into the areas of sentimentality, melodrama, and tragedy. Dickens still retained his powerful and wonderful humorous imagination, but gave himself up to his own name as novelist.

Samuel Clemens, however, remained in the identity of his pseudonym. Indeed, it is no accident that he first "named" himself in the territory. He had gone there as a traitor and a deserter, and, after failing to find silver, had fallen back on writing as if on a last instinctive resort. And he had gone on to San Francisco, where the outlaw in him once again asserted itself (or so he later maintained) in the form of written attacks on the police force. Feeling the displeasure of the representatives of law and order, he evasively turned up on Jackass Hill in Tuolumne County, California. There in Jim Gillis's cabin, he heard the story of the jumping frog which his own great retelling would carry home to the distant East. All this may have been accident, but surely it is essence that, once he came east, he emerged into the foreground of the literary world as the reporter of the first pleasure trip from the New World to the Old. As a kind of interloper among the pious pilgrims, he made his way as a true pilgrim of pleasure-seeking to the Tomb of the Holy Sepulchre. He made excruciating efforts to be reverent in halls of religion and art; he impersonated reverence so well that it would be hasty indeed to conclude that he was joking. Yet the very skill with which he moves from broad humor into the stately periods of reverence evoke skepticism in the wary. And throughout his career there is the presence, amid the earnestness and gravity, of the demonic joker, the old outlaw. Dickens had named his residence Gads Hill as a reminder that his art might not be unrelated to highway robbery. Samuel Clemens, still in the pseudonym of the humorist, had to remind his audiences that he was indeed the highwayman, bilking his hearers and his readers in one way or another—bilking them with jokes as old as the hills, trapping them in confidence games, fooling them with outrageous stretchers, "selling" them on false promises, and reducing them to helpless laughter.

All this was, of course, his "humor," and to sustain it he had to build, behind the humor, the image of a respectable, moral, responsible family man. The "humor" thus became the outlet, the escape valve, the freedom of the more and more pent-up and confined artist. Yet in order for the humor really to be a release, there had to be continual generative pressure in that alter image. The social, responsible moral figure had to feel the stifling quality of society, the contradictions of the moral life, the harrassments of responsibility, and, above all, the "unfortunate" presence of the humorist if he were to *need* continually to free the humorist in him, just as the humorist needed the responsible, moral figure behind—or really *beside*—him in order to sanction the play of the bad boy. The two figures were not separate but intricately bound together in Mark Twain, the name itself coming more and more to be the very authentication of their presence.

This play between the two parts of the self—between man and child, moralist and outlaw, respectable citizen and irreverent joker, philosopher and fool—is nothing less than the mechanism of Mark Twain's humor. And it is just this play which forms the dynamic of his art. Though the primary impulse of the play emerges from the child-outlaw-fool against the adult-moralist-philosopher, the adult in Mark Twain does not die, but forever seems to grow in gravity. That undying adult is as big a miracle in the art of Mark Twain as the magic power of childhood. The adult gains his moral stature from his perception of the outrageous contradictions of the adult world; he gains his cultural stature from his overt willingness to placate rather than merely offend the world of serious art and serious artists; and he gains psychological stature by disclosing increasing restiveness in his identity as humorist. Indeed, there is one joke which Mark Twain can never get out from under—the utterly final fact that he is a humorist and can never *fully* be taken seriously. Helpless before that fatality, he tries to be serious; he wishes he were serious, he earnestly seeks instruction on how to be serious. But either his own demonic impulse to humor thwarts and betrays him at the very moment when he attempts a flight into the realm of high literature, or his unappreciative audience, failing to recognize the poetic dimension of his imagination, bursts into a guffaw in the midst of his highest seriousness as if everything were merely a joke. And so, if he does not bring himself down, he is brought down. That eternal helplessness is a shadow of the power which enables the master humorist to reduce his audiences to helpless laughter.

It was the perfection of this performing personality and the rare capacity to translate the performance into written language which carried Mark Twain forward in his career. The dynamic relation between moralist and humorist, between philosopher and fool, between man and child is what made Mark Twain so much more than an amiable humorist. Indeed there was always implicitly present in Mark Twain the indignation of the abused citizen, the scorn of the satirist, and the outrage of the offended moralist. To discharge these pent-up emotions, the humor had to be broad, extravagant, and primitively clear. Mark Twain's power to transform the savagery of his observations, the violence of his contradictions, and the wildness of his spirit into extended incongruities and digressions of narrative humor gave his style a triumphant casualness and an epic garrulity.

The triumph of Mark Twain's art is, as everybody knows, *Adventures of Huckleberry Finn*. It is his masterpiece, and in encountering its strengths we implicitly deal with Mark Twain's weaknesses, for it, like *Moby-Dick*, *The Scarlet Letter*, and *Walden*, is the kind of achievement which, revealing the author's wholeness in one economic stroke, exposes all the other works by the same author as somehow partial.

Now the first thing to emphasize about *Huckleberry Finn* is that it is a book for everyone—for children, for young adults, for the middle-aged, and for the old. Because it is, everyone can read it at least four times in life, and each time it will be a different book. For the child it will be pure adventure; for the young adult it will be a somber exposure of the evils of slavery; for the middle-aged it will begin to reveal more and more of its humor;

and for the man deep in life it will, I hope, become an act of total humor—a pure pleasure wherein even the ending, which is such a problem for us from youth into the middle years, will no longer be dismaying. At that late time, perhaps Tom Sawyer, so long rejected in favor of Huck, will at last regain his dominion as the necessary, the inevitable companion of Huck.

Now of course this does not mean that the book will be one long guffaw; it does mean that the maturing consciousness will see more and more humor as the adventure of childhood dies into the emerging conscience of the man, and as the conscience itself dies into, or at least is deeply tempered by, the irony of experience. Whatever the outcome, we know that *Huckleberry Finn* will be part of our future as much as it will have been a part of our past. It will always be waiting for us to grow into it even as we have a little sadly grown out of it. There is really no other American book like it—there is probably no book in the world's literature like it. Its capacity to meet us throughout our lives is what makes it a book for everybody, whether educated or uneducated, rich or poor, old or young, sophisticated or plain—and it reminds us that, beyond all his expressed attitudes, his wealth, his resentment, and his ambition, Mark Twain was completely democratic. That seems to me the first and last fact about his achievement. No one can ever quite get over *Huckleberry Finn* any more than anyone can ever quite get beyond it.

That first and last truth about the book brings us irrevocably to the language, the character, and the action of the book. For what Mark Twain was able to do at the height of his career was to let the "low vernacular" of his culture thrust him aside in the person of Huckleberry Finn. Thus, instead of being framed by conventional language, Huck's vernacular implies it; his errors, characterized by his excessive double negative and his ignorance of tense distinctions, evoke as much as they deny the norm from which they deviate. This "bad" language is the expression of a "bad" boy doing a "bad" thing—freeing a slave in the Old South, a triply reinforced vision which secures total audience approval. For Huck, though fictively freeing a slave in the Old South, is acquiring all his virtue from an implied post-Civil War morality. It is just this crucial implication which constantly transforms Huck's bad actions into good ones. The process of inversion embodies what can best be called the moral sentiment sustaining the action of the book.

The moral sentiment is nothing less than the powerful and indulgent wish which Huck's great language and his great journey arouse and which the ending of the novel frustrates. For in those last ten chapters, the novel changes its direction from its seeming high purpose to mere burlesque. Those are the chapters in which Tom Sawyer returns to stage-manage the action of freeing Jim from slavery. It is indeed mere theatricality, for Tom knows what Huck does not know—that Jim is already free. It is Tom's domination of the action which has brought him forever under moral fire just as it has brought Mark Twain under critical fire. Yet if Tom is secretly relying on his knowledge that Jim is legally free, what is every reader of the novel doing but relying on the unquestioned moral security that Jim ought to be free. That security of the moral sentiment makes the reader as safe as, to borrow a line from Mark Twain, a Christian holding four aces. And in scapegoating Tom Sawyer and Mark Twain because of the ending of the novel, the reader is somehow evading the moment when the novel turned against the moral sentiment.

That moment was none other than the very climax of the action—the high-water mark in the novel and surely the high-water mark in Mark Twain's whole career—the moment when Huck utters his grandest line, "All right, then, I'll *go* to hell." Just then, the moral sentiment drowns Huck in applause and sends him to the heart of heaven. Now the only hell there is for Huck to go to in this novel which makes fun of the whole notion of super-stitious hereafters is the hell of adult society, and he is there in five minutes of reading time after his grand asser-tion. For that grand assertion is itself the moment when what had been Huck's instinct becomes his conscience. The very accent and rhythm of the line reveals Huck in the act of beginning to play Tom Sawyer—for he pro-claims the fact that he is acting on principle.

That principle is in reality his Northern or inner con-science in the act of displacing his Southern or social conscience. The Southern conscience had put him in flight from his society; his Northern conscience welcomes him into ours. And either society is hell. Surely that is why we feel that it is so right for Huck to reject civilization at the end of the novel. His rejection is the radically nihilistic action which his doubly negative grammar has been lead-ing toward. Yet if the book is nihilistic—and it surely is—it is humorously nihilistic, which means that it must neither fulminate, satirize, nor complain, but continue to be acted out under the reader's indulgence, affection, and approval. But with Huck's fatal choice, Mark Twain had reached, though he probably could not afford to know how completely he had reached, the limits of his humor: that point at which humor's necessity to gain indulgent and affectionate approval mortally threatened the very identity and character of his humor. Yet even here the form of his masterpiece saved him. For even as Huck elects the Northern conscience, there is a dimension, an inescapable dimension, of his character which chooses to act not heroically because it is the best and right course of action, but *helplessly* because it is the easiest thing to do in a tight place. The good life for Huck has been, and remains, life based not on principle but on comfort, and he leaves civilization not because it is a sham but because it is cramped, smothery, and uncomfortable. Tom and the adult reader are the ones who have all the principle. Moreover, Huck goes into the territory not as an apostle of freedom but as a boy to play. This is not all. The ending leaves all adult readers still in the throes of the moral sentiment, if not in approval of the action, in a state of greater self-approval than at any point in the novel—complacently superior to the author's "failure" and obtusely scornful of their own sentimental surrogate, Tom Sawyer. If it is not a perfect ending it is as good as one can easily imagine for this complete novel of reconstruction which brought not the Old South but an entirely new South back into the union, converting in the process the tragic issues of slavery and Civil War into the very sentiment which would so please the mind that the novel's radical disclosure that the adult conscience is the true tyranny of civilization would pass the rapt censor. That disclosure nakedly seen would be no joke. Yet the book shows that it is under the sign of the conscience that civilized man gains the self-approval to justify the atrocities of adult civilization. And thus man's cruelty is finally his pleasure.

It is just that bleak vision which Mark Twain faced for the rest of his life. It was not that he wanted to reform man and do away with his conscience; he knew that man could not be reformed. He would go on killing and maiming his fellowmen, always with a serious face, as if the whole business were not really pleasure. And he would go on mouthing principles and worshiping the Christian God who was enabling the white man to subjugate the savage peoples of the world. Always man would be a slave to the ruthless Moral Sense; always he would lie the old lie of the adult—the lie which enabled man to conceal from himself that cruelty was his deepest pleasure. The late Mark Twain is full of this vision—so full, I think, that his humor was simplified and weakened. It is true that, when we look at what we have been doing in Asia for the past ten years—and really ever since we made our way there in the nineteenth century—Mark Twain's vision may not be so simpleminded as many have thought it. He was, at the turn of the twentieth century, seeing ruthless subjugation of the colored races by the white Christian. And he was inclined to be less apologetic for civilization than a writer so deep and dark as Conrad. Yet the more directly that he saw the encroachments into Australia, China, and Africa, the less he was able to assimilate his outrage, scorn, and indignation at the complacency of Western man.

There are those, such as Maxwell Geismar, who thrill to Mark Twain's savagery and feel that the incapacity of academic criticism to deal with this prophetic side of Mark Twain amounts to censorship. Now there is no question that Mark Twain realized that in the American antislavery conscience which emerged into the foreground at the end of the Civil War were the seeds of economic exploitation, imperial expansion, technological threat, and unconditional surrender, which have characterized our foreign policy for the twentieth century. Certainly our involvement in Vietnam and our conduct of the war there would have held few surprises for the man who wrote "To the Person Sitting in Darkness" or "In Defense of General Funston."

And yet it seems to me that *Huckleberry Finn* will remain forever the very essence of Mark Twain. In that book he had discovered in a language as rich as that of any writer we have had—and a language somehow more American than that of any writer we have had—the profound destructiveness of conscience and moral intention. True, he had accepted conscience and civilization as, alas, inevitable. So would Conrad. So would Freud. The boy will grow into the man. The one value that he discovered as compensation for the tyranny of conscience and civilization was humor itself.

Now for anyone who thinks that humor is harmless, that it is somehow the safe way out, it is well to remember that *Huckleberry Finn* is the only one of our canonical books which has been subjected to censorship. When it appeared, and was banned by the Concord Public Library, Mark Twain roundly observed that he was glad because the action would sell thirty-five thousand copies. And to-day, the book is again being removed from reading lists in city campuses so as not to offend minority groups. Who has not laughed at the Concord Public Library's censorship? Yet who is really laughing at our own censorship? Who even wishes to mention the fact? Academic criticism used to be fond of patronizing Mark Twain for his assiduous obedience to the sexual conventions of the nineteenth century. Yet now when we can use all the four letter words, it turns out that *Huckleberry Finn* is an embarrassment after all. Mark Twain, who always contended that the truth could not be told, would surely see the joke. If we are to have a sense of humor we had better see it too, and see that it is on us, for how can we say that we have a sense of humor if we cannot take a joke? Mark Twain, who had the greatest sense of humor, could both tell a joke and take one. After all, as Justin Kaplan once observed to me, he began with a publisher named Bliss and ended with a biographer named Paine. He knew that, like the dear old King doing the Royal Nonesuch in *Huckleberry Finn*, man was a naked fraud. And yet he knew also that, like Huckleberry Finn, you couldn't help laughing at him. Huckleberry Finn didn't laugh often. It took the most complete and ancient joke to break him up. That was why when he saw the King wheeling naked across the stage before the "sold" audience, he observed that it would have made a cow laugh to see that old idiot cavorting upon the world's great stage.

Walt Whitman's
Omnisexual Vision

JAMES E. MILLER, JR.

We have not yet come to terms with Walt Whitman's sexuality, and it may be too late. In the current sexual revolution in the arts, Whitman may simply appear obsolete. After all, some would say, he didn't come out of the closet. He wrote in hieroglyphics, and who needs *them*, especially today when discussions of sexuality—auto-, hetero-, homo- —all proceed with the utmost frankness and candor in essays, in novels, plays, and poems, and on talk-shows both morning and midnight.

Yet back in the nineteenth century Whitman's sexual imagery and his descriptions of sexuality and his insistence on sex's importance earned him and his book the wrath of many a prestigious critic. He very early felt the strong pressure from no less a figure than the Master Emerson to fumigate or purify *Leaves of Grass,* and he refused, willfully and stubbornly. Other critics were to offer still greater pressure, and the book was to be banned in Boston, but still the poet persisted in keeping his book the way he felt it had to be, up to the very end.

"A Backward Glance O'er Travel'd Roads," written and published when Whitman was seventy years old and meant to be a permanent afterword to *Leaves of Grass,* contains a description of the book's sexuality that remains perhaps the most acute and the least understood:

From another point of view "Leaves of Grass" is avowedly the song of sex and Amativeness, and even Animality—though meanings that do not usually go along with those words are behind all, and will duly emerge; and all are sought to be lifted into a different light and atmosphere. Of this feature, intentionally palpable in a few lines, I shall only say the espousing principle of those lines so give breath of life to my whole scheme that the bulk of the pieces might as well have been left unwritten were those lines omitted. Difficult as it will be, it has become, in my opinion, imperative to achieve a shifted attitude from superior men and women towards the thought and fact of sexuality, as an element in character, personality, the emotions, and a theme in literature. I am not going to argue the question by itself; it does not stand by itself. The vitality of it is altogether in its relations, bearings, significance —like the clef of a symphony. At last analogy the lines I allude to, and the spirit in which they are spoken, permeate all "Leaves of Grass," and the work must stand or fall with them, as the human body and soul must remain as an entirety [p. 572].[1]

This passage is made up of a combination of deep awareness, untroubled patience, and a dash of prophecy. The prophecy has, in some sense, come true. We would, I think, all agree that there is now a "shifted attitude" toward sexuality—and not just among "superior men and women." But whether the deeper meanings of sex, Amativeness, and Animality have duly emerged, and whether they have been lifted into a "different light and atmosphere" is a highly debatable question. Some would argue to the contrary.

Literary historians of the modern period have not yet disentangled the developments that led to the current liberties and license found in literature. But clearly Whitman contributed much to the movement through his example and presence. He was a direct influence on D. H. Lawrence, as Lawrence himself has testified, and he was much admired by Henry Miller. But any just assessment of the present would have to take into account such disparate figures as James Joyce and Jean Genet, and would, ultimately, have to come to terms with such special and limited writers as William Burroughs and John Rechy. Would Whitman recognize these two writers as some kind of fulfillment of his prophecy? Such a book as John Rechy's *Numbers* (1967), in which the homosexual hero scores thirty-seven contacts, would seem in fact to violate everything Whitman called for: to comprehend the vitality of sex in its "relations, bearings, significance—like the clef of a symphony." Like the Rechy novel, much or even most of contemporary literature of sexuality is reductive, diminishing sex to mere carnality and fleeting sensation, showing a latent contemptuousness close in spirit to that which lay beneath the Victorian prudery.

Today sexuality has become not only a literary but also a political question. The Civil Rights movement first spawned women's liberation, and it in turn spawned the gay liberation, all of these movements borrowing strategies and manifestoes from each other. The major sexual confrontation of our time has been that between Kate Millett and her book, *Sexual Politics* (1969), and Norman Mailer with his *Prisoner of Sex* (1971). Millett's density and Mailer's obtuseness tend to obscure the issues in that exchange, but it seems possible that continuing dialogues and discussions on women's liberation and gay liberation might eventually approach the kind of understanding and "shifted attitude" that Whitman called for. There appears to be in store a more serious examination of the androgyny (the two sexes combined into one) which Virginia Woolf explored and dramatized. And it seems probable that gay liberation will gain in strength and influence as the literature accumulates and revelations are made. Two publications might stand as examples of the revolution in progress —E. M. Forster's posthumously published novel of homosexual love, *Maurice* (1971), and Merle Miller's account of his own long-hidden homosexuality, *On Being Different* (1972). A sign of the times might be indicated in the casual references that Allen Ginsburg and W. H. Auden make to their own homosexuality in public interviews and elsewhere.

Whatever we think of the contemporary movements and discussions and debates involving sexuality, we must recognize that they affect the way we read and respond to Whitman (the situation is different from what it was, say, only twenty years ago—and radically different from the time about thirty years ago when I first read *Leaves of*

Grass). Some readers might assume, hastily, that Whitman has indeed become obsolete and irrelevant. But a second and deeper look at *Leaves of Grass* will confirm that Whitman is remarkably contemporary and often surprisingly relevant. It must first be emphasized that his book is not a sexual manifesto, but a poem; and that it must be read first and always as a poem with a number of themes, sexuality being one that is vital and central. Once this approach to the book is accepted, it is possible to affirm that *Leaves of Grass* offers poetic insight into sexuality that in its depth, vigor, intensity, and subtlety shows up much that passes for insight today to be superficial, thin, and crude. In short, it might be reasonably argued that Whitman had a profounder understanding of the role of the individual's sexuality in his life and experience, personal and national, than many who write so glibly about sex today.

Before examining Whitman's views, the question intrudes as to Whitman's own sexuality, no matter how much we might want to pass over it in silence. Indeed, Whitman criticism has been obsessively burdened with the question in the twentieth century, and it is curious how the question has remained stubbornly unanswered. There are, of course, those who thought they had answered it. There is the notorious story of his old-age confession to John Addington Symonds (who pressed him on the real meaning of the "Calamus" poems) that his life had been "jolly bodily" and that he had had six children. The myth of Whitman's children was nurtured by Whitman's specificity: "two are dead—one living Southern grandchild—fine boy writes to me occasionally—circumstances (connected with their benefit and fortune) have separated me from intimate relations." [2] All the evidence, raked through carefully by many scholars, seems to suggest that Whitman's remarkable assertion was inspired by the need to project an image of a poet virile and potent—an image in biographical fact to correspond with the created image projected in the *Leaves*. It is possible, too, that the assertion was meant to deflect those like Symonds who might have seemed on the trail of discovering a sexual secret which, revealed in those times, might have destroyed what acceptance the *Leaves* had at long last won. Whatever the case, at least one distinguished Whitman scholar, Emory Holloway, long continued to believe in the existence of Whitman's children, and ultimately published an account of an individual he identified as Whitman's son in *Free and Lonesome Heart: The Secret of Walt Whitman* (1960).[3]

Emory Holloway did not find many ready believers. By and large, Whitman scholars and critics have through direct statements, hints, or by discreet silence suggested the view that Whitman's sexuality was probably not heterosexual, certainly not strongly so, and might have been compounded of some kind of autoeroticism or homosexuality, latent or possibly even overt. There have been those who have asserted that the homosexuality of *Leaves of Grass* is as plain as the nose on your (or their) face, and to explain it away is to be deliberately hypocritical or perversely blind. Attempts to supplement this reading of *Leaves* (mainly "Calamus"), however, with biographical evidence have proved largely in vain, but not entirely so. Whitman biographers from the beginning have noted with interest his many friendships with unliterary, unlettered young men, of whom for long the most conspicuous and fully documented example was Peter Doyle, the horse-car conductor Whitman met in Washington during the Civil War. Whitman's letters to him were published as long ago as 1897, under the title *Calamus*.[4] Gay Wilson Allen, when writing his biography, found another documented example in the case of Sergeant Tom Sawyer, whom Whitman met in the hospitals in Washington.[5] And Edwin Haviland Miller, in editing the large body of Whitman correspondence, found still another documented case, perhaps the most convincing of all—Harry Stafford, whom Whitman came to know in the middle 1870s while staying at the Stafford farm in New Jersey (described in *Speci-*

men Days).[6] The letters to Doyle, Sawyer, and Stafford (like many other Whitman letters) are similar in that they express intense emotional and personal involvement, with Whitman assuming a number of roles—father, brother, comrade, and, on occasion, what appears ambiguously to be lover.

It is perhaps noteworthy that all these relationships come late in Whitman's life—in his forties and later. The same is true of relationships that have been reconstructed from a close reading of his manuscripts and texts. The most ingenious of these is a theory of Fredson Bowers based on an early version of the "Calamus" poems which contains only twelve poems and which, according to Bowers's reading, presents "an artistically complete story of attachment, crisis, and renunciation." Through a concrete biographical reading of one of the twelve poems, "When I Heard at the Close of the Day," Bowers attempts to demonstrate that the love affair described in the sequence might be dated some time before the second edition of *Leaves of Grass* (Bowers believes the reference to praise in the Capitol to be a favorable review of *Leaves* in Washington).[7] All of this is highly speculative and generally unconvincing.[8] Similarly speculative and even more unconvincing, I think, is Stephen Whicher's attempt to read "Out of the Cradle Endlessly Rocking" as a homosexual love poem. In his essay, "Whitman's Awakening to Death," he reveals an astonishingly circular method of critical analysis: "[This paper] accepts without argument Schyberg's conjecture of an emotional crisis between 1857 and 1860 and of some sort of homosexual 'love affair' to explain it, and uses this assumption as a basis for the interpretation of some of the poems from which it was first conjectured." [9] If I understand what this sentence says, it indicates that an assumption will be accepted as fact and then used to cast light on the source of the assumption to discover whether it is fact. This procedure might be likened to studying the sun by the use of moonlight.

These are by no means all the attempts to assess Whitman's sexuality, but they are some of the most ingenious. It remains unclear as to just what we might conclude about Whitman. We might speculate, without fear of being very far wrong, that a number of elements entered into Whitman's sexual knowledge and fired his imagination, among them masturbation, homosexual feelings that may or may not have always remained latent, sexual experimentation that may or may not have included intercourse with girls (if not in fact, then certainly in fantasy). We surely do not have to have biographical documentation for assuming these elements to be realities in Whitman's life long before he reached his middle thirties (he was thirty-six when he published the first edition of *Leaves of Grass* in 1855). All of the reconstructions of Whitman's love life concentrate on his middle thirties and later. We all know that he could have lived many sexual lives (and, indeed, probably did) in the first half of his seventy-two years. From what we know about sexuality today, we know that those earlier years determine the nature of the sexuality and largely shape the sexual imagination. To grub around in the biographical scraps of Whitman's middle life and old age for the "crucial" or "critical" love affair that will "explain" *Leaves of Grass* is to indulge in a collossal misdirection of energies in the service of basic misconceptions of poetry and the poetic imagination.

I have said that Whitman refused to revise his book to please his critics, but he did change the *Leaves* often as he shaped his book to leave it a living whole at his death. Two of the passages that he excised are worth glancing at in the context of the speculation just surveyed. The first was dropped from the incantatory last half of "Song of the Broad-Axe":

Their shapes arise, the shapes of full-sized men!
Men taciturn yet loving, used to the open air, and the manners
  of the open air,

Saying their ardor in native forms, saying the old response,
Take what I have then, (saying fain,) take the pay you approached for,
Take the white tears of my blood, if that is what you are after.[10]

The second passage was deleted from "The Sleepers":

The cloth laps a first sweet eating and drinking,
Laps life-swelling yolks—laps ear of rose-corn, milky and just ripened;
The white teeth stay, and the boss-tooth advances in darkness,
And liquor is spilled on lips and bosoms by touching glasses, and the best liquor afterward.[11]

These passages incorporate in many ways some of the best elements of Whitman's verse, and it is difficult to know why he excised them: perhaps because they are "sexual." But of course, Whitman left other equally "sexual" passages in his book. I have copied these passages here because they are typical of many in and out of the finished *Leaves* that offer something of a Rorschach test for the reader. As with a patterned inkblot, the reader may supply an interpretation that comes out of his fantasy and which reveals more about him than the meaning of the lines. I believe that Whitman, at some level of consciousness, counted on his lines acting in this way. In the first of these passages, one reader might well see in the last two lines the suggestion of a series of homosexual encounters. In the second, the same reader might well end up with visions of sodomy dancing in his head. I have no real doubt that Whitman saw these possibilities in the lines. But I have just as much conviction that he saw more, much more: that the first passage presented an image of male virility and potency, with the "white tears" (semen) impregnating a continent and a democracy; the second passage a surrealistic happening in which images of bedclothes, potent phallus, food, and drink all intermingle as they are wont to do in a dream—perhaps even a wet dream.

I for one regret the loss of these lines from the poems, but I regret even more that many readers will use the deletion of the passages as evidence that Whitman was trying to cover something up. The passages "prove" nothing about Whitman, except that he was a good poet with an astonishing range to his sexual imagination. If Whitman was motivated primarily to "covering up," he would never have written *Leaves of Grass,* where he stands creatively, nakedly revealed. And the truth is that we have never looked very carefully at what he has affirmed about sexuality, we have been so busy snickering about this or that inadvertent self-revelation. Whitman simply was not all that dumb. As the paragraph from "A Backward Glance" explaining the sexuality of *Leaves* shows, he knew how this element, though "intentionally palpable in a few lines," actually permeated the whole book, and he realized that the book must "stand or fall" with this pervasive theme. Indeed, he understood the resonance of imagery, and the particular resonance and suggestiveness of sexual imagery, and he fully realized how the sexual resonance of *Leaves* formed a major part of his central intention.

Whatever Whitman's own personal sexual makeup and experience (and I suspect that it was more complex than has yet been guessed), his imagination and vision were omnisexual. He had the artist's capacity to imagine and re-create many sexual roles, and he showed understanding of them and sympathy for them, and flung out his lines in celebration of them all—of sexuality in all its multiple forms as it bestowed being and identity on individuals and helped to form, mold, and shape relationships, societies, nations. The sexual imagery of *Leaves of Grass* does not, to the dismay of its psychoanalytic readers, fall into any single category. It is auto-erotic, hetero-erotic, homo-erotic. Even more, it is projected beyond the human to the natural scene, and beyond nature to the cosmos. It permeates, as Whitman said, the whole book—the whole world that is created in *Leaves of Grass*.

Whitman's omnisexual vision is set forth at the very beginning of *Leaves of Grass*, to serve as the foundation for the rest of the book. "Inscriptions" and "Starting from Paumanok" are, as I have suggested in *A Critical Guide to Leaves of Grass*, introductory in nature, setting forth the basic themes of the entire volume.[12] The body of the book proper begins with three great poems and poem-clusters —"Song of Myself," "Children of Adam," and "Calamus." And it is in these three foundation sections that the sexual imagery dominates even when it is invisible. The autoerotic imagery comes to the fore in "Song of Myself," heterosexual imagery in "Children of Adam," and homosexual imagery in "Calamus." But in no case does one kind of imagery appear exclusively. There is much mingling and merging, and much sexual imagery that cannot be assigned to any one of these categories. Moreover, to identify the predominate imagery is not to locate the major significance—it is only the beginning. It is important at this point to recall Whitman's remark from "A Backward Glance" that sexuality does not "stand by itself" but finds its vitality "altogether in its relations, bearings, significance—like the clef of a symphony." To call "Song of Myself," because of its abundant autoerotic imagery, a poem about self-arousal and onanism would be a kind of madness. But to see the relationship between sexual identity and the concept of selfhood and genuine being and becoming—that is to see the relations Whitman wanted to convey. To see "Children of Adam" as made up of heterosexual imagery and therefore devoted to male-female intercourse would be reductive in the extreme. The heterosexual imagery functions to suggest and imply something about the nature of human relationships, about the mystery of love, and about the miracle of procreation and the continuation in time beyond self of a part of self.

To see "Calamus" as presenting homosexual imagery to describe male-male sexual relationships would be to read it with large blinders. To comprehend the homosexual imagery in its significance for genuine comradeship, for transexual human relationships, for brotherhood, for concepts of the democratic ideal is to comprehend it in the significance that Whitman clearly intended.

Identity, love, friendship—is there any other basis for conceiving a beginning for human society? These great themes are not, of course, original with Whitman, but his insistence on dramatizing their physical and sexual roots makes the themes peculiarly his in *Leaves of Grass*. But the point to make here is that Whitman was not inadvertently revealing anything in this part of *Leaves*. On the contrary he was proclaiming to the world some truths about it and the beings who inhabit it that would not be explored in any depth by the philosophers and scientists until the development of the "new psychology" by Freud and others later at the end of the nineteenth century and the beginning of the twentieth. What the new psychologists were to "discover"—that sexuality permeated every aspect of human behavior and entered every phase of human relationships, male and female, in all their permutations—was something that Whitman had already proclaimed to the world in *Leaves of Grass*. But of course he had proclaimed much more in seeing the vitality of the all-pervasive sexuality in its "relations, bearings, significance." If the opening of *Leaves of Grass* made manifest the sexuality that beat at the heart of being and becoming, of relating and connecting, the large remainder of *Leaves* assumed sexuality as the "clef" of the symphony, as the sounded key to which all life, the world, and the universe were attuned and to which they resonated.[13]

When Whitman said, in "A Backward Glance," that the sexuality must remain in *Leaves of Grass* just as "the human body and soul must remain as an entirety," he was not exaggerating his case. The "enclosing" theme of

Leaves, as Whitman variously and repeatedly described it, was its spiritual or religious theme. Over and over again, he insisted, the soul or spirit gained its identity only through the body ("lacks one lacks both" [p. 31]). A similar relationship exists between the sexuality of *Leaves of Grass* and its spirituality. To remove the one would kill the book. And indeed, the soul takes its sustenance from that very sexuality that permeates every leaf.

Whitman stamps his major thematic premise in large letters all over *Leaves of Grass.* Here is an example, chosen at random, from "Starting from Paumanok":

I will make the poems of materials, for I think they are to be
    the most spiritual poems,
And I will make the poems of my body and of mortality,
For I think I shall then supply myself with the poems of my
    soul and immortality.

(P. 18)

It cannot be stressed too much that such statements are not empty rhetoric or bravado boasting. They are a precise statement of plan and program, and they in effect describe what happens in the body (and soul) of *Leaves of Grass.*

The fundamental poem of the body in *Leaves of Grass* is, of course, "Song of Myself," but it sings the body in order ultimately to affirm and sing the soul. It is difficult to talk about such a richly dense poem without falsifying its astonishing realities, but it is vital to an understanding of Whitman, and absolutely necessary to any understanding of his omnisexual vision. Near the beginning of the poem (sec. 3), as the poet is preparing for his journey, he rejects the talking of the "talkers" and reveals his own insight into the "mystery" that stands by his side:

Urge and urge and urge,
Always the procreant urge of the world.

Out of the dimness opposite equals advance, always substance
and increase, always sex,
Always a knit of identity, always distinction, always a breed
of life.
To elaborate is no avail, learn'd and unlearn'd feel that it is so.

(P. 31)

Always sex. This is a foundation stone of the structure of
Leaves and it stands behind the "mystery" of identity. It
lies at the heart, moreover, of "Song of Myself" in its
exploration of individual identity not in its human relationships (the focus of "Children of Adam" and "Calamus") but in its singleness, aloneness, separateness—its
"myselfness." Stress must be placed on the sexuality of
selfhood; sexual identity, sexual awareness and feeling as
they pervade consciousness, define the "I" of the self, and
delineate and comprehend the world.

The sexual imagery of "Song of Myself" is thus largely
of autoeroticism, the imagery of the beginnings of sexual
awareness and exploration. In the famous passage in section 5, however, describing the sexual union of body and
soul, a passage which launches the sexual-mystical journey
of the poem, the imagery is perhaps more homosexual than
autoerotic.

I mind how once we lay such a transparent summer morning,
How you settled your head athwart my hips and gently turn'd
over upon me,
And parted the shirt from my bosom-bone, and plunged your
tongue to my bare-stript heart,
And reach'd till you felt my beard, and reach'd till you held
my feet.

(P. 33)

This passage has shocked readers (in the way, surely, that
Whitman intended) by suggesting that the body, in the
homosexual embrace of the soul, is held in a state of
ecstatic paralysis. It is a passage that cannot be bypassed
by detour: it sits there in section 5 commanding the

reader's attention, all of the poem before in some real sense leading up to it, and all of the poem that follows flowing out of its drama and meaning. The reader must accept these lines or reject and misread the poem. If the reader carries only the homosexual suggestion away from the lines, he misses their real significance, but there is no need to reject that suggestion to get at the significance. A brief pause with the lines brings the realization that the sexual partner in actuality is the soul, that the tongue plunged through the parted shirt to the "bare-stript heart" is the spiritual tongue informing the heart of the body, and that the grip of the soul on the body from beard to feet signals an infusion of spirit into the flesh, transfiguring it through mystical knowledge. Instant knowledge is bestowed: "Swiftly arose and spread around me the peace and knowledge that pass all the argument of the earth" (p. 33).

Now, to suggest this "meaning" does not imply an attempt (as some think) to "clean up" the lines. The sexual implications are basic to the lines, and in their context in "Song of Myself" where sexual imagery abounds the implications are clearly intended and part of the meaning. Emphasis is not on sexual sharing (again, the focus of "Children of Adam" and "Calamus") but on sexual feeling and transfiguration of a single individual. The "I" in section 5 is entirely passive, and the ecstatic trance is his alone, and the knowledge that follows is his. As the way to identity lies only through the body, so the way to mystical awareness lies only *through* the intensest kind of bodily (and thus sexual) awareness. The sexual ecstasy is the route to mystical and spiritual ecstasy. Thus the soul, who is the metaphorical sexual partner in section 5, is not *sharing* but *bestowing*—for the purpose of launching the long mystical journey.

Section 33 of "Song of Myself" is the longest section of the poem, comprised mainly of a seemingly endless catalogue which attempts to encompass the entire universe.

This is the pivotal section dividing the poem into two halves. It opens:

Space and Time! now I see it is true, what I guess'd at,
What I guess'd when I loaf'd on the grass,
What I guess'd while I lay alone in my bed,
And again as I walk'd the beach under the paling stars of the
    morning.

(P. 61)

What has come before these lines has led to an intensification of awareness that the rest of this section—and the rest of the poem—will try to articulate. Significantly, the poet in each of the scenes recalled in these lines is alone, as he is alone at the beginning and the end of the poem. This song of the self must be sung alone, as identity and the awareness of being can come only from within. But section 33 is pivotal for several reasons. One of the most important is that just before it, the poet has succeeded in establishing his being and becoming through sexual identity and transfiguration, and the cosmic awareness of this central section flows from this "new identity." Thus the sexual imagery of "Song of Myself" is concentrated in the sections before section 33. After section 33, sexual imagery is subordinate to other images as the poet wings his way to deeper, more transcendent, and ultimate knowledge.

As section follows section in the first part of "Song of Myself," the sexual note sounds louder and louder as it moves to the climax that precedes section 33. At one point the poet engages the night itself in sexual passion, as in section 21:

Press close bare-bosomed night—press close magnetic nourish-
    ing night!
Night of south winds—night of the large few stars!
Still nodding night—mad naked summer night.

(P. 49)

Still unsatisfied, the poet turns to the earth: "Smile O voluptuous cool-breath'd earth! . . . Smile, for your lover comes" (p. 49). And after the earth he seeks fulfillment in the sea: "You sea! I resign myself to you also—I guess what you mean,/ . . . Cushion me soft, rock me in billowy drowse,/ Dash me with amorous wet, I can repay you" (p. 49).

Through his love affair with the physical universe, the poet comes to some kind of self-definition, even finding a name and a place: "Walt Whitman, a kosmos, of Manhattan the son,/ Turbulent, fleshy, sensual, eating, drinking and breeding" (p. 24). This is the fully physical Walt Whitman, the body which must exist as a precondition of soul. In his movement toward fullest awareness, the poet translates the natural world into his own sexual terms: "If I worship one thing more than another it shall be the spread of my own body, or any part of it/ . . . Firm masculine colter it shall be you!/ . . . You my rich blood! your milky stream pale strippings of my life!/ . . . Root of wash'd sweet-flags! timorous pond-snipe! nest of guarded duplicate eggs! it shall be you!/ . . . Winds whose soft-tickling genitals rub against me it shall be you!" (p. 53). In these and similar lines the poet merges with and becomes part of nature, in a kind of ubiquitous sexual union. His sexual feelings are reflected and returned to him magnified in every part of the world he looks at, and the universe itself seems to present a challenge.

Something I cannot see puts upward libidinous prongs,
Seas of bright juice suffuse heaven.

The earth by the sky staid with, the daily close of their
    junction,
The heav'd challenge from the east that moment over my
    head,
The mocking taunt, See then whether you shall be master!

                                         (P. 54)

In section 25, the poet accepts the challenge: "Dazzling and tremendous how quick the sun-rise would kill me,/ If I could not now and always send sun-rise out of me" (p. 54). Sections 25–32 of "Song of Myself" are in many ways the poet's response to the sexuality he has in the earlier sections discovered in the world. As heretofore his own sexuality has been diffused in the universe, mingled with night, earth, sea, the heavens and the sun, in these sections his sexuality focuses in the self, and reaches a climax that "quivers" him to a "new identity." He becomes, significantly, passive in section 26: "Now I will do nothing but listen" (p. 55). This listening, as it concentrates on the operatic tenor, leads to the height of sexual arousal:

It wrenches such ardors from me I did not know I possess'd
    them,
It sails me, I dab with bare feet, they are lick'd by the indolent
    waves,
I am cut by bitter and angry hail, I lose my breath,
Steep'd amid honey'd morphine, my windpipe throttled in
    fakes of death,
At length let up again to feel the puzzle of puzzles,
And that we call Being.

                                (P. 56)

But the poet's sexual response to the operator music is not climax and release, but return to the central enigma of this song of the self—the puzzle called Being. If the puzzle is ever to be solved or resolved, the secret will somehow be released through the self's sexuality.

Section 27, which brings us closer to the sexual climax of "Song of Myself" (the climax necessary for the transcendent awareness of sections 33–52), opens with the question of Being restated: "To be in any form, what is that?" It is in this section that the sense of touch moves to the fore: "I merely stir, press, feel with my fingers, and am happy,/ To touch my person to some one else's is about as much as I can stand" (p. 57). The sense of touch at this point assumes the role of hero of the poem, as it will bring a rebirth to the poet. The climactic section 28 opens: "Is this then a touch? quivering me to a new identity[?]" (p. 57).

Section 28 brings sexual climax and simultaneously a transfigured awareness of Being, a "new identity." Sections 29–32 dramatize the gradual downward flow of feeling and subsidence of passion after the climax, along with a new poise, self-assurance, and equanimity that come from the new conception of Being and the new realization of self. The poet is at last prepared for the transcendent flights of section 33 and beyond. Section 28, with its remarkable and fascinating sexual imagery, is one of the sections for which several versions have survived. As these various versions show, Whitman worked his way through several drafts before he hit upon the final imagery and metaphors that make up the published version. These earlier versions are more explicit in relating sexuality to identity, and their interrelationship in the miracle of Being.

One of the most interesting discarded passages suggests that section 28 originated in a sequence of masturbatory images, with emphasis on the performance of the poet's hand.

My hand will not hurt what it holds and yet will devour it,
It must remain perfect before me though I enclose and divide it.

Only one minute, only two or three sheathed touches,
Yet they gather all of me and my spirit into a knot,
They hold us long enough there to show us what we can be,
And that our flesh, and even a part of our flesh, seems more than senses and life.

What has become of my senses?
Touch has jolted down all of them but feeling;
He pleases the rest so every one would swap off and go with him,
Or else she will abdicate and nibble at the edges of me.[14]

The passage is fairly explicit in relating the touch of the hand on the phallus to the discovery of "what we can be," and to the knowledge that "our flesh, and even a part of our flesh [the phallus], seems more than senses and life."

The imagery of section 28 dramatizes sexual ecstasy moving to actual climax and release without introducing anyone other than the poet present, but at the same time evokes a scene in which the poet appears as passive and pursued. The secret is Whitman's dramatization of the senses, all bribed to "swap off with touch and go and graze at the edges" of the poet. These senses ("sentries") might have forestalled the encounter with touch, but they become traitors and let touch through to the "red marauder" (the phallus erect).

The sentries desert every other part of me,
They have left me helpless to a red marauder,
They all come to the headland to witness and assist against me.

I am given up by traitors,
I talk wildly, I have lost my wits, I and nobody else am the greatest traitor,
I went myself first to the headland, my own hands carried me there.

You villain touch! what are you doing? my breath is tight in its throat,
Unclench your floodgates, you are too much for me.

(P. 57–58)

The sexual release at this point is unmistakable, and the knowledge bestowed is left to be explored. In a line from another discarded version, the depth of the experience is suggested: "A touch now reads me a library of knowledge in an instant." [15]

Much more could, of course, be said about "Song of Myself," as it is an inexhaustible poem that creates new patterns

for itself at each reading. But the foregoing account is sufficient to establish the movement and primary meaning of
its generally autoerotic imagery. There will be no need to
devote so many pages to an examination of "Children of
Adam" and "Calamus," as they carry their currents of
imagery and meaning much more clearly on the surface.
(I have, moreover, dealt at some length with both these
clusters and their sexual images and implications in *A Critical Guide to Leaves of Grass*.) [16] A few examples will
suffice to show how these sections relate to "Song of Myself" in the totality of Whitman's omnisexual vision.

In "Children of Adam," the second poem, "From Pent-up
Aching Rivers," is a programmatic poem acting as a kind
of table of contents for the main images of the cluster. The
poet announces that he will be "singing the phallus,/ Singing the song of procreation" (p. 91). And he will be explicit in his celebration of male-female love.

The female form approaching, I pensive, love-flesh tremulous
   aching,
The divine list for myself or you or for anyone making,
The face, the limbs, the index from head to foot, and what
   it arouses,
The mystic deliria, the madness amorous, the utter abandonment.

(P. 92)

Probably the most impressive passage of heterosexual imagery in all of "Children of Adam" appears in "I Sing the
Body Electric," in the middle of the poet's "divine list" or
catalogue of the female body.

Mad filaments, ungovernable shoots play out of it [the female
   form], the response likewise ungovernable,
Hair, bosom, hips, bend of legs, negligent falling hands all diffused, mine too diffused.
Ebb stung by the flow and flow stung by the ebb, love-flesh
   swelling and deliciously aching,

Limitless limpid jets of love hot and enormous, quivering jelly
   of love, white-blow and delirious juice,
Bridegroom night of love working surely and softly into the
   prostrate dawn,
Undulating into the willing and yielding day,
Lost in the cleave of the clasping and sweet-flesh'd day.

(P. 96)

The poet's celebration of the human body, both male and
female, and his celebration of heterosexuality and procreation, are accompanied by an insistence on a dimension beyond the physical:

O I say these are not the parts and poems of the body only,
   but of the soul,
O I say now these are the soul!

(P. 101)

Throughout "Children of Adam," a revitalized and robust
heterosexuality is envisioned as providing the means for
renewal and for return to the natural relationship of the
sexes that existed between Adam and Eve before the Fall:
"To the garden the world anew ascending" (p. 90).

   In "Calamus" Whitman announces in his very title the
image that dominates the cluster—the phallus as it is suggested by the phallic-shaped calamus or sweet flag, either
in its spears or its roots. It is perhaps useful to recall that
Whitman has already, in "Song of Myself," given the image
sexual connotations (in sec. 24, in the middle of a catalogue
of nature-sex images): "Root of wash'd sweet-flag! timorous pond-snipe! nest of guarded duplicate eggs!" (p.
53). It is impossible to read the "Calamus" poems under
the domination of that phallic image without associating
the emotions expressed with homosexual feelings and long-
ings—and it is equally impossible (for me at least) [17] not
to believe that Whitman intended this association. In
"These I Singing in Spring," the poet explicitly identifies
the calamus root with love of comrades.

And here what I now draw from the water, wading in the
pond-side,
(O here I last saw him that tenderly loves me, and returns
again never to separate from me,
And this, O this shall henceforth be the token of comrades,
this calamus-root shall,
Interchange it youths with each other! let none render it
back!)

(Pp. 118–19)

If the calamus-phallic image permeates the entire cluster
of poems, as I suggest, then such a poem as "When I Heard
at the Close of the Day" becomes clearly a poem of homosexual love consummated. It is a poem describing separation and then reunion, and the reunion brings fulfillment:

And that night while all was still I heard the waters roll slowly
continually up the shores,
I heard the hissing rustle of the liquid and sands as directed to
me whispering to congratulate me,
For the one I love most lay sleeping by me under the same
cover in the cool night,
In the stillness in the autumn moonbeams his face was inclined
toward me,
And his arm lay lightly around my breast—and that night I
was happy.

(P. 123)

This narrative of love fulfilled is not typical of "Calamus."
As frequently as not, the poet's passion is secret and silent
and unreturned. Typical of this kind of poem is "O You
Whom I Often and Silently Come":

O you whom I often and silently come where you are that I
may be with you,
As I walk by your side or sit near, or remain in the same room
with you,
Little you know the subtle electric fire that for your sake is
playing within me.

(Pp. 135–36)

That the "Calamus" emotion is one with which the poet struggled is made quite explicit in "Earth, My Likeness":

Earth, my likeness,
Though you look so impassive, ample and spheric there,
I now suspect that is not all;
I now suspect there is something fierce in you eligible to burst
    forth,
For an athlete is enamour'd of me, and I of him,
But toward him there is something fierce and terrible in me
    eligible to burst forth,
I dare not tell it in words, not even in these songs.

                                                    (P. 132)

It would seem obtuse, in view of the omnipresent calamus-phallic image, not to recognize the nature of the male-male attraction in this poem. But this danger of total physical commitment, which might be seen as lurking in all sexuality whatever its manifestation, is balanced by the potentiality expressed again and again throughout "Calamus" of trans-figuring the calamus emotion into a social sentiment that creates and binds a society. "The Base of all Metaphysics" concludes:

The dear love of man for his comrade, the attraction of friend
    to friend,
Of the well-married husband and wife, of children and parents,
Of city for city and land for land.

                                                    (P. 121)

In brief, just as autoeroticism and heterosexuality can be reduced to mere carnality and lust, so can homosexuality. But as autoeroticism can be seen as a basis for identity and definition of Being, and heterosexuality as the basis for a vital and renewed relationship between the sexes (genuine love), so homosexuality can be transfigured into the social ideal of love of comrades and the democratic brotherhood.

    Most people, as we now know, are compounded emotionally of all three sexualities, in some measure, some with more of one component, others with still another. Whitman was one of the first to recognize and explore in depth the complexities and possibilities of sexual feeling with the comprehensiveness of an omnisexual vision. A writer of the twentieth century, also endowed with similar vision— D. H. Lawrence—summed Whitman up in this way:

What a great poet Whitman is: great like a great Greek. For him the last enclosures have fallen, he finds himself on the shore of the last sea. The extreme of life: so near to death. It is a hushed, deep responsibility. And what is the responsibility? It is for the new great era of mankind. And upon what is this new era established? On the perfect circuits of vital flow between human beings. First, the great sexless normal relations between individuals, simple sexless friendships, unison of family, and clan, and nation, and group. Next, the powerful sex relation between man and woman, culminating in the eternal orbit of marriage. And, finally, the sheer friendship, the love between comrades, the manly love which alone can create a new era of life.[18]

But it is not enough, today, to stand on the word of D. H. Lawrence. His authority has been eroded in this day of women's liberation by the attacks on his conception and portrayal of women (see esp. Kate Millett, *Sexual Politics*).[19] Did Whitman, too, speak more for men than for women; was he a prisoner of his maleness? The answer, when it is given, must be, I suspect, in a female voice. But the evidence that must be sifted would include a number of important details and passages. There is, for example, the sensitive feminine nineteenth-century response to Whitman recorded in Ann Gilchrist's "An Englishwoman's Estimate of Walt Whitman" in 1870 (the entire Gilchrist-Whitman relationship would make for interesting exploration).[20] And there are innumerable passages in *Leaves of Grass* that deserve closer scrutiny as they relate to feminine identity—the account of the twenty-eight-year-old woman imaginatively bathing with the twenty-eight young men in section 11 of "Song of Myself"; the eulogy of the female form in "I Sing the Body Electric"; the story of the poet's mother and her "Calamus"-like attachment to a red squaw in "The Sleepers." These and other passages must be examined to determine whether Whitman fulfilled his proclamation in section 21 of "Song of Myself."

I am the poet of the woman the same as the man,
And I say it is as great to be a woman as to be a man,
And I say there is nothing greater than the mother of men.
(P. 48)

Any critical examination that concentrates on sexuality is likely to draw forth the reader's response, "Is that all?" And there will always be skeptics and wags to reduce the omnisexual vision to a simple formula: fornication for mystical vision. The usual disclaimers must here again be entered and emphasized, even though they have been sprinkled throughout the essay. Of course, sexuality is not all, and masturbation does not bestow clairvoyance. For those who have so misread the essay, I can only plead with them to read it (and *Leaves of Grass*) again. Sexuality is a vital part, but only a part, of Whitman's vision. In "A Backward Glance," he described the "purpose enclosing all, and over and beneath all" of his book as follows: "to formulate a poem whose every thought or fact should directly or indirectly be or connive at an implicit belief in the wisdom, health, mystery, beauty of every process, every concrete object, every human or other existence, not only consider'd from the point of view of all, but of each. . . . I fully believe in a clue and purpose in Nature, entire and several; and that invisible spiritual results, just as real and definite as the visible, eventuate all concrete life and all materialism, through time" (p. 573). This is only one of many passages in *Leaves of Grass* (Whitman wanted "A Backward Glance" printed as a permanent part of the poem) that could be cited to suggest its major thematic thrust beyond (and *through*, not *around*) sexuality. For those who remain skeptical, perhaps D. H. Lawrence's words are appropriate: "Whitman put us on the track years ago. Why has no one gone on from him? The great poet, why does no one accept his greatest word? The Americans are not worthy of their Whitman. They take him like a cocktail, for fun. Miracle that they have not annihilated every word of him. But these miracles happen." [21]

Henry James was one of several literary figures who changed their minds about Whitman over a period of years. Unlike Emerson and Swinburne, who moved from ardent response to eventual distaste, James moved from repugnance to grudging admiration.[22] As we now realize, James deplored the placing of sexuality off limits for fiction, and called repeatedly for the Anglo-American novel to open itself to sex as a subject. But he was careful to explain that sex in isolation was not what he had in mind. In a discussion of the work of Gabriele D'Annunzio, he said: "From the moment it [sexual passion] depends on itself alone for its beauty it endangers extremely its distinction, so precarious at best. For what it represents, precisely, is it poetically interesting; it finds its extension and consummation only in the rest of life. Shut out from the rest of life, shut out from all fruition and assimilation, it has no more dignity than—to use a homely image—the boots and shoes that we see, in the corridors of promiscuous hotels, standing, often in double pairs, at the doors of rooms." [23] As far apart as James and Whitman are in talent, taste, and sensibility, they seem fundamentally in agreement about the role of sex in literature. Whitman said, in that passage from "A Backward Glance" quoted at the beginning of this essay, that sexuality does not "stand by itself": "The vitality of it is altogether in its relations, bearings, significance —like the clef of a symphony." In writing *Leaves of Grass*, Whitman sketched out his omnisexual vision at the beginning and then wrote the rest of the book to harmonize with that vision. He was right when he said, "At last analogy the lines I allude to [containing sexual imagery], and the spirit in which they are spoken, permeate all 'Leaves of Grass,' and the work must stand or fall with them." *Leaves of Grass* has not fallen, nor has it become obsolete. The contemporary literary freedom has not brought instant wisdom along with the obsessive portrayal of sexuality, but it has made it possible for us to read *Leaves of Grass* without being distracted by irrelevant questions about propriety and with renewed attention to "relations, bearings, [and] significance" with which Whitman endowed his representations of sexuality. Indeed, we might learn much yet from the good, gray poet. Reading his book can still bestow, imaginatively and metaphorically, the experience of the fulfilled relationship that the poet envisions and celebrates.

> Camerado, this is no book,
> Who touches this touches a man,
> (Is it night? are we here together alone?)
> It is I you hold and who holds you,
> I spring from the pages into your arms.
>
> (P. 505)

Notes–Index

NOTES

2. STEPHEN CRANE IN OUR TIME

1. *Stephen Crane* (New York: William Sloane Associates, 1950), p. xiv.
2. Westbrook and Colvert are well-known Crane scholars. The other two have written theses which no one working seriously at Crane can ignore: Will C. Jumper, "Tragic Irony as Form: Structural Problems in the Prose of Stephen Crane" (Ph.D. diss. Stanford University, 1958); Jean V. E. Whitehead Lang, "The Art of Stephen Crane" (Ph.D. diss. Cornell University, 1944).
3. "Stephen Crane and the Strenuous Life," *English Literary History* 28 (December 1961): 378.
4. *War Is Kind* (New York: Stokes, 1899), p. 41.
5. Lars Åhnebrink, *The Beginnings of Naturalism in American Fiction* (Upsala: University of Upsala Press, 1950), pp. vi–vii.
6. V. L. Parrington, *Main Currents in American Thought*, vol. 3, *The Beginnings of Critical Realism in America* (New York: Harcourt, Brace, 1930), pp. 323–24.
7. Charles Child Walcutt, "Harold Frederic and American Naturalism," *American Literature* 11 (March 1939): 11.
8. See William Dean Howells, "A Case in Point," *Literature* 11 (April 8, 1899): 371; and Donald Pizer, "Frank Norris' Definition of Naturalism," *Modern Fiction Studies* 8 (Winter 1962–63): 408–10.
9. Charles Child Walcutt, *American Literary Naturalism: A Divided Stream* (Minneapolis: University of Minnesota Press, 1956), pp. 20–29.
10. See Sophus K. Winther, "The Realistic War Novel," *University of Washington Chapbooks*, no. 35, ed. G. Hughes (Seattle: University of Washington Bookstore, 1930), p. 15.
11. George J. Becker, "Modern Realism as a Literary Movement," *Documents of Modern Literary Realism*, ed. George J. Becker (Princeton: Princeton University Press, 1963), p. 35. See also Richard Chase, *The American Novel and Its Tradition* (Garden City, N. Y.: Doubleday Anchor Books, 1957), p. 186n.

12. "'Not Men': A Natural History of American Naturalism," *Kenyon Review* 9 (Summer 1947): 433.

13. "Crane's *The Red Badge of Courage*," *Explicator* 8 (December 1949), item 8.

14. Walcutt, *Divided Stream*, pp. 81–82.

15. "Stephen Crane's 'Maggie' and American Naturalism," *Criticism* 7 (Spring 1965): 168–75.

16. *Stephen Crane: Letters*, ed. R. W. Stallman and Lillian Gilkes (New York: New York University Press, 1960), p. 133. In a sketch unpublished during his lifetime Crane states clearly that external conditions never are the cause of moral failure. See R. W. Stallman, "Stephen Crane: Some New Sketches," *Bulletin of the New York Public Library* 71 (November 1967): 560–62.

17. James B. Stronks, "*A Modern Instance*," *American Literary Realism 1870–1910*, no. 4 (Fall, 1968), n.p.

18. Joseph X. Brennan, "Stephen Crane and the Limits of Irony," *Criticism* 11 (Spring 1969): 184.

19. Willa Cather, "When I Knew Stephen Crane," *Prairie Schooner* 23 (Fall 1949): 234.

20. These important stories are *Maggie, The Red Badge*, "A Mystery of Heroism," "The Open Boat," "The Monster," "The Bride Comes to Yellow Sky," "Death and the Child," "The Blue Hotel," "An Episode of War," and "The Upturned Face." The plot of *George's Mother* is the progressive degeneration of the protagonist, apparently used because Crane had studied the end result in the assassin of "An Experiment in Misery."

21. Cather, "When I Knew," pp. 234–35.

22. See *Letters*, pp. 85–120.

23. *War Is Kind*, p. 16.

24. Max R. Westbrook, "Stephen Crane's Poetry: Perspective and Arrogance," *Bucknell Review* 11 (December 1963): 25.

25. *The Black Riders* (Boston: Copeland & Day, 1895), p. 59.

26. See *Letters*, pp. 109–10.

27. Max R. Westbrook, "Stephen Crane's Social Ethic," *American Quarterly* 14 (Winter 1962): 590.

28. See Olov W. Fryckstedt, "Crane's *Black Riders*: A Discussion of Dates," *Studia Neophilologica* 34 (1962): 282–93; *Letters*, pp. 39–40.

29. See Stephen Crane, "Howells Fears Realists Must Wait," *New York Times*, October 28, 1894, p. 20.

30. See *Letters*, pp. 62, 102. An earlier letter to Lily Brandon

Munroe confirms both date and readjustment (*Letters*, pp. 31–33).

31. My view of Crane is presented in detail in *A Reading of Stephen Crane* (Oxford: Clarendon Press, 1971).

3. THE RELEVANCE OF JOHN DEWEY'S THOUGHT

1. John Dewey, "Philosophy and Democracy," *University* [of California] *Chronicle* 21 (1919): 43; reprinted in *Characters and Events*, ed. Joseph Ratner (New York: Henry Holt and Co., 1929), 2:841–55.
2. Sidney Hook, "Philosophy and Public Policy," *Journal of Philosophy* 67 (1970): 461–70.
3. Dewey, "Science as Subject-Matter and as Method," *Science*, n.s. 31 (1910): 217; reprinted as "Science and the Education of Man," in *Characters and Events*, 2:765–75.
4. See Dewey, *The Public and Its Problems* (New York: Henry Holt and Co., 1927), pp. 212–13.
5. Karl Marx, *The Eighteenth Brumaire of Louis Bonaparte*, in *Karl Marx and Frederick Engels: Selected Works in Two Volumes* (Moscow: Foreign Languages Publishing House; London: Lawrence and Wishart, 1950), 1:228.
6. Dewey, *Freedom and Culture* (New York: G. P. Putnam's Sons, 1939), p. 175.
7. I have discussed this in two related essays: "The Ideologies of Violence," *Encounter* 34 (1970): 26–38, and "Reason and Violence—Some Truths and Myths about John Dewey," *Humanist* 29 (1969): 14–16.
8. Dewey, *Freedom and Culture*, p. 170.

4. MR. EMERSON—OF BOSTON

1. According to Edward Washburn "at Andover they sell shelves full of Coleridge's 'Aids to Reflection' in a year." *The Journals and Miscellaneous Notebooks*, ed. William H. Gilman et al. (Cambridge: Harvard University Press, Belknap Press, 1960–), 8:278 (hereafter cited as *JMN*).
2. A. Robert Caponigri's article "Brownson and Emerson: Nature and History" (*NEQ*, 18 [Sept. 1945], 368–90) sets forth lucidly Emerson's inferable doctrine, but Emerson himself certainly never saw it so clearly and did not suppose himself to be engaged in polemic.
3. John Edward Dirk contrasts Emerson and Parker in his

The Critical Theology of Theodore Parker (New York: Columbia University Press, 1948). Joel Arthur Myerson's chronicle of Parker's relationship with *The Dial* reveals the contrasting views of Emerson and Parker, "A History of *The Dial*" (Ph.D. diss. Northwestern University, 1971), pp. 406–22.

4. Letter of 17 October 1838, *The Correspondence of Emerson and Carlyle,* ed. Joseph Slater (New York: Columbia University Press, 1964), p. 196.

5. "Literary Ethics" (Dartmouth, 24 July 1838), *Collected Works,* ed. Alfred Ferguson and Robert E. Spiller (Cambridge: Harvard University Press, 1972), 1:102.

6. Frank B. Sanborn, "Journal . . . 1854–55," ed. Kenneth W. Cameron, *Transcendental Climate,* 3 vols. (Hartford: Transcendental Books, 1963), 1:212. Charles J. Woodbury, *Talks With Ralph Waldo Emerson* (London: Kegan Paul, Trench, Trübner Co., Ltd., 1890) cites, p. 13, an unlocated letter to "Miss Peabody" [Elizabeth, I take it]: " 'My special parish is young men inquiring their way of life.' "

7. Emerson treats the subject of being an example in a conventional way in Sermon 3 (23 Dec. 1827), MS, Ralph Waldo Emerson Memorial Association (hereafter cited as RWEMA), Houghton Library; see also *JMN*, 3:81–82. In 1830 he offers a different view, Sermon 63 (24 Jan. 1830), MS, RWEMA; see also *JMN*, 3:175.

8. Thomas Hamilton, *Men and Manners in America,* 2 vols. in one, Reprints of Economic Classics (New York: A. M. Kelley, 1968), 1:166, 167, 168. Hamilton visited the United States in 1831; his book was published in London and in Philadelphia in 1833.

9. Letter to his mother, 28 Mar. 1840, *The Letters of Ralph Waldo Emerson,* 9 vols., ed. Ralph L. Rusk (New York: Columbia University Press, 1939), 2:266. Emerson is making an in-joke. His mother would recall his father's posthumous *An Historical Sketch of the First Church in Boston* (Boston: Munroe & Francis, 1812). In it William Emerson reviews the stories of Ann Hutchinson (pp. 28–61) and the Great Awakening (pp. 184–93) and names his ancestors, Samual Moody, Joseph Emerson, and Daniel Bliss, as among those who "zealously cooperated" with George Whitefield. In spite of manful attempts to be liberal in his judgments, he sides with Charles Chauncy in the latter's debate with Jonathan Edwards. Emerson's

sympathies with enthusiasts is expressed frequently enough to need no documentation; for an example, see JMN, 3: 207.

10. *The Great Awakening,* ed. Alan Heimert and Perry Miller (Indianapolis: Bobbs-Merrill Company, Inc., 1967), p. 258.

11. See Norman Kemp Smith, *The Philosophy of David Hume* (London: Macmillan and Company, Ltd., 1966), pp. 547–53, where the difficulties in Hume's use of "feeling," "belief," "the moral sentiment," etc., are described. Smith's book is concerned largely with Hume's *Treatise,* which Emerson knew apparently only at second hand, and only incidentally with the *Enquiry,* but the difficulties are inherent in all Hume's speculative writings and would leave Emerson with an ambiguous and shifting terminology and without a ground for his convictions. He did read Hume's "Dialogues Concerning Natural Religion" (see note 36 below); if he knew the view prevailing in his day that Cleanthes represents Hume's opinion and is the winner in the debate, he would be the more unsettled. See Smith's edition (second) of the *Dialogues* (London: Thomas Nelson and Sons, Ltd., 1947), p. 58 and pp. 97–123.

12. William Paley, *Natural Theology* in *Works,* (Boston: Joshua Belcher, 1810), chap. 16, entitled "Compensation," pp. 192–202. Beginning, "It is a happy world after all," Paley's passage describing joyful insects includes aphids in a "state of gratification" (p. 311). The joyful fish that follow (p. 312) include bounding shrimp. Emerson refers to both this passage and the chapter on compensation in a journal entry of 1829 (*JMN,* 3:152): "I say to myself shall Paley pretend to derive fervour to his piety & fire to his faith from an ↑microscopic↓ examination of the tendons, muscles, & the nerves of an animal [,] ↑the leap of a shrimp or the economy of a bee↓? or shall Newton nurse & enlarge a lofty mind by tracking the paths of the stars in heaven?" Paley had denigrated the use of astronomy in the argument from design (p. 260). See note 28 below for the Federalists' preference for astronomy as a nobler science than biology. Paley's *Natural Theology* was borrowed from the Boston Library Society in March 1822: Kenneth W. Cameron, "Books Borrowed from the Boston Library Society . . . (1815–1845)" in *Emerson the Essayist,* 2 vols. (Raleigh: The Thistle Press, 1945), 2:159 (hereafter cited as *EtE*). For "compensation" as a "watchword," see *Letters,* 1:330.

13. A.l.s. Ruth Haskins Emerson to Mary Moody Emerson, 12, 17 March, 8 April, 1818 (RWEMA). See Smith, *The Philosophy*, pp. 3–8, 343–45, 519–26 for Hume's reputation.

14. *JMN*, 1:342–43. David Hume, *Essays and Treatises on Several Subjects*, 2 vols. (London: Printed for J. Jones 1822), 1:3. I cite this edition here and hereafter because it includes the "Dialogues," which were not printed until 1779 and not added to the collected essays until 1787. The American edition, *Philosophical Essays on Morals, Literature, and Politics*, 2 vols., ed. Thomas Ewell, M.D. (Philadelphia: Printed for the editor by Edward Earle, 1817), does not include the "Dialogues." See notes 11 above and 36 below.

15. "The Present State of Ethical Philosophy," in Edward Everett Hale, *Ralph Waldo Emerson* (Boston: Brown & Company, 1899), pp. 120–23. The equivocal character of Emerson's comments is noted by Alexander Kern, "The Rise of Transcendentalism," *Transitions in American Literary History*, ed. Harry Hayden Clark (Durham, N. C.: Duke University Press, 1953), pp. 265–66. An undated letter by Mary Moody Emerson, endorsed 1821 by Emerson (RWEMA), offers a pseudo-quotation from Hume; see Emerson's copy in *JMN*, 1:336. Possibly he had already expressed his admiration to his aunt or she had inferred it from his essay.

16. *JMN*, 1:260.

17. Letter to John Boynton Hill, 28 February and 8? April? 1823, *Letters*, 1:131.

18. Ralph L. Rusk, *The Life of Ralph Waldo Emerson* (New York: Charles Schribner's Sons, 1949), p. 80, citing (p. 515) a letter by Mary Moody Emerson to Emerson, 24 February 1821.

19. A.l.s., to William Withington, 21 November 1822, Library of Congress. (Printed inaccurately by Mary Withington in "Early Letters of Ralph Waldo Emerson," *The Century* 26 [July 1883]: 456–57.) Journal entries of June 1822 (*JMN*, 1:141–46, 147–49, 152–53) and a letter to Emerson from Aunt Mary, 25, 26 July [1822] show some exposure to scepticism before November. Miss Emerson's letter begins: "That some of the best intellects have been infidels is certain"; and further: "For you seemed ignorant of that host of Recluses who in [attitude?] have neither been 'peevish nor selfish.' But if He. [Hume?] condemns those 'illustrations,' you mention, then he condemns all reasonings *apriori* [*sic*] it seems??" She recommends, apparently

as an antidote, Thomas Brown, *Lectures on the Philosophy of the Mind*, adroitly and tactfully suggesting that Brown is easy reading. (This MS and others hereafter are quoted by permission of the Ralph Waldo Emerson Memorial Association and the Harvard Library.) Emerson borrowed from the Boston Library Society two volumes of Brown, vol. 1 in September and vol. 2 in December 1822 (*EtE*, 2:159–60).

20. Emerson recommends Stewart to his students; a.ll.s., 6 January 1825 to Elizabeth Parsons; 18 February 1825, to Elizabeth B. Francis; the first is in Houghton Library, the second in private hands. See *JMN*, 3:198 for an impression of Stewart's failure to live up to promise.

   For Stewart as preparatory for Coleridge, see Merrill R. Davis, "Emerson's 'Reason' and the Scottish Philosophers," *NEQ* 17 (June 1944): 209–28. If while reading Hume, Emerson read all the way through Brown's first volume (see note 19 above) he would find Stewart's mentor Thomas Reid and Hume described as holding identical views as to the impossibility of proving the existence of the material world by reason and the impossibility of denying a natural belief in its existence: "The sceptic, and the orthodox philosopher of Dr. Reid's school, thus come precisely to the same conclusion. . . . The difference, and the only difference is, that . . . the sceptic pronounces the first in a loud tone of voice, the second in a whisper,— while his . . . antagonist passes rapidly over the first, and dwells on the second, with a tone of confidence." Brown, *Lectures . . .* , 3 vols. (Andover: M. Newman, 1822), 1:430–31. In the third volume of Brown (pp. 452–53) he would find Paley's happy insect passage quoted.

21. Letter to John Boynton Hill, 19 June 1823, *Letters*, 1:135. Emerson is speaking here of Hume's history, but I believe the idolatry extended to the philosophical writing too and evoked imitation, not easily proved; see, however, "True Epicureanism," *JMN*, 2:283–85.

22. *Letters*, 1:138.

23. *JMN*, 2:161–62; the language of the journals is stronger; *JMN*, n. 37, quotes the relevant passage from Hume.

24. Copy entered in MS Journal 18 [A], pp. 7–8; printed in part by Edward Emerson in his edition of the *Journals*, 10 vols. (Boston: Houghton Mifflin Co., 1909–14, 1:324–27 [hereafter cited as *J*]). Emerson's copy is headed: "Canterbury Nov 11, 1823." The editors of *JMN* take the heading to be the date of entry, but Mary Moody Emerson's un-

mistakeable reply to the letter is addressed to Emerson at Roxbury to which the Emersons moved 24 May 1823 (Rusk, p. 97); Miss Emerson's answer, "24 Jan. n.y." (RWEMA) cannot be earlier than 1824 and is so endorsed by Emerson. She refers to the letter of 11 November by date and quotes (inaccurately) from it.

He had already described himself in his October letter: "I ramble among doubts to which my reason offers no solution." *Letters*, 1:137.

25. *Letters*, 1:141; Rusk's suggestion that Emerson is entertaining his aunt is taken from Mary Moody Emerson herself, 13 April 1824 (RWEMA), where referring to the letter of 1 February she says: "I read it again, and supposed the *Humism* assumed for the purpose of amusing." An eighteen-year-old may show off without being any the less serious. Emerson is still talking "Humism" two years later. Letters of 1826 from Aunt Mary (RWEMA) show her less inclined to suppose him to be merely amusing her. Her letter of 24 September 1826 exposes her nephew's inconsistencies. Apparently he has written her of feeling *"how strong the sentiments of moral beauty are"* (her italics) while his " 'feelings of piety are cold'! and to the desert the letters came with cold speculations of Humism." See Stephen Whicher, *Freedom and Fate* (Philadelphia: University of Pennsylvania Press, 1953), pp. 8–12 for a recognition that the doubts are serious.

26. A.l.s., 20 January [1824], (RWEMA). She will also belittle his admiration of Sampson Reed and Coleridge.

27. Harry Hayden Clark, "Emerson and Science," *Philological Quarterly* 10 (July 1931): 225–60.

28. See Linda Kerber, *Federalists in Dissent* (Ithaca: Cornell University Press, 1970), pp. 67–94, chap. 3, "The Object of Scientific Inquiry." Mrs. Kerber demonstrates that Federalists regarded astronomy as the respectable science and mocked Jefferson and Jeffersonians for their eclectic interest in the trivial sciences of biology and botany. See the passage from Emerson quoted in note 13 above. Note that he chooses astronomy as the subject for a sermon (157, 27 May 1832), printed by Arthur Cushman McGiffert, Jr., *Young Emerson Speaks* (Boston: Houghton Mifflin Co., 1938), pp. 170–79, 252–53.

See also Mrs. Kerber's account (pp. 126–29) of John Quincy Adams's conviction of the relation between eloquence and liberty.

It is perhaps suggestive that Thomas Ewell (M.D. of Virginia) who was responsible for the first American edition of Hume should have dedicated the volumes to James Monroe.

For a history of the argument from (and to) design, see Robert Hurlbutt, III, *Hume, Newton and the Design Argument* (Lincoln: University of Nebraska Press, 1965).

29. Hume, 2:446–48; the poet is Homer and the allusion is to the *Iliad*, bk. 24, ll. 527–33.

30. Hume, 2:448.

31. Ibid., pp. 449–50. Emerson may have taken in also Hume's "Note [G]" (Hume, 2:502–3) to the essay in which he affects to write as "The Sceptic." In the list of "philosophical reflections" that are in the note attributed to the skeptic appears: "2. Everyone has known ills; and there is compensation throughout. Why not be contented with the present?" and "7. Every good must be paid for. . . ." The conclusion of the note lists for reading Plutarch (for his learning) and Montaigne (for his gaiety) among others. Emerson's serious reading of these life-long favorites post-dates his reading of Hume. (The Montaigne borrowed in 1820 from the Boston Library Society was returned in two days, *EtE*, 2:157.)

32. See note 24 above. Emerson's copy plainly reads: "countries of barbarism," but "centuries" makes more sense.

33. *JMN*, 2:71.

34. Ibid., pp. 116–17, 144–46.

35. Ibid., p. 340; a part of the essay which follows goes into Sermon 4 (see note 39 below).

36. *JMN*, 2:413–20. Emerson cites here, p. 417, the "Dialogues." He borrowed Hume from both Harvard, 20 February 1825, and the Boston Library Society, 11 September–30 December 1824, 30 December 1824–3 February 1825 (Kenneth W. Cameron, *Ralph Waldo Emerson's Reading*, Raleigh: The Thistle Press, 1941, p. 46 [hereafter cited as *ER*]; and *EtE*, 2:161). It is possible that Emerson later bought a copy; see *Letters*, 1:206 and 215 where in August 1827 he has done up Hume's essays to be sent to his Aunt Mary and in October finds that they have not gone; he proposes to lend them to her for three months.

37. See Quentin Anderson's provocative book *The Imperial Self* (New York: Alfred A. Knopf, 1971).

38. I use here phrases from that portion of Coleridge's poem

"Limbo" that Emerson would have encountered in *The Friend* (ed. Barbara E. Rooke, *Collected Works* 4, London: Routledge & Kegan Paul, 1969), 1:494.

39. MS Sermon 4, 17 June 1827 (RWEMA), p. [5]; Emerson is quoting Ecclesiasticus 42:24; *JMN*, 2:340–41. For an account of the further history of the Law of Compensation, see Henry F. Pommer, "The Contents and Basis of Emerson's Belief in Compensation," *PMLA* 77 (June 1962): 248–53.

40. Emerson, "The Present State of Ethical Philosophy," Hale, p. 117. The tryannical father does not figure in Boston biography.

41. A.l.s. Thomas Wren Ward to Joshua Bates, 25 April 1844, Massachusetts Historical Society.

42. Emerson's copy, tipped in Blotting Book Y (RWEMA); see note 44 below; printed in *J*, 2:276–79.

43. Emerson is answering her letter of 10 November (a.l.s., RWEMA); in her reply of 28 December (a.l.s., RWEMA) she intensifies her attack.

44. See description of this journal, *JMN*, 3:163, 165, n. 6; Emerson includes his letter in the pagination of the journal.

45. MS Sermon 43 (11 July 1829), p. [12] (RWEMA). He will give a better expression to his intuition in Sermon 160 (2 Sept. 1832), pp. [21]–[22] (RWEMA): "It is not our soul that is in God, but God is *in* our soul. . . . This pure & holy inmate of every human breast, this Conscience, this Reason,—by whatever name it is honored—is the Presence of God to man." He will continue to use Sermon 160, delivered nineteen times up to 25 September 1836.

The *Biographia* was withdrawn for two days from the Boston Library Society in 1819 (*EtE*, 2:155). The next recorded withdrawal is of 1826 from Harvard (*ER*, p. 46) again of the *Biographia*. But it is not until the opening of Blotting Book Y that notes from Coleridge become frequent.

The continuing presence of Hume in his mind is attested by his struggles with Sermon 102 (13 Jan. 1831), on the miracles (McGiffert, pp. 120–26, and notes, pp. 239–40). He ends his sermon with an unctuous passage from Coleridge, but the whole sermon is haunted by Hume. Many years later Emerson would juxtapose the two; in MS Journal GH (RWEMA) in an entry of 1847, p. 33, he writes: "The useful the badge of the true. What profits

Coleridge or Hume?" A variation (p. 47) substitutes Kant for Coleridge.

46. Mary Moody Emerson to Emerson, 25, 26 July [1822], cited above in note 19, charges him with saying " 'that instead of intellectual excellence you hoped to be a good man.' "

47. *JMN*, 4:86.

48. Ibid., p. 27.

49. Ibid., p. 30.

50. See *The Early Lectures of Ralph Waldo Emerson*, 3 vols., ed. Stephen Whicher and Robert E. Spiller (Cambridge: Harvard University Press, 1959), 1:79–83, for the abstract of Coleridge; cf. *The Friend*, 1: 464–71. Paley's happy aphids appear on p. 77; see note 12 above.

51. *The Early Lectures*, 1:377–80.

52. 31 May 1834, *Letters*, 1:412–13.

53. A.l.s., 24 January 1835 (RWEMA).

54. Letter of 11 November 1823 to Mary Moody Emerson, cited above note 24; this portion of the letter is quoted in *Letters*, 1:139.

55. *JMN*, 4:42.

56. 31 May 1834 to Edward Bliss Emerson; see note 52 above.

57. *Complete Writings*, 12 vols. Centenary Edition (Boston: Houghton Mifflin Co., 1903), 2:222–23.

5. CONSISTENCY IN THE MIND AND WORK OF HAWTHORNE

1. See George Parsons Lathrop, *A Study of Hawthorne* (Boston: James R. Osgood, 1876), pp. 167–68.

2. Julian Hawthorne, *Nathaniel Hawthorne and His Wife*, 2 vols. (Boston: James R. Osgood, 1884), 1: 186–87.

3. Ibid., 1:432–33.

4. Ralph Waldo Emerson, *The Journals and Miscellaneous Notebooks*, ed. William H. Gilman et al. (Cambridge: Harvard University Press, Belknap Press, 1960–), 7 (1969): 21; *The Journals*, 10 vols., ed. Edward Waldo Emerson and Waldo Emerson Forbes (Boston: Houghton Mifflin Co., 1909–14) 6:240; 10:39–40.

5. See Poe's review of Hawthorne's *Twice-Told Tales* in *Godey's Lady's Book*, November, 1847; in Poe's *Complete Works*, 17 vols. ed. J. A. Harrison (New York: T. Y. Crowell, 1902), 13:55.

6. In "Chiefly About War Matters," *The Writings of Na-*

thaniel Hawthorne, 22 vols. (Boston: Houghton Mifflin, 1900), 17:297–398.

7. See James C. Austin, *Fields of the Atlantic Monthly: Letters to an Editor, 1861–1870* (San Marino, Calif.: Huntington Library, 1953), p. 231.

8. See F. B. Sanborn, *Hawthorne and His Friends: Reminiscence and Tribute* (Cedar Rapids, Iowa: Torch Press, 1908), p. 61.

9. See Moncure D. Conway, *Life of Nathaniel Hawthorne* (New York: Scribner and Welford, 1890), pp. 147–48, and *Autobiography: Memories and Experiences,* 2 vols. (Boston: Houghton Mifflin Co., 1904), 1:126.

10. Emerson, *Journals,* ed. Emerson and Forbes, 10:39–40.

11. Preface to the *Twice-Told Tales,* 1851.

12. Undated fragment in the Huntington Library.

13. Hawthorne to Henry Bright, March 10, 1860 (in the British Museum, printed in *Nathaniel Hawthorne and His Wife,* 2:241–42).

14. This letter is at the Huntington Library.

15. In Malcolm Cowley, *The Portable Hawthorne* (New York: Viking Press, 1948), pp. 622–24.

16. In Lawrence S. Hall, *Hawthorne, Critic of Society* (New Haven: Yale University Press, 1944), pp. 16–17.

6. WILLIAM DEAN HOWELLS: PERCEPTION AND AMBIVALENCE

1. "Fears Realists Must Wait / An Interesting Talk With William Dean Howells," *New York Times,* 28 October 1894, p. 20.

2. For a study of Howells's awareness of inner mind of his characters and his attempts to penetrate their consciousness see Gordon O. Taylor, *The Passages of Thought: Psychological Representation in the American Novel 1870–1900* (New York: Oxford University Press, 1969).

3. Reference is to a MS letter in the Ohio State Historical Society collection quoted by Clara M. and Rudolf Kirk, *William Dean Howells* (New York: Twayne, 1962), p. 70.

4. *Life in Letters of William Dean Howells,* 2 vols., ed. Mildred Howells (New York: Russell & Russell, 1968), 1:162.

5. *Book Buyer* 14 (1897): 558–59.

6. In *Years of My Youth* (New York: Harper & Brothers, 1916), p. 178, Howells claimed an "instinct of actuality,"

well illustrated, as Clara Kirk notes in "Reality and Actuality in the March Family Narratives," *PMLA* 74 (March 1959): 138, "by the exactness with which he dated the events in his imaginary world." See also John Reeves introduction to the CEAA ed. of *Their Wedding Journey* (Bloomington and London: Indiana University Press, 1968), pp. xvi–xviii, for a discussion of Howells's use of diary entries, and Edwin H. Cady, *The Road to Realism: The Early Years 1837–1885 of William Dean Howells* (Syracuse: Syracuse University Press, 1956), p. 159.

7. *North American Review* 114 (1872): 444–45.
8. CEAA ed., p. 3. Subsequent citations are to this text.
9. Reeves, p. xvi.
10. Kirk, "Reality and Actuality in the March Family Narratives," p. 137.
11. CEAA ed. of *A Chance Acquaintance* (Bloomington and London: Indiana University Press, 1971), p. 99. Subsequent references in text are to this edition.
12. Cady, p. 183.
13. Edwin H. Cady, *The Light of Common Day: Realism in American Fiction* (Bloomington and London: Indiana University Press, 1971), p. 43.
14. See Taylor, pp. 37–38.

7. WASHINGTON IRVING: NONSENSE, THE FAT OF THE LAND AND THE DREAM OF INDOLENCE

1. Until the badly needed CEAA edition of Irving, now beginning to appear, is fully published, we lack a readily available "standard" text of his works. My quotations from those works, except for the first, are brief. I have identified them therefore not by citing page numbers but by citing particular stories, essays, chapters, etc. I have in every case quoted from texts published by Putnam, his American publisher. And I have always used the "author's revised" version of a work, except where none exists. The revisions were published 1848–50. *Salmagundi* was not revised. Neither was *Wolfert's Roost*, which came out in 1855, after the revision.
2. "Letter from Mustapha," *Salmagundi*, no. 7.
3. Vernon L. Parrington, *Main Currents of American Thought*, vol. 2, *The Romantic Revolution in America* (New York: Harcourt, Brace, 1927), p. 193.

4. *Form and Fable in American Fiction* (New York: Oxford University Press, 1961), pp. 83–96.

5. Heller, *Catch-22* (New York: Simon and Schuster, 1961), p. 91.

6. "The Author's Account of Himself," *The Sketch Book of Geoffrey Crayon, Gent.*

7. "The Pride of the Village," *The Sketch Book.*

8. "Washington Irving," in *Literary History of the United States,* 3 vols., ed. Robert E. Spiller et al. (New York: Macmillan Co., 1948), 1:249.

9. "From the Elbow-Chair," *Salmagundi,* no. 1.

10. Pierre M. Irving, *The Life and Letters of Washington Irving,* 4 vols. (New York, 1863–64), 1:393.

11. "Preface to the Revised Edition" (1848), *The Sketch Book.*

12. Williams, *The Life of Washington Irving* 2 vols. (New York: Oxford University Press, 1935), 1:288; Pierre M. Irving, 2:240–41.

13. *Letters of Henry Brevoort to Washington Irving,* 2 vols., ed. George S. Hellman (New York, 1916), 2:185–86.

14. "The Creole Village" (1837), republished in *Wolfert's Roost.*

15. *Journals and Notebooks, Volume I, 1803–1806,* ed. Nathalia Wright (Madison: University of Wisconsin Press, 1969), pp. 7–8.

16. Martin Roth, ed., *Washington Irving's Contributions to "The Corrector"* (Minneapolis: University of Minnesota Press, 1968), p. 7.

17. *Journals and Notebooks,* pp. 15–16.

18. "A Tour on the Prairies," chapters 29–30, *The Crayon Miscellany* (originally published, 1835).

19. *Knickerbocker,* bk. 2, chap. 2.

20. "The Author's Farewell to Granada," *The Alhambra.*

9. WILLIAM GILMORE SIMMS

1. *Main Currents in American Thought: Volume Two: The Romantic Revolution in America, 1800–1860* (New York: Harcourt, Brace, 1930), p. 128. Originally published as a separate volume in 1927.

2. *Dictionary of American Biography,* 17 (New York: Charles Scribner's Sons, 1933), p. 173.

3. *The American Novel, 1789–1939,* rev. ed. (New York: Macmillan Co., 1940), pp. 54–55.

4. *The South in American Literature* (Durham, N. C.: Duke University Press, 1954), pp. 588, 597.

5. *Mississippi Quarterly* 15 (1962): 127. Wilson's judgments about Harris and his creation are preserved in *Patriotic Gore: Studies in the Literature of the American Civil War* (New York: Oxford University Press, 1962).

6. Ridgely, *William Gilmore Simms* (New York: Twayne, 1962), p. 67.

7. Ibid., pp. 29–30.

8. *The Letters of William Gilmore Simms*, 5 vols., collected and edited by Mary C. Simms Oliphant, Alfred Taylor Odell and T. C. Duncan Eaves (Columbia: University of South Carolina Press, 1952–56), 2:477, 492–93. The letters are dated 7 February and 7 March 1849.

9. Ibid., 3:427.

10. Published in Madison, Ga., in 1843, it was issued in the Library of Humorous American Works by Carey & Hart in 1847.

11. See Simms, *Letters*, 2:132 n.

12. *The Raven and the Whale* (New York: Harcourt, Brace, 1956), p. 30.

13. *Letters*, 1:263.

14. Ibid., 1:265.

15. "William Gilmore Simms in His Letters," *South Atlantic Quarterly* 53 (1954): 412.

16. *DAB*, 17:173.

17. *South in American Literature*, p. 590.

18. *Letters*, 1:lii.

19. For example, many of the pieces in *The Wigwam and the Cabin* (1845–46); portions of *As Good as a Comedy* and *Paddy McGann;* the posthumously published "How Sharp Snaffles Got His Capital and His Wife" (*Harper's Magazine*, Oct. 1870); and the unpublished sketches, notably "Bald-Head Bill Bauldy, and How He Went Thru the Flurriday Campaign." Volumes 2 and 3 of the South Carolina edition of Simms (out in 1972) make these and other uncollected stories available; volume 9 will reprint *Wigwam and Cabin*, which has been available in the Gregg reprint series since 1968.

20. Simms's statement; he considered the earlier *Martin Faber*, which had hard-cover publication, only a tale. *Letters*, 2:223–24.

21. *Guy Rivers*, new and rev. ed. (New York: Redfield, 1855), p. 500. For information, I have checked this version

against the first edition; there are many revisions, most of them apparently authorial.

22. Ibid., p. 77.

23. Ibid., p. 79.

24. Ibid., pp. 84–85.

25. *American Fiction* (New York: Appleton-Century, 1936), p. 122. Quinn, too, apparently prefers local color realism. "Perhaps, after all," he writes, "the material [of the frontier] was not so good for fiction, for when life is illogical a novelist must treat it as Bret Harte knew how to do, but as Simms did not." Ibid.

26. *Guy Rivers*, p. 156.

27. *Letters*, 2:228. Simms's Indians also express an attitude toward the land that becomes an important element in the writing of William Faulkner. Sanutee says, "He [the white man] wants our lands. But we have no lands to sell. The lands came from our fathers—they must go to our children. They do not belong to us to sell—they belong to our children to keep." *The Yemassee*, new and rev. ed., (New York: Redfield, 1853), p. 97. There are also apparent authorial changes between the passages in this edition and in the 1835 first edition.

28. *The Yemassee*, p. 294.

29. Ibid., p. 395.

30. *The Cassique of Kiawah* (New York: Redfield, 1859), p. 53. This is the first edition of this text.

31. *DAB*, 17:172.

32. *Richard Hurdis* (New York: Redfield, 1855), p. 66. Differences between passages from the new and revised edition and the first are not significant in the present case. In his "Notes of a Small Tourist," Simms had written from Mississippi to the Charleston *City Gazette* in 1831, "I cannot but think the possession of so much territory [the newly opened Indian purchase], greatly inimical to the well being of this country. It not only conflicts with, and prevents the formation of society, but it destroys that which is already well established. It makes our borderers mere Ishmaelites, and keeps our frontiers perpetually so." *Letters*, 1:37. Simms's view, antithetical to F. J. Turner's thesis about the frontier, holds some truth; some historians, at least, have believed the frontier to have left a dark stain on American character: a heritage of brutality, lawlessness, racism, and a penchant for running away from the pressing problems of creating a viable civilization.

33. *Richard Hurdis*, pp. 279–80.
34. Simms's forthrightness appears in his unfavorable comments in the novel about the acting of Edwin Forrest, remarks he was forced to explain later to his—and Forrest's—good friend, the New Yorker James Lawson. Simms always wanted to put a play into Forrest's repertory, but he never succeeded. See *Letters*, 1: 187–88.
35. *The Theatrical Apprenticeship and Anecdotal Recollections of Sol Smith* became vol. 1 of the Carey & Hart Library of Humorous American Works in 1846.
36. *Border Beagles*, new and rev. ed. (New York: Redfield, 1855), p. 412. Considerable revision in this passage, from the first edition, seems to be authorial.
37. *Letters*, 1: li–lii.
38. William Charvat, *The Profession of Authorship in America, 1800–1870*, ed. Matthew J. Bruccoli (Columbus: Ohio State University Press, 1968), pp. 49–67.
39. *Letters*, 1: lxxxix.

10. HENRY THOREAU AND THE REVEREND
    POLUPHLOISBOIOS THALASSA

1. "Thoreau," in *The Complete Works of Ralph Waldo Emerson*, 12 vols., Centenary Edition (Boston and New York: Houghton Mifflin, 1903–4), 10:476.
2. *Walden*, ed. J. Lyndon Shanley (Princeton: Princeton University Press, 1971), p. 17.
3. *The Writings of Henry David Thoreau*, 20 vols., Walden Edition (Boston and New York: Houghton Mifflin, 1906), 15:121.
4. Ibid., 4:121.
5. Ibid., 7:236, 234.
6. Ibid., 1:315.
7. Gaston Bachelard, *The Poetics of Reverie*, trans. Daniel Russell (Boston: Beacon Press, 1971), pp. 14, 8.
8. *Writings*, 1:316.
9. Ibid., 7:381.
10. Henry David Thoreau, *Excursions*, ed. Leo Marx (New York: Corinth Books, 1962), p. 201.
11. Ibid., p. xiii.
12. Ibid., p. 161.
13. Henry Nash Smith, *Virgin Land: The American West as Symbol and Myth* (Cambridge: Harvard University Press, 1950). See also Edwin Fussell, *Frontier: American Litera-*

ture and the American West (Princeton: Princeton University Press, 1965), pp. 181 ff.

14. Gaston Bachelard, *The Psychoanalysis of Fire*, trans. Alan C. M. Ross (Boston: Beacon Press, 1964), p. 109.
15. *Excursions*, pp. 205, 162.
16. *Writings*, 1:70; *Excursions*, p. 185.
17. *Excursions*, pp. 167, 188–90.
18. *Walden*, p. 98.
19. *Frontier*, p. 177.
20. Gaston Bachelard, *The Poetics of Space*, trans. Maria Jolas (Boston: Beacon Press, 1969), p. 8.
21. *Excursions*, p. 207.
22. Ibid., p. 186.
23. *Walden*, p. 312.
24. For another Keatsian passage on the robin, see *Writings*, 9:450.
25. *Walden*, p. 186.
26. *Writings*, 9:486.
27. Ibid., 8:19; 10:190; 11:292.
28. Ibid., 10:190; 11:169.
29. Ibid., 12:39, 225.
30. Ibid., 1:94; 11:254–55.
31. *Walden*, p. 87.
32. *Writings*, 11:292–93.
33. *Excursions*, p. xiii; *Frontier*, p. 181.
34. William Ellery Channing, *Thoreau: The Poet-Naturalist* (Boston: C. E. Goodspeed, 1902), p. 341.
35. A notable exception, however, is a thoughtful essay by Jonathan Bishop, "The Experience of the Sacred in Thoreau's *Week*," *ELH* 33, no. 1 (March 1966): 66–91.
36. Cf. Sherman Paul, *The Shores of America: Thoreau's Inward Exploration* (Urbana: University of Illinois Press, 1958), p. 198: "To ascend the river to its fount was to get to the beginning or youth of time, to the summit where water was mist and mingled with light, and all was a golden age."
37. *Writings*, 1:335.
38. Ibid., pp. 86, 133.
39. *The Psychoanalysis of Fire*, p. 71.
40. *Writings*, 1:320.
41. *Walden*, p. 249; *Writings*, 1:249–50.
42. *Writings*, 1:250. Thoreau tells us not only that the water of the Merrimack is yellow but also that his boat is painted green below to correspond with the element in which it

rides. Walden Pond, seen "near at hand," is both yellowish and green. Jonathan Bishop remarks that "the bittern represents the mysterious past of Greece, geology, and the two testaments as well, and to look into its eye would be to learn the secret of Nature and of one's own green soul" ("Experience of the Sacred," p. 80).

43. Gaston Bachelard, *L'Eau et les Rêves: Essai sur l'imagination de la matière* (Paris: Corti, 1942), p. 5; translation supplied.
44. *The Psychoanalysis of Fire*, p. 90.
45. A useful (though somewhat abstract) comparison of the symbolic use of water in Emerson and Thoreau is Nina Baym, "From Metaphysics to Metaphor: The Image of Water in Emerson and Thoreau," *Studies in Romanticism* 5, no. 4 (Summer 1966): 231–43.
46. *Writings*, 4:62, 103, 177.
47. Ibid., pp. 32, 127, 188.
48. *Excursions*, p. 167; *Writings*, 4:273, 127.
49. *Writings*, 4:186, 68, 189, 66, 177.
50. Ibid., pp. 66–67.
51. *The Shores of America*, p. 381.
52. *Thoreau: The Poet-Naturalist*, p. 77.
53. *The Poetics of Space*, p. 198.
54. *Writings*, 4:67.
55. Wallace Stevens, *The Collected Poems* (New York: Alfred A. Knopf, 1957), pp. 29, 30. Thoreau's tendency in the direction of a kind of language mysticism was undoubtedly reinforced by his acquaintance with the writings of Charles Kraitsir, a Polish émigré and protégé of Elizabeth Peabody, who was a sort of linguistic genius for the Transcendentalists. In his *Glossology . . . A Treatise on the Nature of Language and on the Language of Nature* (1852), from which Thoreau copied extracts into his Fact Book, Kraitsir elaborated concretely on the Emersonian notion that the harmony between man's spirit and nature is expressed directly through words. In his "apocalyptic phraseology," Kraitsir went so far as to assign colors, feelings, and shapes to vowels; and in a long chapter on "Germs and Roots," he cites Plato's *Cratylus* at great length concerning the "natural propriety" of Greek. Homer is used as Socrates' principal example of the God-given natural force of words. In fact, Thoreau's interest in *Poluphloisboios Thalassa* might have been stimulated by his reading here that Phi and Sigma "denote blowing,"

with Lambda "the tongue glides," Alpha is "great," and Omega "round." For a brief general treatment of the Transcendentalists' interest in linguistic theories, see John B. Wilson, "Grimm's Law and the Brahmins," *New England Quarterly*, 38, no. 2 (June 1965): 234–39. Gaston Bachelard concludes *L'Eau et les Rêves* by attempting to prove "que les voix de l'eau sont à peine métaphoriques, que le langage des eaux est une réalité poétique directe, que les ruisseaux et les fleuves *sonorisent* avec une étrange fidélité les paysages muets, que les eaux bruissantes apprennent aux oiseaux et aux hommes à chanter, à parler, à redire, et qu'il y a en somme continuité entre la parole de l'eau et la parole humaine" (p. 22).

56. *The Collected Poems of Wallace Stevens*, pp. 29, 30, 28.
57. *Complete Works*, 10:453, 479.
58. *Writings*, 4:211.
59. *The Collected Poems of Wallace Stevens*, p. 24.
60. *Writings*, 4:123.
61. *Walden*, p. 98.
62. Ibid., p. 330.
63. Thoreau copied into his Fact Book the following passage from M. F. Maury's *The Physical Geography of the Sea* (1855): "the greatest depths at which the bottom of the sea has been reached with the plummet are in the North Atlantic Ocean, and the places where it has been fathomed do not show it to be deeper than twenty-five thousand feet." (See *Thoreau's Fact Book*, annotated and indexed by Kenneth Walter Cameron [Hartford: Transcendental Books, 1966].) One wonders just what sort of consolation Thoreau found in learning that the North Atlantic was scarcely five miles deep when he himself had discovered that the "bottomless" Walden Pond had a "remarkable depth" of one hundred and seven feet! The alert reader of *Cape Cod*, by the way, will notice that the crucial question of *bottomlessness* is central also to Thoreau's comparison between Christian theology and the preaching of the sea. Thoreau devotes a portion of "The Plains of Nauset" to a summary of the life and work of Nauset's first minister, the Rev. Samuel Treat. Thoreau openly admires the rigor and consistency of this "Calvinist of the strictest kind" who proclaimed "the doctrine of terror"; and we are offered an impressive sample of Reverend Treat's pulpit rhetoric from a discourse on Luke xvi. 23 beginning "Thou must ere long go to the bottomless pit" (*Writings*, 4:48–52).

64. *The Collected Poems of Wallace Stevens*, p. 30.
65. Cf. Sherman Paul, *The Shores of America*, p. 201: "Like his experience on Ktaadn, his experience with the ocean gave him a terrifying sense of otherness, of a primordial nature apart from the interests of man, and not easily conquered by thought."
66. *Writings*, 4:77.
67. Ibid., pp. 77–78.
68. It seems to me likely that Melville's animadversions on the failure of charity owe something to Thoreau, for this part of *Cape Cod* was first published in the August 1855 number of *Putnam's Monthly* magazine, which Melville undoubtedly noticed since it contained his own "The Bell-Tower." Melville began to write *The Confidence-Man* sometime in the late fall or early winter of 1855.
69. *Paradise Lost*, 2:891–96. It is interesting to note that Thoreau, in describing another confrontation with unmediated wildness in "Ktaadn," alludes to this same "illimitable Ocean" passage from *Paradise Lost:* "This was that Earth of which we have heard, made out of Chaos and Old Night" (see *Writings*, 3:78–79).
70. *The Poetics of Space*, pp. 5, 32.
71. *Walden*, p. 194.
72. For fire, compare the poems by Thoreau and Ellen Sturgis Hooper in "House-Warming"; for the pond, compare "It is no dream of mine . . ." and Thoreau's statement in "The Ponds" that Walden is "earth's eye; looking into which the beholder measures the depth of his own nature." Bachelard cites this sentence in his chapter on "intimate immensity" in *The Poetics of Space*, pp. 209–10.
73. See, e.g., Walter Harding, *The Days of Henry Thoreau* (New York: Alfred A. Knopf, 1965), p. 361.
74. George Santayana, *Winds of Doctrine* (New York: Harper & Brothers, 1957), pp. 213–15.
75. *Writings*, 1:316.

12. WALT WHITMAN'S OMNISEXUAL VISION

1. Numbers following quotations in the text refer to Walt Whitman, *Leaves of Grass: Comprehensive Reader's Edition*, ed. Harold W. Blodgett and Sculley Bradley (New York: New York University Press, 1965), a volume in *The Collected Writings of Walt Whitman*.
2. For an account and Whitman's letter, see Gay Wilson

Allen, *The Solitary Singer* (New York: Macmillan Co., 1955), pp. 535–36.

3. Emory Holloway, *Free and Lonesome Heart: The Secret of Walt Whitman* (New York: Vantage Press, 1960).

4. Walt Whitman, *Calamus*, ed. Richard Maurice Bucke, M.D. (Boston: Laurens Maynard, 1897).

5. Allen, *Solitary Singer*, pp. 297–99.

6. Walt Whitman, *The Correspondence: Vol. III, 1876–1885*, ed. Edwin Haviland Miller (New York: New York University Press, 1964). See introduction, pp. 2–9.

7. Fredson Bowers, *Whitman's Manuscripts: "Leaves of Grass" (1860)* (Chicago: University of Chicago Press, 1955), pp. lxvi–lxx.

8. See James E. Miller, Jr., *A Critical Guide to Leaves of Grass* (Chicago: University of Chicago Press, 1957), pp. 56–58, for an expression of my skepticism.

9. Stephen E. Whicher, "Whitman's Awakening to Death: Toward a Biographical Reading of 'Out of the Cradle Endlessly Rocking,'" *The Presence of Walt Whitman* (New York: Columbia University Press, 1962), p. 2.

10. Walt Whitman, *Leaves of Grass: Inclusive Edition*, ed. Emory Holloway (New York: Doubleday, Doran, 1926), p. 116.

11. Ibid., p. 683.

12. See James E. Miller, Jr., *Critical Guide*, pp. 188–96.

13. For deeper exploration of this point, see James E. Miller, Jr., "Walt Whitman and the Secret of History," *Start with the Sun* (Lincoln: University of Nebraska Press, 1960), pp. 15–28.

14. James E. Miller, Jr., ed., *Whitman's "Song of Myself"— Origin, Growth, Meaning* (New York: Dodd, Mead, 1964), p. 103.

15. Ibid., p. 102.

16. Miller, Jr., *Critical Guide*, chaps. 2 and 3.

17. My discussion of "Calamus" in chap. 3 of *A Critical Guide* would be changed in emphasis were I writing it today (it was written almost twenty years ago). Much of the analysis I would let stand, and I would want to continue my defense of "Calamus," but I would now want to discriminate more carefully among the multiple themes, allowing more prominence to the conscious sexuality of the poems and their symbolism.

18. D. H. Lawrence, *The Symbolic Meaning: The Uncollected Versions of Studies in Classic American Literature*, ed.

Armin Arnold (London: Centaur Press, Ltd., 1962), pp. 262–63.

19. Kate Millett, *Sexual Politics* (New York: Doubleday, 1970; rpt. Avon Books, 1971), pp. 237–93.

20. "An Englishwoman's Estimate of Walt Whitman" appeared in the *Boston Radical*, May 1870. It is reprinted in Edwin Haviland Miller, ed., *A Century of Whitman Criticism* (Bloomington: Indiana University Press, 1969).

21. D. H. Lawrence, *Symbolic Meaning*, p. 264.

22. James reviewed Whitman's *Drum-Taps* in 1865, and *Calamus: Walt Whitman's Letters to Peter Doyle* in 1898. See Edwin Haviland, ed., *A Century of Whitman Criticism*, pp. xxi–xxiii.

23. James E. Miller, Jr., *Theory of Fiction: Henry James* (Lincoln: University of Nebraska Press, 1972), p. 150. See chap. 7, "Sex: An Immense Omission."

INDEX

Adams, Henry, 122
Adventures of Captain Bonneville, U.S.A., 158
Adventures of Huckleberry Finn, 181, 218, 224, 225, 229, 230
Afloat and Ashore, 15
Agee, James, 170
Åhnebrink, Lars, 31, 33
Aids to Reflection, 79, 92
Aldrich, Mrs. Thomas Bailey, 220
Aldrich, Thomas Bailey, 220
Alger, Horatio, 79
The Alhambra, 153, 159
Allen, Gay Wilson, 237
All That Money Can Buy, 170
American Democrat, The, 23
American Novel, 1789–1939, The, 176
American Prose Masters, 213
American Renaissance, 105
American Tragedy, An, 37
American Turf Register, 178
"Armchair of Tustenuggee, The," 189
Arnold, Matthew, 33
Arouet, François Marie. *See* Voltaire
As Good as a Comedy; Or, the Tennessean's Story, 178
Astor, John Jacob, 155, 158, 159
Astoria, 158
Auden, W. H., 235
Austin, Jane, 220
Autobiography of a Pocket Handkerchief, 19

Bachelard, Gaston, 192, 194, 197, 200, 201, 203, 208

"Backward Glance O'er Travel'd Roads, A," 233, 241, 242, 243, 257, 258
Baldwin, Joseph Glover, 178, 179
Balzac, Honoré de, 23
"Bartleby the Scrivener," 38, 169, 170
"Base of all Metaphysics, The," 255
Baudelaire, Charles, 79
Bayle, Pierre, 85
Beggar's Opera, The, 32
"Bell Tower, The," 170
Benét, Stephen Vincent, 170
"Benito Cereno," 170
Bernard of Clairvaux, Saint, 91
Berryman, John, 27, 34, 51
Bible, 100
Billy Budd, 28, 170
Biographia Literaria, 92
Black Riders, The, 46, 49
Bliss, Elisha, 230
Blithedale Romance, The, 101, 109, 110, 114, 116, 186
Blotting Book Y, 90
"Blue Hotel, The," 28, 40
Bohn, Erven F., 167
Border Beagles, 176, 184, 186, 187, 188
Bostonians, The, 219
Bowers, Fredson, 238
Boz. *See* Dickens, Charles
Bracebridge Hall, 153, 155
Bradbury, Ray, 170
Bravo, The, 7, 8, 9
Brooks, Van Wyck, 216, 219
Brown, John, 103
Brown, William Hill, 187
Brownell, W. C., 213, 214

Bulkeley, Peter, 82
Bunyan, John, 79, 219
Burr, Aaron, 147
Burroughs, William, 234
Butler, Bishop, 89

Cady, Edwin H., 27, 135
Cain, 181
Calamus, 237
"Calamus," 236, 237, 242, 243, 245, 246, 252, 253, 254, 255, 257
Cape Cod, 192, 193, 201, 203, 205, 206, 208, 209
Capek, Karel, 32
Carlyle, Thomas, 80, 92, 93, 102
Carolina Sports by Land and Water, 179
Cassique of Kiawah, The, 184, 185, 186
Catch-22, 150
Cather, Willa, 39, 42
"Celestial Railroad, The," 102
Chainbearer, The, 21
Chance Acquaintance, A, 120, 121, 127, 128, 129, 130, 132, 133, 134, 137, 139
Channing, Ellery, 102, 203
Channing, William Ellery, 81, 89
Charvat, William, 189
Chasles, Philarète, 164
"Children of Adam," 242, 245, 246, 252, 253
"Clean, Well-Lighted Place, A," 38
Clemens, Samuel. *See* Twain, Mark
"Closing Up Peepers According to 'The Science,'" 188
Coleridge, Samuel Taylor, 79, 80, 82, 89, 90, 91, 92, 93
Columbus, Christopher, 154, 159
Colvert, James B., 27
Comly, James M., 121

Confidence Man, The, 170, 188, 207
Conrad, Joseph, 14, 168, 229
Conway, Moncure, 103
Cooper, James Fenimore, ix, xiii, 176, 180, 183, 213
Cooper, Judge William, 3, 4
Corrector, The, 157
Cotton, John, 82
Cowley, Malcolm, 31, 34
Cramer, William, 168
Crane, Jonathan Townley, Rev., 44
Crane, Stephen, ix, x, xiii, 190
Crater, The, 22
Crime and Punishment, 171
Critical Guide to Leaves of Grass, A, 242, 252
Crockett, David, 176
Crouse, Nellie, 43, 49
Cyclopedia of American Literature, 179

D'Annunzio, Gabriele, 258
"Dark-Brown Dog, A," 36
Davenport, James, 82
Davidson, Donald, 180, 181, 188, 189, 190
"Death and the Child," 50
Deerslayer, The, 5, 13, 19, 24
De Lancey: family of Cooper's wife, 4, 7
Desor, Edouard, 202
Dewey, John, ix, xi
Dial, The, 80
Dickens, Charles, 221, 222
Dickinson, Emily, 217
Dictionary of American Biography, 176
Diedrich Knickerbocker's History of New York, 144, 145, 147, 148, 149, 150, 151, 158
"Discipline," 88
"Doctor of Geneva," 204
Doolittle, E. S., 166
Dostoyevsky, Fyodor, 167
Doyle, Peter, 237, 238
Dreiser, Theodore, 35, 37

Duchess of Malfi, The, 32
Duck Soup, 150
Dupin, Amadine Aurore Lucie. *See* Sand, George
Duyckinck, Evert, 179

"Earth, My Likeness," 255
"Earth's Holocaust," 109, 115
Edwards, Jonathan, 79
Eliot, T. S., 213, 214
Elliott, William, 178, 179, 180
Emerson, Charles, 83
Emerson, Edward, 93
Emerson, Mary Moody, 85
Emerson, Ralph Waldo, ix, x, xiii, 102, 103, 104, 110, 113, 137, 193, 203, 204, 210, 213, 217, 220, 233, 258
"Encantadas, The," 170
"Endless Study, The," 165, 167
English Notebooks, 99
"Englishwoman's Estimate of Walt Whitman, An," 256
"Essay on Necessary Connection," 86
"Essays on the Principles of Method," 92
Experience and Nature, 71
"Experiment in Misery, An," 36, 39, 42

"Fancy's Show Box," 116
Fanshawe, 112
Faulkner, William, 159, 160, 180, 182, 213
"Fenimore Cooper's Literary Offenses," 23
Fichte, Johann, 81
Fields, James T., 101
Fitzgerald, F. Scott, xii, 159
Flush Times of Alabama and Mississippi, 179
Fly, E. J. M., 169
Forster, E. M., 235
"Four Men in a Cave," 41
Frank Forrester's Field Sports of the United States, and British Provinces, of North America, 179
Franklin, Benjamin, 79
Free and Lonesome Heart: The Secret of Walt Whitman, 237
Freud, Sigmund, 229, 243
"From Pent-up Aching Rivers," 252
Frost, Robert, 213
Fuller, Henry Blake, 37
Fuller, Margaret, 110
Fussell, Edwin, 197

Gauguin, Paul, 168
Geismar, Maxwell, 229
Generation of Vipers, 38
Genet, Jean, 234
"Genteel Tradition in American Philosophy, The," 209
"Gentle Boy, The," 102
George's Mother, 28, 41, 48, 51
George IV, 16
Gibbon, Edward, 85
Gilchrist, Ann, 256
Gillis, Jim, 222
Ginsburg, Allen, 235
Goethe, Johann Wolfgang von, 80, 92, 93
Golden Christmas, The, 177
Grapes of Wrath, 33
"Grayling," 189
Great Gatsby, The, xii, 159
"Greatness," 88
Greene, Herman Melville, 169
Greene, Toby, 169
Green Hills of Africa, xii
Guy Rivers, 181, 182, 183, 188

Hamilton, Thomas, 81
Hamlet, 100
Hamlet, The, 159
Hanover, House of, 15, 16
Harris, George Washington, 177, 180, 186
Hawthorne, Elizabeth, 102, 107, 109
Hawthorne, Julian, 107

Hawthorne, Nathaniel, ix, xii, xiii, 79, 163, 167, 184, 186, 190, 213, 214
Hawthorne, Sophia Peabody, 101, 102
Hawthorne, Una, 107
Hazard of New Fortunes, A, 120, 140
Headsman, The, 7
Heart of Darkness, 28
Heidenmauer, 7
Heller, Joseph, 150
Hemingway, Ernest, xi, 213
Heraclitus, 200
Herbert, George, 200
Herbert, Henry William, 179
Hilliard, John Northern, 43
Hitler, Adolph, 61, 63
Hoffman, Daniel, 150
Hoffman, Josiah Ogden, 157
Hoffman, Matilda, 149
Holloway, Emory, 237
"Hollow of the Three Hills, The," 106
Holman, C. Hugh, 177, 190
Holmes, Oliver Wendell, 220
Home as Found, 10, 12, 13, 23
Homer, 199, 202, 203
Homer, Winslow, 163
Homeward Bound, 10, 11, 12, 24
Hooper, Johnson Jones, 178, 179, 186
House of Hanover. *See* Hanover, House of
House of Stuart. *See* Stuart, House of
House of the Seven Gables, The, 107, 114
Howells, William Dean, ix, xiii, 32, 37, 47, 48, 177, 218, 219, 221
"How to Tell a Story," 150
Hubbell, Jay B., 177, 180
Hudson, W. H., 168
Hume, David, 82, 83, 84, 85, 86, 87, 88, 89, 91, 93, 94

Hurdis, John, 186
Huston, John, 170
Huston, Walter, 170

Iliad, 202
"In Defense of General Funston," 229
"Inscriptions," 242
International Episode, An, 23
"Intrigue," 50
"In Wildness is the Preservation of the World," 195
Irving, Peter, 146, 147
Irving, Washington, ix, xiii, 3
Irving, William, 143
"I Sing the Body Electric," 252, 257
Israel Potter, 163

Jackson, Andrew, 10
Jackson, Lydia, 93
Jack Tier, 19, 20, 22
James, Henry, 13, 19, 22, 23, 100, 104, 119, 213, 214, 217, 219, 220, 258
James, William, 75, 81
Jefferson, Thomas, 10, 64, 67, 146, 147, 157
Jennie Gerhardt, 35
Jonathan Wild, 176
Jonson, Ben, 221
Joyce, James, 234
Jumper, Will C., 27, 46

Kafka, Franz, 14
Kant, Immanuel, 71, 81, 85, 204
Kaplan, Justin, 230
Katz, Joseph, 50
Keats, John, 198
Kipling, Rudyard, 46
Kirk, Clara, 124

Lafayette, Marquis, de, 7, 9
Lang, Jean Whitehead, 27
L'Assommoir, 31
Last of the Mohicans, The, 5, 18

"Last Wager, The," 189
Lathrop, George Parsons, 100
Lawrence, D. H., 234, 256, 258
Leander, 126
Leather-Stocking Tales, 5, 20, 23
L'Eau et les Rêves, 192, 201
Leaves of Grass, 233, 234, 235, 236, 238, 239, 240, 241, 242, 243, 244, 245, 256, 257, 259
Lectures on Witchcraft, Comprising a History of the Delusion in Salem in 1692, 101
"Legend of Sleepy Hollow, The," 150, 152, 153
"Legend of the Mor's Legacy," 159
Leibnitz, Gottfried von, 81, 85
Letters from an American Farmer, 28
Letter to His Countrymen, A, 9, 10
Life and Voyages of Christopher Columbus, 154
Life of Scott, 16
Lincoln, Abraham, 215
Lionel Lincoln, 5, 6, 7, 9, 13
Little Lord Fauntleroy, 33
Littlepage Manuscripts, The, 20, 21
Locke, John, 85
Lockhart, John Gibson, 16
Logic: The Theory of Inquiry, 72
Longfellow, Henry W., 220
Longstreet, A. B., 178, 180
Loti, Pierre, 168
Lounsbury, Thomas Raynesford, 20
Loved One, The, 38
"Loves of a Driver," 180
Lowell, James Russell, 213
Lynskey, Winifred, 31, 34

Maggie, 28, 35, 36, 46, 48, 49
Mailer, Norman, 235
Main Currents in American Thought, 175

Major Barbara, 16
Major Jones's Courtship, 179
Marble Faun, The, 100, **109**, 114
Mardi, 164
Martin Faber, 183, 186
Marx, Karl, 65, 67, 68, 73
Marx, Leo, 195
Mather, Edward, 108
Matthiessen, F. O., 105
Maurice, 235
"Maypole of Merry Mount, The," 102
Mellichampe, 186
Melville, Herman, ix, x, xii, xiii, 3, 38, 79, 113, 128, 179, 186, 188, 190, 201, 207, 213, 214, 220
Melville, Stanwix, 168
Melville, Thomas, 169
Melville Log, The, 165, 167
"Men in the Storm, The," 36, 39
"Mesmeric Mountain, The," 41
Michelangelo, 220
"Midnight Sketches," 38
Miles Wallingford, 15, 19
Miller, Edwin Haviland, 237
Miller, Henry, 234
Miller, Merle, 235
Miller, Perry, 179
Millett, Kate, 235, 256
Milton, John, 90
"Minister's Black Veil, The," 114
Miss Lonelyhearts, 38
Moby-Dick, 166, 170, 171, 185, 186, 209, 224
"Modern Aspects of Letters," 92
Modern Instance, A, 120, 121, 140
"Modest Man, A," 108
Modest Proposal, A, 38
Modigliani, Amedeo, xiii
Moll Flanders, 32
Monikins, The, 10

Montaigne, Michel Eyquem de, 79
Montcalm, Louis Joseph, Marquis, de, 138
Mumford, Lewis, 163
Murray, Henry, 169
Murray, John, 167

Nagel, Ernest, 72
"Natural History of Religion, The," 87, 88, 89
"Naturalist, The," 92
Natural Theology, 83
Nature, 88, 93
"New Adam and Eve, The," 116
New Testament, 45
Newton, Isaac, 88, 94
Nietzsche, Friedrich, 79
Norris, Frank, 32, 37
Norton, Andrews, 82
Notions of the Americans: Picked up by a Travelling Bachelor, 7, 10
Numbers, 234

Oak Openings, The, 22
Odysseus, 33
"Of the Delicacy of Taste and Passion," 84
Old Manse, The, 102
Old Testament, 32
Oliver Twist, 32
Omoo, 167
On Being Different, 235
"Open Boat, The," 44, 50
Ordeal of Gilbert Pinfold, The, 38
Ordeal of Mark Twain, The, 216
Othello, 145, 146
Our Old Home, 99, 103, 110
"Out of the Cradle Endlessly Rocking," 238
"O You Whom I Often and Silently Come," 254

"Pace of Youth, The," 42
Paine, Albert Bigelow, 218, 230
Paley, William, 81, 83, 92, 93
Paradise Lost, 207
Parker, Hershel, 166
Parker, Theodore, 80
Parrington, Vernon L., 31, 148, 175, 176, 177, 185, 190
Partisan, The, 184, 185
Pathfinder, The, 5, 13
Paul, Sherman, 203
Paulding, James Kirke, 143, 145
Peabody, Elizabeth Palmer, 99, 101, 102, 110
Peabody, Sophia. *See* Hawthorne, Sophia Peabody
Peale, Norman Vincent, 79
Peck, Gregory, 170
Pendleton, Philip C., 180
Pierce, Franklin, 99, 103, 109, 110
Pilot, The, 5, 6
Pioneers, The, 4, 5, 6, 8, 10, 11, 21, 24
Pirate, 5
Pizer, Donald, 31, 35
Plato, 66, 90
Plotinus, 79
Poe, Edgar Allan, 3, 103, 104, 189, 201, 213
Porter, W. T., 179
Power of Sympathy, 187
Prairie, The, 5
Precaution, 3, 8
Prisoner of Sex, 235
"Prudence," 94

Quinn, Arthur Hobson, 182

Rahv, Philip, 13
Raven and the Whale, The, 179
Rechy, John, 234, 235
Red Badge of Courage, The, xii, 28, 29, 32, 38, 44, 46, 48, 49

Red Rover, The, 7, 19, 20, 22
Redskins, The, 15, 21, 22
Reed, Sampson, 93
Richard Hurdis, 176, 184, 186
Richard II, 16
Richard III, 32
Ridgely, J. V., 178, 186
Rimbaud, Arthur, 167
Ripley, Samuel, 83
"Rip Van Winkle," 152, 153
Rise of Silas Lapham, The, 120
"Roger Malvin's Burial," 114
R.U.R., 32
Russell, Lillian, 36

Sainte-Beauve, Charles Augustin, 22
Salley, A. S., 190
Salmagundi; or, the Whimwhams and Opinions of Launcelot Longstaff, Esq., and Others, 143, 114, 145, 146, 147, 149, 150, 155
Sanborn, Frank, 103
Sand, George, 23
Santayana, George, 66, 81, 155, 209
Satanstoe, 14, 20, 24
Sawyer, Tom, Sergeant, 237, 238
Scarlet Letter, The, 107, 108, 115, 224
Schelling, Friedrich von, 81
Schyberg, Frederik, 238
Scott, Sir Walter, 4, 5, 6, 16, 112, 155, 156, 180, 220
Sea Lions, The, 22
Second Dissertation, 85
Sexual Politics, 235, 256
Shakespeare, William, 146, 164
"Sights from a Steeple," 115
Sister Carrie, 35
Sketch Book, The, 150, 151, 153, 155, 159
"Sleepers, The," 240, 257
Smith, Henry Nash, 195
Smith, Joseph Edward Adams, 168

Smith, Sol, 188
"Snake of the Cabin, The," 189
Snopes trilogy, 33
Snow, C. P., 56
Socrates, 85
"Song of Deborah," 33
"Song of Myself," 242, 244, 245, 246, 247, 249, 251, 252, 253, 257
"Song of the Broad-Axe," 239
South in American Literature, The, 177
Specimen Days, 237, 238
"Sphinx, The," 193
"Spring," 198
Spy, The, 4, 19
Stafford, Harry, 237, 238
"Starting from Paumanok," 242, 244
Statesman's Manuel, 92
Steinbeck, John, 33
Stevens, Wallace, 204, 206
Stewart, Dugald, 85
Stewart, Randall, 104
Stranger, The, 170
Study of Hawthorne, A, 100
Stuyvesant, Peter, 147
Sullivan County Sketches, The, 39, 41
Sumner, Charles, 111, 112
"Sunday," 200
"Sunday at Home," 115
Swan, Robert, Rev., 169
Swan Lake, xiii
Swift, Jonathan, 38
Swinburne, Algernon Charles, 258
Symonds, John Addington, 236, 237

Tales of a Traveller, 152, 153
Telemachus, 33
Thalassa, Poluphloisboios, 204, 209
Thales of Miletus, 200
Their Wedding Journey, 120,

121, 122, 123, 124, 126, 127, 129, 135, 136, 139
"These I Singing in Spring," 253
Thompson, William Tappan, 178, 179, 180
Thoreau, Henry David, ix, xii, xiii, 110, 113, 213
"Threefold Destiny, The," 116
Ticknor, William D., 109, 110
Tillich, Paul, 79
"To the Person Sitting in Darkness," 229
"Tour on the Prairies, A," 158
Trent, William P., 175, 185, 190
Twain, Mark, ix, xi, xiii, 23, 38, 104, 150, 181, 188, 190
Two Admirals, The, 16, 17, 24
Two Cultures, The, 56
Typee, 167, 170

"Unappropriated Land," 200
Undiscovered Country, The, 120
"Unity of God," 89
Upham, Charles W., Rev., 101
"Upturned Face, The," 39, 50

Van Buren, Martin, 156
Van Doren, Carl, 176, 177, 180, 185
Vinci, Leonardo da, 220
Virgin Land, 195
"Virtuoso's Collection, A," 115
Voltaire, 85
Voltmeier, 188, 189

Walcutt, Charles Child, 31, 32, 34, 35
Walden, 193, 196, 198, 199, 200, 201, 205, 206, 208, 224
"Walking," 194, 195, 196, 197, 202
Ward, Samuel Gray, 89
Ward, Thomas Wren, 89
War Is Kind, 29

"War Memories," 39, 42, 50
Warren, Robert Penn, 171, 180
Washington, George, 155
Water-Witch, The, 7, 8, 19
Waugh, Evelyn, 38
Waverley, 6
Waverley novels, 6
Ways of the Hour, The, 22
Weaver, Raymond, 163
Webster, Daniel, 156
"Wednesday," 200
Week on the Concord and Merrimack Rivers, A, 194, 196, 200, 201
Welles, Orson, 170
Wept of Wish-Ton-Wish, The, 18
Westbrook, Max R., 27, 44
"When I Heard at the Close of the Day," 238, 254
Whicher, Stephen, 238
"Whitman's Awakening to Death," 238
Whitman, Walt, ix, xiii, 100, 201, 213, 214, 215, 216, 217, 220
Whittier, John Greenleaf, 220
Wide World: pamphlet, numbers 10 and 11, 88
Wigwam and the Cabin, The, 189
"William Gilmore Simms and the 'American Renaissance,'" 177
Williams, Stanley T., 54
Wilson, Edmund, 177
Wing-and-Wing, The, 17, 18
Wings of the Dove, The, 19
Winters, Yvor, 24
Withington, William, 85, 88
Wittgenstein, Ludwig, 71, 72
Woodberry, George Edward, 104
Woolson, Constance Fenimore, 23
Wordsworth, William, 92

Worth, Captain, 166
Wounds in the Rain, 36
Wyandotte, 19

Yemassee, The, 183, 184, 185

"Young Goodman Brown,"
102, 113

Zola, Emile, 31

CEAA EDITIONS OF AMERICAN AUTHORS

James Fenimore Cooper
State University of New York Press
Stephen Crane
The University Press of Virginia
John Dewey
Southern Illinois University Press
Ralph Waldo Emerson
*Harvard University Press and
the Belknap Press of Harvard University Press*
Nathaniel Hawthorne
Ohio State University Press
William Dean Howells
Indiana University Press
Washington Irving
University of Wisconsin Press
Herman Melville
Northwestern University Press
William Gilmore Simms
University of South Carolina Press
Henry David Thoreau
Princeton University Press
Mark Twain
University of California Press
Walt Whitman
New York University Press

CENTER FOR EDITIONS OF
AMERICAN AUTHORS
An Approved Apparatus
MODERN LANGUAGE
ASSOCIATION OF AMERICA

®